S0-BAN-146

**Mass Society
and the Extension
of Welfare**

1960–1970

Kirsten A. Grønbjerg

Mass Society and the Extension of Welfare

1960-1970

The University of Chicago Press
Chicago and London

KIRSTEN A. GRØNBJERG is assistant
professor of sociology at Loyola
University, Chicago, and has taught at
the State University of New York at
Stony Brook.

The University of Chicago Press,
Chicago 60637
The University of Chicago Press, Ltd.,
London

Library of Congress Cataloging in Publication Data

Grønbjerg, Kirsten A
  Mass society and the extension of welfare,
1960-1970.

  Bibliography: p.
  Includes index.
  1. Public welfare—United States. 2. Public
welfare—United States—States. I. Title.
HV95.G75   362'.973   76-8101
ISBN 0-226-30964-9

Til mine forældre
Jens og Christine Grønbjerg
med tak
for deres støtte og tillid

Contents

Foreword

This is a sociological study of welfare in the United States. It is concerned with crucial aspects of welfare as a national system and with its recent growth and transformation. A monograph of this variety is not the definitive sociological analysis of the contemporary welfare system, but it can definitely be said that with its publication the sociological analysis of welfare has been transformed.

This is sociology in the grand manner. Sociology in the grand manner is not "mere" speculation or even "profound" speculation, but it has by tradition rested on a fusion of theoretical concerns with detailed empirical research. In this tradition, sociology is concerned with social responsibility and with social policy. In this study of the growth of welfare, Kirsten Grønbjerg continues this style of endeavor. Her analysis is rooted in the central and persistent issues of the theoretical study of macrosociology and the analysis of the process of societal change; at the same time, it makes use of a careful analysis of a massive body of statistical data. Its relevance for social policy is direct and obvious and hardly contrived.

She addresses the basic question of the root causes of the increase in welfare recipients and the broadening of welfare policies. She is fully aware that the public debate about the "welfare crisis" is cast in narrow and polemical terms. Unfortunately, much of the thrust of empirical research is a response to the form of this public debate rather than a reflective pursuit toward deeper understanding.

It is, of course, appropriate and essential that the analysis of the expansion of the welfare system be grounded in an analysis of the pressures of economic reality and of personal and family dependency. In this sociological perspective, the expansion of the welfare system is a direct—but resisted—response to poverty. Since poverty has both economic and social dimensions, Kirsten Grønbjerg calls this theoretical perspective the "social stratification" approach. In this view we would expect the expansion of the welfare system to be more marked in circumstances and locales where impact of poverty is greatest—here the notion of social and economic need is central.

The alternative—or, if you will, the supplementary—explanation is based on the idea of citizenship and the political extension of the social rights of citizenship under a parliamentary democracy. Here the emphasis is on moral and political rights. This is the "mass society" conception of sociopolitical change. The idea of mass society in this frame of reference focuses on incorporating excluded groups into the cultural and political body. Industrialization and urbanization in the United States—as in other Western parliamentary systems—reflects the expansion of citizen rights; these initially were political rights in the eighteenth and nineteenth centuries and progressively became social and economic rights in the twentieth century. The expansion of both the incidence and the magnitude of welfare payments in recent years represents another step in the expansion of citizen rights; this is the mass society approach.

The strength of this research monograph rests in part on the originality and effectiveness with which these explanatory theories are operationalized. The empirical result is that the two explanations are empirically distinct and separate. The analysis of the development of welfare requires both explanations; rather, part of the expansion is related to the one set of factors and part to the other. But the striking and central finding is that in more recent years—with the passage of time—the mass society theory has become more relevant than the social stratification model for explaining the continued movement of the United States toward the welfare state.

The research strategy is designed to deal with the reality that the welfare system is a composite of a national and a state-by-state system. The research task is to identify the factors associated with the different levels of state welfare efforts. In order to examine recent social trends, the basic comparisons are for the years 1960 and 1970. The crucial measures are both the eligibility rules and the active level and incidence of payments for AFDC (Aid to Families with Dependent Children) on a state-by-state basis for 1960 and 1970. As a result, the approach has the advantage of a detailed comparative analysis in a framework which deals with the large sociopolitical system.

Kirsten Grønbjerg has collected a mass of data on both eligibility and actual payments. The sociological study of welfare—based on economic measures—requires the collection of hitherto unavailable information; it is not possible for sociologists to test their hypotheses on the basis of a limited number of published indicators. The state-by-state analysis makes possible a concern with the ecological perspective in the national system; the focus on state eligibility rules and standards links the analysis to normative concerns. As a result of the materials assembled, we have a composite quantitative measure of state-by-state eligibility standards, which have changed over time. One of the striking findings is the limited impact of eligibility requirements in controlling the levels of welfare expenditures. This is not to deny the importance of eligibility standards as political and moral goals, but rather to point to their limitations as devices for budgetary control.

Therefore, the research keeps in focus both the eligibility requirements and actual expenditures, as reflected in the number of people

receiving welfare benefits and in their level of support. The core of
the analysis rests on an energetic effort to test both models—the
social stratification and the mass society approaches. The analysis
helps to explain the fact that the incidence and level of welfare payments have risen faster in the most industrialized and most wealthy
states. The goal of the statistical analysis is hardly that of a rigid
cost-benefit analysis, but rather the testing on a state-by-state basis
of the sources of increased expenditures. The goal is to understand
the sociopolitical context in which welfare expenditures have grown.
Moreover, the results also highlight those structural variables which
already operate to inhibit and limit this pattern of growth and will
do so more powerfully in the future.

Morris Janowitz
The University of Chicago

Abbreviations

AB	Aid to the Blind
ABD	Aid to the Aged, Blind, and Disabled
ADC	Aid to Dependent Children
AFDC	Aid to Families with Dependent Children
AFDC-U	Aid to Families with Dependent Children—Unemployed Fathers
APTD	Aid to the Permanently and Totally Disabled
CPI	Consumer Price Index
FAP	Family Assistance Plan
FFP	Federal Financial Participation
GA	General Assistance
OAA	Old Age Assistance
OASDHI	Old-Age Security, Disability, and Health Insurance (Social Security)
PL	Public Law
SPCU	State Program Characteristics Unit of the United States Department of Health, Education, and Welfare
SSA	Social Security Administration
SSI	Supplemental Security Income
TES	Total Eligibility Score
UF	Unemployed Fathers (program)
WPA	Work Projects Administration
WRO	Welfare Rights Organization

**The Welfare
Crisis in the
United States**

The Burden of
Responsibility

1

In recent years both the number of welfare recipients and the amount spent on welfare have increased dramatically. So great has been this increase that some have called it a "welfare crisis." Much time and effort has been spent in attempting to explain this rapid increase in dependency despite a general rise in the national standard of living. A multitude of books and articles attempting to find the right solution to the "crisis" have been published since the early 1960s.[1] Clearly, the welfare crisis is as much a crisis of explanation as of financing or managing the growth in dependency. One might even argue that an "explanation" of this crisis is as essential as, say, finding new funds to support the dependent or new administrative procedures to control who becomes eligible for assistance. No single interpretation of the welfare crisis has won public or academic acceptance so far, although, as we will see, there are many contenders.[2]

The primary purpose of this book is to restate the problem of the welfare crisis so as to place it in a larger perspective. In the process of describing and analyzing the quantitative data collected for this purpose I will also arrive at several conclusions which bear on the origin, development, and future of the "welfare crisis" and on its social significance as well. But the central objective is to show that understanding the "welfare crisis" requires us to go beyond the current proponents of the debate and place the issue squarely in the global processes of modernization.

Briefly, haltingly, the United States took another step toward the welfare state in the 1960s. The reasons for and the consequences of this movement are complex, but the findings of this study strongly point to a glacial and uneven shift toward the democratization of social rights. As the most primary forms of citizenship rights—those of civic and political participation—have developed, they have expanded to include those of economic citizenship as well: a vaguely defined right to share in the collective product of national achievement. My interpretation of the growth of public assistance in the United States sees in the expansion of welfare rolls an extension of citizenship—an extension which benefits not only the very poor, but other elements of society as well. Welfare rolls, then, have not grown because there are more poor people in America, for by any objective measure there are relatively fewer poor people today than ever before. Welfare rolls have grown not just because the poor have become more demanding, which may or may not be the case, but because broader concepts of citizenship have been drawn into the discussion of who is deserving and a wider range of people have thus become eligible for welfare. At the same time, then, those who are less desperately poor are receiving welfare, and poverty has come to be seen as the occasion for greater public concern.

Naturally, there are certain limits to this development. There are reasons to think that the 1960s was a period of unusual activity in expanding the social and economic rights of Americans. Also, persistent factors in the American society, particularly its cultural fragmentation into mutually suspicious groups and the resultant prejudice and discrimination, make it unlikely that citizenship in the fullest sense of the word will be extended to all members of the American society within the foreseeable future (for a further analysis of some of these limiting factors, see Grønbjerg, Street, and Suttles, forthcoming, chaps. 1, 2, 3).

In short, my hypothesis is that during the 1960s the United States has made only another halting step toward the modern welfare state—extending the primary rights of national citizenship to include the secondary rights of economic citizenship. In the process, the definition of public welfare has been enlarged to encompass situations of more than drastic and utter deprivation. I shall try to clarify these statements as I go along.

Popular and Sociological Conceptions of Poverty

There are two basic questions which beset discussions of public assistance in the United States: (1) Why are people poor and in need in the first place? and (2) What has been the collective response to these needs? Some writers seem to have assumed that change in the amount of support for the poor or needy is only a reflection of their changing numbers—that the magnitude of poverty determines the response to it. However, these two questions have different answers and need to be answered separately, although they clearly are related. At the very least, any given explanation of the causes of poverty has implications for the decision whether any action need be taken as well as for the level at which such intervention should occur and the type of policy which would be most effective.

The problem of explaining the causes of poverty and need, of course, has long been of concern to economists, politicians, journalists, historians, political scientists, psychologists, psychiatrists, social workers, and philanthropists. Historically, however, there have been and still are essentially two arguments concerning the causes of poverty in advanced industrial society.[3] The first and earliest is that the causes of poverty must be sought out in the individual characters of those who are poor. The second and more recent explanation[4] is that there are certain structural and systemic causes of low income and unemployment which lie outside the control of the individual and can be ameliorated through proper economic and social policies. The two arguments derive from folk theories of poverty, but each has received major support in the social science literature.

At the same time it should be emphasized that each of these theories and its respective policy implications is accepted and endorsed by segments of the population and sizable proportions of politicians, administrators, and social scientists today. Although there is a clearly discernible trend in favor of one of these theories—at least among the social scientists—many, if not most, state, local, and federal public policies still rest to a large extent on the foundation of the other theory.

Individual Responsibility

Although the first of these two explanations of poverty is the earlier, its remnants are still prevalent outside of academic circles in the United States. Originally the argument emphasized laziness and immoral behavior as the causes of destitution (Rainwater's [1970b, pp. 16-17] moralizing perspective). This viewpoint was most clearly stated very early in the writings of Malthus (1817) and Ricardo (1821). Later the argument shifted somewhat, especially after the introduction of psychiatry in the 1920s (the medicalizing perspective, Rainwater 1970b, pp. 17-19). This new argument essentially substituted characterological shortcomings for moral ones as the primary reason for poverty. More recently, the explicit formulation of the culture of poverty theory has transformed the argument of characterological shortcomings into an emphasis on culturological[5] or even biological ones[6] (the naturalizing perspective, Rainwater 1970b, pp. 19-21).

Although each of these related perspectives still has supporters, during the 1960s the culture of poverty theory received the most attention. This theory has explicitly or implicitly been endorsed by Frazier (1957), Oscar Lewis (1966, 1968), Moynihan (1965, 1966), Miller (1958), Banfield (1968), Henriques (1953), and Mizruchi

(1967). The culture of poverty theory tends to see poverty as perhaps originally the creation of the social structure, but as soon becoming an integral function of the personal characteristics of the individual. These characteristics are transmitted to him through his distinctive and local social environment, milieu, or culture, thus producing apathy, isolation, or a preference for casual associations and an indifference toward achievement in the larger society. The accompanying absence of interest in improving oneself through education hinders one's ability to climb the social ladder in terms of occupation, income, and prestige. For some writers, the culture of poverty theory also includes the notion that those entrapped in this cycle are satisfied with their life, in fact that they are enjoying their casual social relationships, their lack of responsibility, their time for recreation, sexual license, and so forth.[7] Thus the satisfaction of the poor provides a positive barrier to changing their lives (Banfield 1968; Miller 1958).

The ability of the culture of poverty theory to explain the existence of poverty in the United States is questionable. Most empirical studies do not lend support to the theory,[8] and its conceptual framework has also been questioned (Valentine 1968). My presupposition in this study is that structural and situational factors are basic causes of poverty and as such lead people to seek some form of financial assistance.

However, the culture of poverty theory and its antecedents have provided the major foundations for responses to poverty, dating back to the Elizabethan Poor Law of 1601. On one hand, the argument has been made that since poverty is self-imposed and perhaps even a "natural" phenomenon (biological or cultural), nothing can or should be done about it. At most, only the barest necessities, with adequate safeguards against misuse, should be made available to those whose poverty may be seen as a matter of fate or God's will, or whose conditions are truly desperate and life-threatening. This is the type of government response Piven and Cloward (1971), Elman (1966), and Bell (1965) have amply described and documented. On the other hand, if government is to take extensive action, as we have increasingly come to believe it must, these theories indicate that antipoverty policies must both be comprehensive and involve concerted (and usually expensive) attempts to make the poor better-adjusted members of society. This was, of course, one of the major goals of the War on Poverty. Ironically, its widely accepted failure may inadvertently have lent further support to its theoretical foundation, the culture of poverty theory, because the failure could be attributed to the strength of the culture of poverty and the correspondingly inadequate funding of the antipoverty programs (Pilisuk and Pilisuk 1973). In the process, the War on Poverty discredited most major government responses to poverty, at least in the opinion of the most ardent supporters of the culture of poverty theory (Banfield 1969).

The degree of governmental involvement in antipoverty efforts has been much less problematic for the other major explanation of poverty, which emphasizes the societal and economic creation of poverty and the unfortunate victims of these processes.

Societal Responsibility

Beginning with factory and wage-and-hour legislation during the Progressive Era around 1900, and especially since the Great Depression, an increasing number of writers have pointed to a series of structural factors in industrial societies which create needs that cannot be met through income from wages.[9] Such circumstances as climatic conditions, natural disasters, political considerations, or the absence of a subsistence economy to fall back on may create or exacerbate these structural factors. Indeed, unhealthful working conditions, industrial accidents, occupational diseases, automation, regional depressions, economic cycles of boom or bust, and occasional shortages of various forms of raw materials may create poverty even though everyone attempts to provide for himself. Unemployment, for instance, can no longer be considered just a matter of individual choice. Instead, it is largely the result of aging, the economic depression of some regions, the consequences of discrimination, or many other selective criteria outside the control of the individual. Furthermore, changes in the economic structure have led to greater demand for highly skilled, well-educated employees, which of course has meant less room for the low-skilled, poorly educated person. The effects of discrimination have therefore become more crucial and the result may in fact be a more permanent and more dependent poor population.

Many of these problems are directly linked to the process of industrialization, which implies that their solution must also be of a structural nature. Especially since the Great Depression, the responsibility for such solutions has increasingly been placed at the feet of successively more central levels of government. And as urbanization and industrialization have progressed, government has become increasingly capable of undertaking such responsibilities (Almond and Powell 1966, pp. 207-12). As a result, federal fiscal and monetary policies play a direct role in the production of both employment and unemployment in the United States today.

There seems to be sufficient evidence on these causes of poverty to warrant the conclusion that most poverty in the United States is linked to structural needs created by the industrial society. However, these needs have not been met by either private or public funds to the extent that they eliminate poverty or a sense of the gross injustice about how material benefits are distributed. Nor have any other industrial countries completely accomplished these goals, although many have been more successful than the United States.

The Ideological Uses of Poverty

For our purposes, the question of why people are poor in the United States is important primarily because the answers have been the basis for the response to poverty, a topic of primary concern in this book. In particular, the two arguments outlined above have been important in shaping policies of eligibility for the various public assistance programs.

Arguments on the causes of poverty have tended to move in one of two directions to account for both the causes of poverty and the growth of welfare: (1) the improvidence of the poor, along with the carelessness of those distributing welfare; (2) the permanency and increase of poverty owing to structural conditions and their increasing impact on the most unfortunate, along with the assumptions that welfare rates may be either only a reflection of how many are poor or a result of government manipulations in making welfare available to the poor for political reasons. The first of these arguments has generally been adopted by those with a conservative political persuasion (Governor Reagan of California, Senator Goldwater of Arizona, columnist William F. Buckley), and their argument rests to a large extent upon theoretical propositions similar to those belonging to the culture of poverty theory (especially those of Moynihan [1965] and Banfield [1968]). Any effort to combat poverty and rising welfare rolls, then, must begin with rehabilitating and changing the poor, since they are assumed to be deficient or at fault.

The second argument has in its more extreme forms been adopted by the radical left (for example, Stokely Carmichael) but, in general, those who are usually characterized as liberals have adopted similar points of view (e.g., liberal Democrats). Here the argument has been that since low incomes and unemployment are due to structural and systemic elements of the social structure, these inequities can be alleviated only through proper structural changes and economic and social policies. In this case, social reform involves at the very least changing the economic and employment policies of the central government. However, in most cases this has included an insistence upon some restructuring of the economic system, especially the elimination of discrimination and its effects. In a more extreme form the argument has been extended to the demand for a complete overthrow of the economic system in favor of a more collectivist form, or at the very least a universalistic approach to public welfare. This second argument rests on the theoretical foundation provided by some economists, but the sociological basis has most recently been formulated by Valentine (1968) and by Piven and Cloward (1971).

Neither of these basic types of reforms may eliminate poverty or the need for welfare programs. The United States, with its emphasis on individualism, has large pockets of poverty and a variety of social welfare programs. However, even the most collectivist of the modern industrial societies with their extensive welfare systems have not been able to eliminate poverty.[10] A comprehensive system of social welfare programs seems necessary to meet the endemic failures of industrialized societies. The United States is a heavily industrialized society, but the integral need for a more comprehensive and less stigmatizing welfare system has not yet been as fully appreciated or endorsed here as it has in Great Britain and the Scandinavian countries.

The Extension of Social Citizenship in Modern Society

The movement towards the welfare state has been slow and halting in the United States because of the profound difficulties Americans have had in interpreting the meaning of poverty and dependency. Nevertheless, increasing industrialization and urbanization have brought some realization that the responsibility for coping with poverty cannot be left to the individual or private charity alone (see Grønbjerg, Street, and Suttles, forthcoming, chaps. 2 and 3; Wilensky and Lebeaux 1965). Although industrialization and urbanization created many social problems, especially those associated with old age, unemployment, disability, blindness, and child dependency, these processes also promoted other changes which made some sorts of solutions possible. In particular, a greater demand for well-educated employees, higher incomes, and a more national scale of organization, which facilitated economic growth, were very important in providing the necessary resources and capacities for attempted solutions (Almond and Powell 1966). It should be recognized, of course, that each of these changes also tended to intensify the problems of poverty for those who did not share in the improvement in education or rise in income. Large-scale economic organizations furthered economic interdependence and concentration and in time gave birth to large-scale government as a way of counteracting some of their disruptive effects. As a result, the problems of the industrial society, especially those of poverty and inequality, have increasingly been located within the political economy and have come to be thought of as the responsibility of state and federal governments (Briggs 1961).

The expansion of government activities is of course a commonly accepted observation. However, it is less frequently emphasized that such government duties are only the counterpart of citizen's rights. A number of observers have noted the way in which these changes in the economic structure due to industrialization have significantly increased the range of government capacity and responsibility and expanded the rights of the individual vis-à-vis the state.[11] Over time, the widely recognized "modern" societies have actually seen a broadening of citizens' rights and increasing popular participation in both political affairs and central cultural institutions.[12] The history of the United States has been one of a more or less continuous trend in this direction (Huntington 1973).

Citizenship, however, involves several different elements. Marshall singles out three as the most important: political, civil, and social citizenship (1964, pp. 71-72). Undoubtedly all three forms of citizenship have expanded in the United States. Originally the vote was granted only to property-holding white males.[13] In recent years, only felons, the insane, and the mentally incapacitated have been legally restricted from participating in the political life of the nation. Thus, by 1960 about 60 percent of the total United States population was estimated to be eligible to vote, an increase of 43 percentage points over the past one hundred years. (Gendell and Zetterberg 1964, p. 5; Bendix 1968, p. 75).

Historically the movement toward increasing participation in political affairs was preceded by (but overlapped to some extent) the movement toward more inclusive rights of civil citizenship (Marshall 1964, p. 71): the rights necessary for individual freedom; liberty of the person, freedom of speech, thought, and religion, the right to own property and to enter into contracts, and the right to equal justice. Neither political nor civil forms of citizenship, however, have yet been fully realized by all members of American society, and the degree to which these rights have been achieved varies among the states.

The extension of both civil and political citizenship has been followed more or less closely by the granting of what Marshall (1964, p. 72) has called "social citizenship," that is, "the whole range from the right to a modicum of economic welfare and security to the right to share to the full in the social heritage of a civilized being according to the standards prevailing in the society." Obviously, this third form of citizenship is even less realized in the United States than the other two forms.

This secular drift in terms of increasing participation in the economy and polity is similar to Shils's notion of changes in the center-periphery division of society, or the extent to which the central belief system and common associational forms come to be shared by larger proportions of the population (Shils 1975). The "center" is not to be understood in a geographical or physical sense but indicates the central institutions of a society, where authority is exercised and cultural symbols are created and diffused. The society is most effective when the central value system, shared by elites, is also in accordance with the central authority structure. The "periphery," in contrast, includes those who are less in touch with the center and are recipients of influence, commands, and beliefs originating in the center. Such members of a society are less affected by the central culture and authority structure (Shils 1975, pp. 3–16, 34–47).

According to Shils (1975, pp. 91–107), the expansion of the center has occurred primarily through the expansion of education and mass communication, thus presupposing an economically developed society. Education and mass communication make possible closer interaction between members of a society, and the culture of the center can be more widely diffused. However, it is only in democracies with representative institutions that there is a strong possibility of expanding the center to include members of the periphery on a more equal basis. In such societies, the distance between the center and the periphery may consequently be reduced and a sense of common identity and mutual responsibility promoted. These societies Shils calls "mass societies,"[14] and I have found it preferable to use this term rather than "modernization" to indicate that economic development by itself is not sufficient.

In the mass society, where the center, or the elite, includes a wide selection of the population, and where the distance between the center and the periphery is diminished, the well-being and disposition of the periphery becomes a criterion for policy. This perception of equal "civil quality" of the elite and the masses (Shils 1975, pp. 304-6) is one of the most important foundations of the modern welfare state. And it is when the civil quality of the masses comes to be fully recognized as comparable or equal to that of the elite that Marshall's three types of citizenship rights are likely to be equally and fully extended. For this reason, it is Marshall's third form of citizenship in which I am mainly interested as a dependent variable. Social welfare and public assistance are forms of income which originates from such social and economic citizenship rights. On a national level, however, the actual extension of these social rights has been rather slow and uneven, although a major step forward was taken with the adoption of the Social Security Act in 1935.

The movement toward the extension of citizenship in the United States has been complicated by the fact that for a highly industrialized nation the American political system is relatively decentralized (Huntington 1973). States have jealously guarded their constitutional prerogatives to set policies in areas where the constitutional authority does not rest exclusively with the federal government (as it does, for example, in areas of defense, customs, immigration and naturalization). The degree of state and local autonomy which persists in the United States is extensive and can be seen as a remnant from a preindustrial era, when the economic systems of the different states or localities were not as interdependent as they are today.[15] In strictly economic terms the states are no longer rational geographic units. Economic spheres surrounding some of the larger cities in the United States cut across state and sometimes regional boundaries (e.g., the Greater New York metropolitan area, the Greater Chicago metropolitan area). However, the widespread suspicion of government, and especially of big government, which has been an integral element of the American culture since before the Revolution has helped maintain the political viability of the state as a unit of government. Because of their relative independence from the federal government, state governments have been seen as a possible check on the power of "big government."

Ironically, the federal government itself has been instrumental in maintaining and perhaps even increasing the political autonomy of the states. Thus states have been encouraged, prodded, and pushed to establish a variety of new programs or to expand existing ones into areas previously not considered the responsibility of government at all, or into areas under local government control (Stephens 1974). Much of the encouragement for such state action can be traced to federal grants-in-aid to specific state (and local) programs.[16] The states also have long historical claims to independent political action, sanctioned by the Constitution. In the words of one political scientist, although they are part of the overall American civil society, the states are also civil societies in their own right (Elazar 1972, p. 2). The states have, in fact, succeeded in preserving their integrity as political units, as is indicated by the high salience of state politics to the attentive public (Jennings and Zeigler 1970). Perhaps for these reasons, state politicians and administrators often complain of undue federal interference in state affairs through the strings attached to grants-in-aid (Break 1967; Derthick 1975).

The regulation of public assistance is no exception to this state-federal rivalry in the division of political power. At present, the federal government offers a series of public welfare programs in which the states may elect to participate to obtain federal financial support for public assistance. In return, the states agree to operate according to federal regulations for the administration of these programs. However, there is considerable room for state-by-state variation, and the states have been granted considerable autonomy in their operation of welfare programs, sometimes beyond the intent of the federal government (Break 1967; Derthick 1970, 1975; Advisory Commission on Intergovernmental Relations 1964).

The continuing ambivalence about the significance of poverty in the United States, evident in the difference between culture of poverty and structural interpretations of dependency, must be reemphasized at this point. The different approaches to explaining the problem of poverty have necessarily affected government responses to conditions of poverty. Each of the different explanations of poverty has been associated with certain political ideologies and, to some extent, with particular political administrations. Consequently, the changing public assistance policies have reflected theories of both individual and structural causes of poverty. Perhaps more important, federal policies have deliberately left room for state interpretations in order to entice the states to participate in the programs. In short, exponents of both types of explanation have had to be placated. We are likely, then, to observe the effects of both explanations in the diverse policies the states have adopted to deal with conditions of poverty and dependency.

This is particularly true since the political subdivisions in the United States are unlikely to move equally fast in the direction of mass society or modernization. In Shils's formulation, some states are more likely to be included in the national center while others are more nearly part of the national periphery. Not only may the states be seen as more or less integrated into the national society in this manner, but the states themselves have centers of varying sizes, with longer or shorter distances to the periphery. Consequently, states most nearly approaching the mass society type would be expected to extend primary and secondary citizenship rights to the masses most fully, while those states with small centers and great distance between the elite and the masses would be expected to evaluate policy more nearly in terms of how these protect the elite. Political scientists will recognize this type of categorization of the states as similar to Elazar's attempt (1972) to identify state political cultures. What I call mass society states correspond most clearly with Elazar's moralist state culture, while states least characterized by mass society traits correspond most closely to Elazar's traditionalist state cultures (Elazar 1972, pp. 93-102).

By any of the conventional measures of economic development—industrialization, urbanization, education, wealth, and so forth—there is great variation among the fifty states in terms of how "modern," or mass-society oriented they are. This is a point which political scientists and economists have documented well and have related to the *ability* to undertake public programs.[17] They have not, however, clearly emphasized the degree to which states would be expected to differ in their approaches to granting certain forms of citizens' rights—that is, *willingness* to undertake public programs apart from availability of financial resources.

One would expect to find the greatest collective support for the economic, political, and social rights of citizens in the states with the highest overall mass society status—that is, in the urbanized, industrialized states with large professional and occupational elites, high levels of education, and high voter participation. States that are progressive in some ways may be expected to be progressive in their welfare programs as well. In other words, such states should have high standards of welfare payments, lenient, less punitive eligibility requirements, little stigma attached to public assistance, and therefore more people receiving such aid. The major point to emphasize here is that in the mass society states public assistance itself may become a way of extending citizenship to a larger proportion of the population.

Conversely, we would expect least support for the social rights in states least characterized by mass society status. In these states public assistance is likely to be granted only or primarily to those who are already members in good standing—that is, "citizens," or people who are included in the "center" but are poor. To a large extent this would mean that aid would be provided primarily to those who are white, native-born, and who previously have been hard-working and not destitute. Bell (1965) argues that this approach not only was prevalent very early in the Aid to Dependent Children (ADC) program but was necessary to make the program acceptable to the population at large, at least in some states.[18]

Those who are in need but do not fall in the category of favored "citizens" have for some time, in some states, been left to care for themselves, or at least have had to be in greater need before they were likely to be considered deserving. Thus aid may be available primarily or only to the respectable poor and the destitute poor. The criteria for providing assistance, then, is the person's place in the stratification system—not economic need alone, although that may be seen as a convenient index, for if economic need is very extensive the poor are likely to include some very respectable people. The best approximation to identifying such an approach to public assistance among the states may be to examine "potential need" or "potential pressure" on the welfare rolls.[19]

This concern with who is to be provided with aid is particularly important if there are present in the state any groups (usually racial and ethnic groups) which are not thought to be "deserving" or "full members" of the society but which are part of the periphery. If the civil and political rights of such groups are limited in a society, the social rights almost always will be limited as well. This type of discrimination may be seen as basically a premodern pattern which (presumably) declines with modernization and the development of the mass society. It is the continuation of such forms of discrimination which makes it difficult at present to classify the United States as a truly "modern" society (Shils 1975, pp. 91–107). Furthermore, the continued presence of such "guest groups" and uncertainties about their full inclusion in society are likely to place ultimate limitations on the potential for further movement of the United States toward higher mass society status and full extension of social citizenship rights.

In poor states, as well as in those with large numbers of people whose citizenship status is in doubt, there is likely to be great pressure on public assistance rolls (needs), but also a stratification approach to granting such aid—that is, restrictive policies to limit aid to those of appropriate status and to conserve scarce fiscal resources. In addition, the level of welfare benefits may also be set low in order to limit their attractiveness and discourage "misuse." Because many of those considered "good citizens" are also likely to be poor in states with widespread need, as well as for humanitarian reasons, states with low mass society status have found themselves extending public assistance to sizable proportions of their populations. The role of the federal government in providing special incentives for poor states to extend low levels of benefit to large numbers of poor people should not be ignored.[20]

In summary, then, we have two general, somewhat different propositions about how and why states differ in their responses to conditions of poverty and need. In backward states the absolute need for assistance is likely to be great, and therefore welfare rolls can be expected to be relatively large. In turn, welfare policies should be less generous and more restrictive in these states so as to insure that only those in great need obtain assistance. On the other hand, the more modernized and wealthy a state, the more likely it is that its standards of need will be high, and the more people are likely to have extensive notions of what their rights are. Therefore, public assistance rolls will also be high, but welfare policies should be lenient.

There is no confounding of these propositions in regard to welfare policies alone. The two hypotheses lead to similar predictions for the same states. However, both propositions suggest that welfare rolls will be high in both backward and mass society states—in the wealthy as well as the poor states. There are two ways of separating out the implications of these two hypotheses. First, these theoretical perspectives represent two different *approaches* which states or their populations may take in responding to conditions of need. A state may take a very restrictive view of the purpose of public assistance and grant aid only to those considered desperately in need. Or it may consider public assistance a way of responding equitably to broader needs than absolute destitution, such as temporary unemployment and the need to finish higher education. The two models of responding to poverty then represent a continuum of options of how and to what extent the state will respond to conditions of need. At any given time, the "mass society" approach may predominate in some states, while in other states the "stratification" approach may be emphasized.

Another way of separating out the implications of these two propositions is to look at changes over time. Since the United States as a whole has become increasingly modernized, so have the different states. Over time, then, states should move in the direction of mass society, or, to put it differently, their approaches should move further toward the "ideal" mass society approach—the welfare state.

If that is indeed the case, we have found a plausible explanation for the "welfare crisis" discussed earlier. It is not that more people are poor or increasingly find welfare the easy way out, or that public assistance officials have let more people onto the rolls because they are careless or fear public disorder. Instead, changing notions of what constitutes need and deservedness have increased both the number of people who may be eligible for some form of assistance despite a general improvement in individual incomes and the number of people aware of and willing or eager to obtain such benefits. In some states, this movement has been drastic; in others it is less noticeable. But all states have moved in this direction, placing a severe strain on government resources and public comprehension as well. Both seem to be major ingredients in the crisis.

One must not lose sight of the countervailing forces in American society which retard the movement toward a mass society and welfare state: the continuation of mutual suspicions between various ethnic and racial groups, the extent to which some members of the society continue to be seen as a threat to cultural ideals, as well as the need to maintain some measure of inequality to instate the differential importance of social values and their achievement (Dahrendorf 1974). The first two of these factors are likely to limit severely the extent to which social citizenship may be extended within relatively short periods of time. The last factor places ultimate limitations on the development of the welfare state.

This study is an attempt to examine some of these issues: not only whether and how the states respond to conditions of need in their respective populations, but how that pattern may have changed over time. In the process I will also provide an interpretation of the welfare system which at crucial points departs from the explanation provided by Piven and Cloward (1971) in their widely read study. In particular, I will argue that their interpretation of public assistance as primarily, if not exclusively, a mechanism for social control of the poor is too simple-minded. Their account not only does violence to the data, where such data exist, but fails to recognize—or refuses to accept as genuine—real social facts. The system of welfare, I will argue, has changed; it is less restrictive and does provide assistance to those less desperately poor than was previously the case. The changes may not be equally great everywhere or as large and drastic as Piven and Cloward and many others, including several influential politicians, would like, but they are real nevertheless. I will return to this issue and to my disagreement with Piven and Cloward in greater detail in the last two chapters of this book.

Chapter 2 will examine some of the previous studies of state welfare programs and outline the structure of the present study. In chapter 3 the nature of state eligibility policies and their relationship to welfare rolls will be examined. This chapter will present the nontechnical reader with the background material necessary for understanding how the AFDC (Aid to Families with Dependent Children) program operates. Chapter 4 looks in detail at the two approaches to public assistance: stratification and mass society, and outlines the major hypotheses of the study. In chapter 5 the relative strengths of the two approaches in explaining the size of AFDC rolls for 1960 are examined. Chapter 6 deals with the same issue for 1970 and arrives at a somewhat different conclusion. Some of the reasons for finding a different pattern in the approach to AFDC in 1970 as compared with 1960 are explored further in an examination of the uneven growth in AFDC rolls between 1960 and 1970. This changing pattern is also the major focus of chapter 7, which looks at the issue from the perspective of how state welfare policies are translated into welfare rolls. Finally, chapter 8 places the findings of this study in the larger perspective of mass society and extension of social citizenship. The limitations on a continued extension of such rights, especially in the United States, are discussed, and some of the policy implications of the study are examined.

Mass Society
in the States

Overview and
a Framework
for Analysis

2

The United States is one of very few countries in which a direct study of the mass society theory is possible. The division of the country into fifty relatively autonomous political units provides the special opportunity for assessing the relative importance of economic development. The impact of mass society on policies which are directly related to the extension of social rights can thus be determined within an overarching national framework. Because federalism in the United States provides cultural, historical, and administrative uniformity while allowing for considerable diversity in socioeconomic development and policy execution, the states can be considered something of a natural laboratory.[1]

Certainly, many of the problems that beset cross-national studies—such as data of questionable comparability and unequal quality, as well as unique historical and political traditions[2]—are diminished, although not avoided. Each of the fifty states is unique in some ways; however, each is also intimately connected not only to other states,[3] but to the national center as well. The relationship between a state and the national center may be more or less tenuous, but it has become increasingly significant. Not only have the states become more integrated into a national economy, but over time the federal government has played an increasingly important role in supporting and shaping state and local policies.[4]

Because the federal government is charged with sole responsibility for some of the most expensive social policy areas, especially national defense, most state and local policies have concentrated on what may be broadly defined as social welfare policies: health, education, housing, transportation, and of course income maintenance. One of the most durable problems facing researchers, politicians, and to some extent the general public has been the question of why the states differ in their welfare policies. The outcomes of public assistance policies, such as the relative size of welfare rolls and the level of welfare payments and expenditures have been a prime subject of concern. Most of the studies of state-by-state welfare policy variation have been done by political scientists, a few economists, and even fewer sociologists. The findings and interpretations of these studies have remained rather fragmentary. In fact, the cross-fertilization between the various disciplines has been surprisingly limited. There has been little attempt to develop a larger theoretical perspective which could comprehensively evaluate the various findings. I have attempted to provide such a perspective, and I will test its adequacy in explaining state welfare policies and their outcomes.

Welfare Policies and Political and Economic Conditions in the States: A Review

Because the state is not a distinct, rational, or well-contained economic unit, most economists have focused on welfare policies at the national or international level.[5] Researchers accordingly have tended to limit themselves to two major areas of investigation: (1) the relative or absolute size of public welfare expenditures, which have then been examined in relation to Gross National Product (in national and international studies), forms and degrees of taxation, per capita income, urbanization, and so forth, and (2) the relationship between welfare payments and work incentives.[6]

Most of the economists' studies of state variations in welfare expenditures for the United States have involved rather complicated quantitative analyses of the relationship between welfare expenditures and social and other economic conditions in the states studied. In general, the findings can be summarized as follows: (1) increasing industrialization and economic development (usually measured by per capita income, urbanization, and density) have been accompanied by increasing expenditures on the problems produced by such economic development;[7] (2) the effect of federal aid on state expenditures is probably important but is difficult to assess;[8] and (3) the best predictor of a state's welfare (or other) expenditure at any point in time is the previous level of expenditure for that function.[9]

Recently other outcomes of state welfare policies, such as the number of people on welfare and the level of payments provided those recipients have also been examined by economists.[10] When these components have been included, they have been of interest mainly because of their relationship to welfare expenditures. Collins's study (1967) is the outstanding example here, although it also is one of few which recognize the possible importance of eligibility rules in influencing the number of recipients and thus welfare expenditures. I will return to some of the shortcomings of Collins's study later on, but I wish to emphasize her conclusion, shared by other writers, that level of per captia income and urbanization are positively related to welfare expenditures and level of benefits. Collins sees this as reflecting both the fiscal ability of the states to pay high benefits and higher standards of need in richer states. The theory of mass society would of course predict that pattern: the more industrialized and urbanized the state, the more it would be expected to spend on those programs most likely to benefit the periphery. However, as I shall show, this is in some ways too "easy" a conclusion, because favorable economic conditions are not necessarily closely associated with more favorable welfare policies. This is particularly the case if the periphery is composed of population groups whose membership is suspect because of ethnic or racial characteristics.

In many ways, the political science literature on state welfare policies is at least as relevant to the study of the mass society model. The recent publications in particular provide more revealing evidence for pieces of the mass society model. Only occasionally, however, have conclusions to that effect been made explicit.

The early studies by political scientists seem to provide almost a complete justification for the economists' assumption that only economic conditions[11] are important in predicting the level of state public welfare expenditures or payments.[12] Not surprisingly, the pre-eminence of economic development as an explanatory variable has been an uncomfortable finding for political scientists. It has also led them to the conclusion that state political structures, such as degree of party competition, malapportionment, democratic control, and voter participation seem to have little or no consistent influence on welfare policies independent of economic development.[13]

The consternation with which political scientists have met these conclusions[14] is perhaps understandable, since each finding seems to refute a widely endorsed theoretical argument by Key (1949, 1956) to the effect that the degree of party competition, and by extension malapportionment, is crucial in determining policy outcomes because it reflects the extent to which politics are organized or unorganized in the state. Organized politics are assumed to lessen the difficulty of lower status groups in sorting out political actors and issues, thereby enabling them to promote their own interests more effectively—that is, to increase welfare expenditures. Similarly, democratic party control and voter participation are thought to be related to competition for lower-class votes and thus should tend to increase welfare expenditures.

Obviously, welfare expenditures and payments are the result of some political process, and just as clearly, factors other than sheer economic capacity enter into that political process. However, our discussion of the two different approaches to public assistance (mass society and stratification) also suggests that an explanation of welfare policies in the United States much more complex than the one presented by Key and his followers must be developed. Parts of that explanation have been documented already in the recent political science literature, although the aim of these studies often has been to reestablish the importance of the traditional political variables.

As expected, much of the effort by political scientists has focused on developing better, more inclusive[15] measures of state political structures that are more closely related to policy outputs. On the assumption that socioeconomic developments can have only very indirect effects on the development of a given policy (Uslaner and Weber 1975; Morss 1966; Coulter 1970), political scientists have attempted to include factors that are more directly related to political decision-making. Thus a number of writers have emphasized that the political power structure (Hofferbert 1970; Morehouse 1973) and the characteristics and opinions of state legislators themselves (Uslaner and Weber 1975) may be crucial in shaping state politics. The results of most of these studies indicate that the argument by Key (1949, 1956) needs revision or at least elaboration. However, basic socioeconomic factors are still important in all these studies, although they have been pushed into the background or at least are considered less "interesting." These findings provide support, however indirect, for the extension of a mass society approach at the expense of the stratification approach.

A second series of studies has been more relevant to my concern with the degree to which social rights are extended in the states. A number of writers (Coulter 1970; Gary 1973; Jacob and Lipsky 1971; Elliott 1965; Walker 1969; Crew 1969; Fry and Winters 1970) have argued that by their very nature state public expenditures and public assistance payment levels are closely related to economic conditions. The level of benefits and especially the level of expenditures clearly are functions of how much a state can pay—that is, how economically developed it is. A selection of dependent variables which are so closely and obviously related to economic conditions may well explain why so many political scientists have found economic conditions such powerful determinants of state policies, to the exclusion of political conditions.[16]

The average payments provided various public assistance recipients have usually been interpreted as indicating how "pro-welfare" a state is. However, average payments need not bear any direct relationship to the economic liberalism of the welfare programs, since some states may allow recipients to have considerable income from work and other sources, which is not reflected in average payments. Furthermore, states may be very generous with the few recipients they do let onto the rolls, but this does not suggest a clear pro-welfare attitude either. Thus the average level of benefits may have some relationship to a state's commitment to those to whom it does extend aid, but it does not necessarily reflect the number of people to whom such assistance is made available. The extension of social rights is greatest when the largest number of people are provided with assistance and the standards of support are highest. The average payment levels therefore cannot alone measure the extension of social rights or the relationship between that extension and conditions of mass society or stratification.

In an attempt to look at noneconomic policy outputs Walker (1969) examined the diffusion of innovation in public programs among the states. His general conclusion, based on a longitudinal study of the adoption of eighty-eight different policies, is that the larger, wealthier, more industrialized states—those most likely to have high mass society status—adopt innovative policies more quickly than other states. Walker argues that most of these innovative programs have diffused as similar standards have become widely adopted throughout the nation. He also indicates that many of these innovative policies have benefited the poor.

Other writers have examined policies which primarily benefit the poor and which also can be separated analytically from the economic capacity to undertake welfare programs. Thus Crew (1969) found that socioeconomic development was positively related to the proportion of all state expenditures going to a broad category of welfare programs: health, public assistance, libraries, and veterans' service. The proportion of all expenditures used for welfare measures the relative importance a state gives to its welfare programs, which is not necessarily related to its fiscal capacity. Crew's findings are important because they indicate the extent to which economic development (or mass society status) is associated with spending disproportionately large funds on welfare programs.

Fry and Winters's (1970) study, as well as that of Baer and Jaros (1974), examines the net effects of state policies on the well-being of low-income groups. Each looked at indexes of redistribution for the lowest three income classes by comparing how much this group contributed to state revenues with how much it received in state expenditures. While their recognition that welfare benefits may barely outweigh what the poor pay in taxes is important, there are serious problems with some of the assumptions underlying their calculation of the redistribution index.[17] The findings of the two studies are nevertheless suggestive. Both found that redistribution (i.e., net benefits to the lowest 60 percent of the population) varies directly with economic development. However, a study of the net redistribution to the lowest 20 percent of the population might have been more useful since this is the group for whom redistribution is likely to be most crucial.[18]

Two other studies (Dye 1969*b*; Prothro 1972) are much more directly related to my concern with mass society. Both examined policies which are direct indications of how willing a state is to grant full citizenship status to peripheral groups. Prothro (1972) studied the extent of school desegregation in southern states and found it to be inversely related to the percentage of the population which is black. This study thus suggests that, at least in extending educational opportunities in the South, the stratification approach was still prevalent in the mid-1960s.

Dye's study (1969*b*) also examines the situation of blacks, but with regard to civil rights policies in all states. As we would expect, based on the mass society model, Dye finds that the most extensive civil rights policies exist in the wealthy, urban, industrial states with high levels of education, voter turnout, and party competition. Civil rights policies reflect the extension of civil and political rights to blacks, and thus Dye's study clearly falls into the traditions of both T. H. Marshall and Edward Shils. Dye did include some measures of the extension of social rights to blacks by examining black-white ratios in income, unemployment, education, and high-level occupations. He finds that where civil rights policies are most extensive, black-white differentials are smallest—that is, blacks are most likely to have the same incomes and occupations as whites. However, Dye treats black-white status differentials as determinants of civil rights policies rather than as results of them.

In Aid of the Poor: Welfare
Rolls in the States

Blacks are a minority in the United States, although they are overrepresented among the poor and welfare recipients. While the extent to which blacks are included as full members of the society is a crucial test of the mass society model, the primary emphasis must be on the position of the poor. The presence of large numbers of blacks in a state may result in a stratification approach to public assistance, but that is a hypothesis which must be carefully examined.

The primary emphasis should be on the poor and the programs most directly benefiting them, especially public assistance.[19] The size of public assistance rolls and the policies that determine who is eligible for such aid are the most crucial factors to consider if a distinction between the mass society and the stratification approach to public assistance is to be evaluated. Most studies that have examined this type of state policy have focused on the size of welfare rolls, usually but not always[20] adjusting for the number of people falling below the official poverty level (Sharkansky 1970a; Dawson and Gray 1971; Dye 1965, 1966, 1969c; Collins 1967; Paulson, Butler, and Pope 1969; Gold 1969).

In those studies where poverty, or the level of need, is included in a study of state welfare policies the following three hypotheses generally have been tested: (1) the greater the level of need or poverty in the state, the greater the welfare effort;[21] (2) the higher the level of wealth (ability) and urbanization and education (positive attitudes toward welfare), the greater the welfare effort; and (3) the more representative or advanced the political structure, the higher the welfare effort. Of these hypotheses, only the first has not been considered in most of the studies discussed so far. It is an obvious expectation if one is interested in welfare rolls, but not if the focus is on welfare payments. Perhaps the early and pervasive preoccupation with the level of welfare payments and the per capita welfare expenditures may account for the belated consideration of need, or demand, as a determinant of welfare policy.

The hypothesis that welfare effort is related to need has almost come in by the back door. Most of the political scientists and the few economists (Collins 1967; Paulson, Butler, and Pope 1969; Gold 1969) who have included need in their analyses have done so without second thoughts. The hypothesis is an important one, however, for it is closely related to the stratification approach. As I indicated in chapter 1, when absolute need is extensive the poor will include some people whose citizenship status is well attested. Furthermore, the hypothesis stands in direct conflict with the most widely observed finding: the greater the level of wealth and other indicators of socioeconomic development (or mass society status), the greater is the welfare effort (hypothesis number 2, above). Only rarely have political scientists and economists recognized that contradiction. Thus Dawson and Gray (1971) simply ignored the distinction and entered both their equations as a single control. Others seem to have assumed that economic development would determine welfare expenditures and payments, but not welfare rolls. The latter usually are assumed to be determined primarily by the level of need. Still others (Collins 1967) claim a direct relationship between economic development and need by arguing that the reason urbanization and per capita incomes are positively related to welfare rolls is that these factors produce social disorganization and economic maladjustment, especially for the unskilled, poorly educated, and aged. In reality, however, poverty is most concentrated in the poorest, most agricultural states.

Only Sharkansky (1971b) has emphasized the need to distinguish between the two hypotheses and to make clear which is operating in a given state. Sharkansky's focus is on the linkages between per capita income and welfare benefits. His analysis is particularly interesting because he specifies some of the assumptions political scientists have made about two approaches to the study of policy: resource-policy analysis and need-policy analysis. In resource-policy analysis citizens' demands are assumed to be equal, and only the level of resources explains the differences among the states. Need-policy analysis, on the other hand, assumes that demands vary directly with conditions of absolute need and that politicians will respond to these demands almost irrespective of resources. I disagree with both these assumptions. My assumption is that demand is neither constant nor necessarily in direct proportion to the level of absolute need. Poverty is a relative concept, subject to the larger society's evaluation of what is "necessary" for a minimum standard of living, while the poor themselves may find welfare so traumatic that they would rather go without.

Sharkansky's oversimplifications are curious, because in an earlier study (1971a) he casually mentioned that in some cases citizens may desire minimum service, not maximum as is usually assumed. This is exactly the point I emphasized in the discussion of the stratification approach. Furthermore, such desires, presumably less likely to be shared by the poor, are only one of a number of factors which act as intervening variables between rates of poverty and rates of dependency—that is, welfare rolls.

The most obvious of these intervening factors are of course the rules of eligibility which determine who among the "needy" will obtain assistance. Only one study (Gary 1973) has examined state-by-state differences in eligibility requirements. In the process Gary does confirm the earlier conclusion that benefit levels are tied much more closely to economic development than are other forms of welfare policies such as eligibility requirements. Although Gary's evidence provides only limited support for his conclusions, he suggests that both eligibility requirements and welfare payments may be more lenient in states with high economic development (measured by education, industrialization, urbanization, and per capita income). Conversely, eligibility requirements, but not welfare payments, are most restrictive in states with high levels of need (children in broken homes, low education, income inequality, and unemployment). This latter argument is in direct conflict with the hypothesis that a high level of need will encourage greater welfare effort. Gary gets around this by suggesting that eligibility requirements are restrictive in states with high levels of need because these states have only limited revenue available. However, since he does not relate restrictiveness of eligibility rules to the size of welfare rolls, it is difficult to determine exactly whether these requirements do serve the function of preventing excessive drain on state resources.

Because the nature of eligibility requirements is to prevent certain types of people from obtaining assistance, the rules must be interpreted as distinguishing between the "deserving" and the "undeserving." As such they become an indispensable tool which can be used to distinguish between mass society and stratification approaches to public assistance. Their relationships to poverty, mass society status, welfare rolls, and the presence of suspect groups then become crucial for understanding public assistance in the United States.

In some sense eligibility requirements, along with other policies, may be assumed to reflect the political climate or public opinion in a state. This latter condition then may also operate as an intervening factor between rates of poverty and rates of dependency. Albin and Stein (1971) thus have pointed to what they call the minimal sensitivity of the states to the real distribution of needs, the political unpopularity of welfare expenditures, and the arbitrariness and harshness often employed in administering the welfare programs. Bell (1965) arrived at a similar conclusion in her study of how the states have administered the suitable home clause in the AFDC program. The Piven and Cloward (1971) analysis is also useful here because it points to some of the ways in which welfare policies may reflect political beliefs. Their analysis also indicates that the size of public assistance rolls may influence views about the poor and attitudes toward poverty and dependency.

Very little, if any, systematic work has been done on how such attitudes vary between the states. Nor do we know much about how populations of different states view public policy matters,[22] have a certain attachment and loyalty to the state, are politically socialized, or participate in wide areas of political life. We do know the extent to which they tend to vote in political elections, but not to what extent they contribute time and money to political issues or to what extent they have strong feelings of civic obligation (Patterson 1968).[23]

All these state variations in popular attitudes and activities undoubtedly influence both welfare policies and the realization of these policies in welfare rolls. Nie, Powell, and Prewitt (1969) have argued in an international comparison that such forms of citizen involvement are highly related to economic development. Similar points have been made by Almond and Verba (1965), Benjamin, Blue, and Coleman (1971), Heffernan (1969), Inkeles (1969), and Olsen (1968). Such arguments go well beyond the notion that citizen participation is a reflection of party competition or malapportionment. All these authors point to the significance of economic development in a somewhat different light, emphasizing especially the relationship between economic development (i.e., the movement toward mass society), the capacity of the government to undertake public policies, and the definition and entailment of citizenship.

None of the explanations provided by the studies of state welfare policies adequately explain the facts of the "welfare crisis" by themselves. They remain a series of discontinuous studies, composed of somewhat discrete propositions. Furthermore, even these propositions may be valid only for a particular time period, as is suggested by the works of Hofferbert (1968) and Morgan and Lyons (1975). My own effort has been to move toward an explanation of the halting movement toward expanding social rights through welfare, the general movement toward mass society, and the crisis in understanding the growing welfare rolls in this society.

In any event, it is not sufficient to blame the recent expansion in welfare on the quest for votes, as most political scientists and Piven and Cloward (1971) seem to have done. Nor can the "crisis" be adequately explained by increased economic capacity to undertake welfare programs, more professional or efficient administrative procedures, or the more sociological, but not necessarily more valid, arguments[24] about diminishing work incentives, breakdown of family life (caused by a culture of poverty, the economic structure, or the system of welfare itself), migration of the poor to states with lenient eligibility requirements, more lenient administration of welfare programs (for whatever reason), or increased legitimacy of welfare.

Each of these "explanations" has been supported by different studies, and most of these processes may in fact have been in operation in recent years. However, we need to place them in a more integrated and comprehensive perspective. The studies themselves are important pieces of data: more or less successful attempts at coming to grips with a changing society. In the process, some writers, especially the political scientists, have pointed to some of the factors I consider crucial in understanding the "welfare crisis," especially the movement toward mass society and the limitations of that movement.

Study Design

This study will attempt to establish not only whether and how the various states respond to conditions of need among their populations, but also how that pattern may have changed over time. It is especially important to discover whether the United States has moved in the direction of mass society, as I have hypothesized, by extending public assistance to broader categories of eligible populations.

Some political scientists have approached the problems of developing a more complex explanation of state public policies by suggesting that certain statistical techniques are more appropriate for the study of state politics than the partial regression analysis[25] used in the earliest studies. While some of these suggestions are probably misleading[26] and of limited importance,[27] others have been more relevant to the current problem of assessing the prevalence of mass society and stratification approaches to public assistance. The argument that only certain limited conditions are crucial in determining a given state policy (Cnudde and McCrone 1969) is important because it suggests that a particular factor related to one policy issue may not have much theoretical or factual relationship to other policies. Thus we would not necessarily expect the number of high-school graduates in a state to be determined by exactly the same factors as the level of old-age assistance benefits. Nor would we expect the number of unemployed in a state to be as important in determining expenditures for aid to the blind as in determining unemployment issurance payments. Those authors who have been more discriminating in their use of variables have therefore been able to develop more refined hypotheses as to why a particular state condition should be related to a given state policy. Their methodology is therefore especially relevant to this study, since I want to examine which of two different approaches is the prevalent one without assuming that both must operate.

The design of this study must include, then, both a cross-sectional analysis allowing us to determine the type of approaches used by the states, and a time-series analysis to examine how this pattern changes over time. To fulfill the first of these requirements, I have selected stepwise regression analysis[28] to determine the consequences of both the stratification and mass society approaches at two different points in time. This allows us not only to examine the pattern of approaches in either year, but to compare the two patterns for these two years and thus detect changes in the set of factors that determine these policy outcomes. Several other procedures will be used to evaluate these changes over time.

For practical and theoretical considerations I chose to do my analysis for the years 1960 and 1970. It was important to select years for which census data was available, since much of the information I wanted to consider was available on a statewide basis only in the census years. Second, I found it difficult to get fully adequate data for 1950, especially data on state welfare policies. I have therefore restricted myself to material from 1960 and 1970.

There are also theoretical reasons for choosing this particular period for analysis. It was not until the 1960s that the "welfare crisis" really bloomed and attracted the attention of the general public as well as of politicians, administrators, and social scientists. Second, the 1960s was a period of intense concern with the meaning of citizenship and clarification of the rights and duties associated with it. This concern was probably reflected in the civil rights movement of the early 1960s, but by the end of the decade it had come to include numerous other groups in addition to blacks: women, Indians, Mexican-Americans, homosexuals, draft-resisters, and welfare recipients also began to press for their rights as citizens. If the interpretation that public assistance is a way of extending social citizenship is correct, we can expect telling differences between the approaches of the states to the problem of poverty in 1960 and 1970.

AFDC Rolls and Policies

Our analysis is restricted to the AFDC program.[29] There are several reasons for this choice: AFDC is probably the program among the public assistance programs which has been the least influenced by previous expansion and growth of other public or private income maintenance programs, particularly the OASDHI program (Social

Security), at least since 1950 when survivors became eligible for Social Security benefits. Second, in contrast to the programs for the old, blind, and disabled, whose recipients are almost all involuntarily out of the labor market and unlikely to draw social criticism, AFDC includes a number of people who are often thought of as being either employable (especially fathers) or responsible for their own predicaments (unwed mothers).[30] It is the AFDC program which is most apt to juxtapose mass society and stratification approaches to the question of public support. Partly for these reasons AFDC has been the most controversial of all public assistance programs[31] and AFDC has been especially the subject of many scandals and investigations (Steiner 1966), particularly in the 1960s.

AFDC has also been the fastest-growing program, especially in the 1960s,[32] and this has been another source of public consternation. Knowing that incomes have been rising and that Americans in general are better off than residents of most other nations, it is not unreasonable that many people have come to believe that fraud and laziness are the major explanations for the rising welfare rolls.

Finally, by 1970 the AFDC program accounted for about 70 percent of all public assistance recipients, compared with 43 percent in 1960 and 37 percent in 1950. It is thus now both the largest and the fastest-growing of all the public assistance programs, which alone marks it as a worthy subject for analysis.

In this study we were also able to look directly at the size of AFDC rolls and their relationship to the restrictiveness of AFDC policies. This information is in the files of HEW, and some of it has not been previously available, but a fortunate opportunity to consider each of the eligibility requirements was provided by personnel in the United States Department of Health, Education, and Welfare. The material consists of records of communications between the Assistance Payments Administration of HEW and the various states and includes all changes in eligibility standards since about 1960.[33]

The size of AFDC rolls has been measured by the average monthly percentage of families in the state who received some form of AFDC benefits in 1960 and 1970,[34] rather than by the percentage of children receiving AFDC, since the latter variable is likely to be highly correlated with family size. The number of individual recipients could only bias the results in a state-by-state comparison, since family size is an important factor in determining need and should be used as an independent variable.

Since the stratification approach suggests that high incidence of economic dependency should be associated with high public assistance rolls and restrictive eligibility requirements, information was collected on the incidence of various forms of poverty or situations of dependency: low income, unemployment,[35] large family size, broken homes. All of these factors are likely to be associated with people in need—that is, potential welfare recipients.

The mass society perspective suggests that factors other than income and economic dependency are important in explaining the relative size of welfare rolls and restrictiveness of welfare policies. Shils (1975), for example, points to level of education and size of occupational elites as the important factors in determining the size of the "center" or, in my conceptualization, the degree to which the state is a mass society. The extension of political citizenship is most directly measured by the percentage of the population of voting age who vote in elections. In addition to these particular variables I included the more standard measures of economic development: degree of urbanization and industrialization. But the trend towards mass society is not a uniform trajectory without obstacles, especially when we consider the cultural fragmentation of the United States. For this reason I have considered the threat posed by cultural fragmentation, or the extent to which there are groups in the state who have been viewed with suspicion and the fear that they would misuse the rights of social citizenship.

The extent to which the state governments themselves have high "incomes," as distinct from the incomes of their residents, was also thought to be an important consideration, particularly for determining how much the state is able to pay welfare recipients. Consequently, information on state finances was collected and the per capita revenue and per capita taxes calculated for each state. I have listed all the independent variables included in this study in table 1. These variables will be more fully discussed in chapter 4.

This is a very long list of variables. Part of the methodology of this study involves examining the way each of these variables enters the prediction equations of the various dependent variables. This will allow us to construct a more complex model of determinants than has usually been the case. My intent, then, is not to say that every one of the independent variables is related separately and directly to

Table 1   **Independent Variables**

Category   Independent Variables, 1960 and 1970

Stratification
   Percentage of families with incomes below SSA poverty level
**Percentage of families with incomes more than 25% below SSA poverty
   level
 *Percentage of males aged 14 and over who did not work full year, 1959
**Percentage of males aged 16 and over who did not work full year, 1969
 *Percentage of females aged 14 and over who did not work full year, 1959
**Percentage of females aged 16 and over who did not work full year, 1969
 *Percentage of females aged 14 and over who worked only part year, 1959
**Percentage of females aged 16 and over who worked only part year, 1969
 *Percentage of females aged 14 and over who did not work at all, 1959
**Percentage of females aged 16 and over who did not work at all, 1969
   Nonworker-worker ratio
   Percentage of all families which are not husband-wife families

Mass society
   Median level of education for population aged 25 and over
   Percentage of population aged 25 and over who finished at least high
      school
   Percentage of all employed working in upper white-collar occupations
   Index of urbanization
   Industrial index for males with earnings
   Industrial index for females with earnings
 *Percentage of population of voting age who voted in presidential election
**Percentage of population of voting age who voted in U.S. congressional
      election
   Percentage of all employed working in nonfarm occupations

Threat
   Percentage of population which is black
   Percentage of population which is nonwhite
   Percentage of native population born in the South
 *Percentage population increase between 1950 and 1960
**Percentage population increase between 1960 and 1970
 *Percentage total in-migration between 1955 and 1960
**Percentage total in-migration between 1965 and 1970
 *Percentage nonwhite in-migration between 1955 and 1960
**Percentage nonwhite in-migration between 1965 and 1970
 *Percentage total out-migration between 1955 and 1960
**Percentage total out-migration between 1965 and 1970
 *Percentage nonwhite out-migration between 1955 and 1960
**Percentage nonwhite out-migration between 1965 and 1970
 *Percentage total net migration beween 1955 and 1960
**Percentage total net migration between 1965 and 1970
 *Percentage nonwhite net migration between 1955 and 1960
**Percentage nonwhite net migration between 1965 and 1970

Table 1 (continued)

Fiscal capacity
  Per capita state revenue
  Per capita state taxes

Note	All variables not used in both 1960 and 1970 analyses are so indicated. See chapter 4 for more detailed descriptions.
*	Variables used only in 1960 analysis.
**	Variables used only in 1970 analysis.

welfare rolls or policies. Indeed, this sort of approach is exactly what has led to the welfare crisis: an incapacity to explain, justify, or administer the growth in welfare rolls except by an indiscriminate piling up of assertions. I hope to simplify the explanations, to reduce the number of factors under consideration and to order others into a more indirect relation to welfare rolls. To do this we also need to consider most of those variables which have been mentioned by investigators, or for that matter, by an angry and confused public.

Conclusion

The techniques of stepwise regression analysis will allow us to select the mix of variables from the list of independent variables in table 1 which best predicts AFDC rolls and policies in 1960 and 1970. There are three questions which this study design will allow us to examine and, I hope, to answer. First, we will be able to evaluate the extent to which states employ the stratification or mass society approaches to welfare. Second, we will be able to determine whether their approaches have changed over time, or at least during the 1960s. Third, by looking at and comparing the set of factors which determines AFDC eligibility policies and the set which determines AFDC rolls we will be able to say something about how the eligibility requirements may or may not determine the size of welfare rolls. This last question is one I have not previously stressed, but it involves a process which is basic to the crisis of explanation surrounding the rising welfare rolls. If neither liberal nor repressive policies have worked to relieve the gross problems of need, then an alternative explanation is needed—one other than that provided by the stereotypic version of Moynihan or those of Piven and Cloward.

Symbols of
Deservedness

Eligibility
Requirements in
the States

3

The varying responses of the separate states to conditions of economic need should be most directly observable in their welfare policies. The restrictiveness or leniency of the formal eligibility requirements is important because, at the very least, they are the legal conditions under which aid is granted. As we shall find, however, they are also the symbolic indicators of how public assistance programs and recipients are viewed collectively in the various states. The requirements reveal whether the states are concerned with limiting their programs to those most desperately in need or use their public assistance programs to respond to broad social needs. Even if they are not enforced, the eligibility requirements are often seen by the public as effective tools by which legislators and public assistance officials can control the volume and characteristics of welfare recipients and separate those judged deserving of public assistance from those who are not. We will examine, therefore, the symbolic nature of the eligibility requirements as well as the extent to which these formal aspects of state welfare policies actually directly control the relative size of welfare rolls.[1]

The Federal Framework

The AFDC program was established as Title IV of the Social Security Act of 1935. That act included administrative and statutory requirements which the states had to fulfill in order to be eligible for federal matching funds in the public assistance programs of OAA, AB and ADC. Two of the most important requirements were (1) participation had to be on a statewide basis, and (2) the operation of any of the specific programs had to be administered by a single state agency.[2]

The result of these two requirements has been to create and enforce uniform legislative standards of eligibility and payment within each state. The states have considerable latitude in the welfare policies they can implement, but once the policies have been set the federal statutes leave little room for formal variation among sub-state jurisdictions. It is primarily for this reason that the state is the most appropriate unit of analysis if one is to find the systematic determinants of the variation in welfare rolls in the United States. Previous research has failed to reveal much systematic or substantial variation in welfare policies for smaller units of analysis such as municipalities or regions. In several studies of welfare administration within one state, little variation has been found among different cities (Derthick 1968) or agencies (Handler and Hollingsworth 1971). Handler and Hollingsworth (1971, p. 11) argue that the uniformity observed in the operation of different agencies,[3] in spite of considerable differences in agency size and location, is a reflection of the similar problems encountered by the different agencies. Other studies looking at welfare policies in several municipalities over time also have found few systematic differences (Hodge and Zald 1963).

The uniformity of formal (and possibly informal) welfare policies within states is the more significant since uniform state standards were not the most frequent method of organizing and delivering state public assistance in the decades before the enactment of the Social Security Act in 1935. In those relatively few states where state public assistance programs existed before 1935, some counties had no provisions at all for distributing public aid, while there were wide variations in restrictions and payments among the remaining counties within any given state.[4] Previous differences between county and municipal programs for public welfare thus diminished as each state adopted the provisions of the Social Security Act. The federal government, then, has been instrumental in creating state-wide bureaucratic systems of welfare administration designed to treat all potential recipients alike wherever they live in the state (Derthick 1970, pp. 193–218).[5] Undoubtedly this conclusion is also supported by the increasing centralization of state authority and erosion of local autonomy after the 1930s reported by Stephens (1974).

Federal Incentives for the States

The states have been surprisingly willing to accede to federal directives, primarily because of economic incentives. The formula for calculating the federal share in financing public assistance programs is designed to encourage the participation of states in each program and to extend uniform coverage to as large a proportion of the needy population as possible. Since 1965 there have been two alternative formulas for calculating the federal share of money payments to AFDC recipients: the two-step formula[6] and the alternate formula.[7] The alternate formula sets no maximum for the federal share, as does the two-step formula, and is therefore potentially more generous toward the states. However, the alternate formula may be used only if the state operates medical assistance programs under Title XIX of the Social Security Act ("Medicaid") and is an incentive by which the federal government encourages the states to participate in the medical assistance programs. In July 1971 Arizona and Alaska were the only two states that had not initiated a program under Title XIX (U.S. Social and Rehabilitation Service 1972, p. 4); all other states were eligible to use the alternate formula. However, only twenty-nine states made use of it, mainly those with the highest level of payments.

The federal government also pays 50 percent of all administrative costs of the AFDC program (President's Commission on Income Maintenance Programs 1970, pp. 273–74). Since the 1962, and especially the 1972 amendments to the Social Security Act, the federal government has also paid 75 percent of the costs of providing "social services" to welfare recipients (Derthick 1975, pp. 7–14). The result has been that more states have elected to participate in a wider range of federally controlled and supported programs. There seems, in fact, to have been a virtual run on joining the ADC program and other federally supported public assistance programs as soon as they were established.[8] Thus thirty-nine states plus Washington, D.C., had adopted the ADC program by March 1938, or within three years of its establishment (Ernst 1938).[9] In the late 1960s and early 1970s several states developed considerable ingenuity in redefining their existing services so they could be included under the 75-percent matching grant for social services, rather than the 50-percent matching grant for administrative costs (Derthick 1975, pp. 29–34).

One indication of the extent to which states have been willing to transfer their welfare costs to the federal government is that the state and local government share in public assistance expenditures dropped from 55.8 percent of the total public assistance expenditures in 1950 to 39.9 percent in 1971.[10] Of the combined state and local public welfare expenditures, local jurisdictions pay a relatively small percentage: 22.9 percent in 1950 and 30.2 percent in 1969.[11] In several states local jurisdictions contribute nothing to public assistance, especially to the federally supported programs.[12]

All these monetary incentives encourage states to participate in the federally supported public assistance programs and to establish relatively uniform standards within their boundaries. Fiscal considerations are clearly the important factor in a state's decision to join a program or extend an existing program to include new recipient groups.[13] This pattern of fiscal concern is also evident in cases where extending public assistance would entail new or greater financial outlays for the state. Thus Alaska indicated at one point that it had no interest in adopting the Unemployed Parent part of the AFDC program, since this would only pick up a large proportion of the present General Assistance recipients of the Bureau of Indian Affairs, which is financed by the federal government. Adopting the program would thus transfer part of the cost of supporting these recipients from the federal government to the state of Alaska (SPCU Reports). Similarly, Idaho indicated no interest in the Unemployed Parent program because it feared that such a program "would make substantial increases in the number of eligibles" (SPCU Reports). The same officials from Idaho argued that adopting AFDC-U would only lead to a decrease in General Assistance; but since these were county programs, the state was not interested in accepting the new financial responsibility. Similar arguments were used by New Jersey until 1969 when that state finally adopted the Unemployed Parent program (SPCU Reports). In general, then, the states have been quite mercenary in selecting the programs they are willing to superintend, but the federal government has been equally generous in giving the states incentives for participating, so long as they do so within the federal guidelines.

The Character of Eligibility Requirements

The thrust of federal legislation thus has been to reduce variations within the states. However, there is room for substantial variation in welfare policies among the states and, in fact, the states vary greatly in the extent to which they limit the size of their potential recipient populations (Derthick 1968). There are two sources of this type of variation in welfare policies among the states: (1) some states have eligibility requirements that other states do not have (e.g., some states require that the home must be suitable, while other states do not), and (2) those states which have the same types of eligibility requirements, for example, limitations on real property, may differ in the restrictiveness of these requirements (e.g., some states allow recipients to own real property valued at no more than $500, while in other states recipients may own real property valued at up to $1,000).

The role of the federal government in public assistance consists mainly in establishing the statutory requirements for public assistance programs and in seeing that the states fulfill these requirements. Two of the most important federal requirements have already been discussed: statewide participation and a single state agency. The federal directions about state eligibility requirements, however, are of more direct importance to potential recipient groups. Most of those standards of eligibility, for which the federal government has set limits of maximum and minimum restrictiveness within which states may vary, deal with demographic characteristics of the recipients, such as age, residency, and family status. The areas where states are left virtually free to impose eligibility requirements, and over which the federal government has little or no control, concern social and economic characteristics of recipients. Over the years, however, federal administrative rulings and Supreme Court decisions have encroached on even these areas of state control.

The direct influence of federal legislation is clearest in the demographic eligibility requirements. Thus the federal government has set an upper age limit for children receiving aid under AFDC. States may have a higher age limit, but no federal matching grants are available for children who exceed the federal age limit. This has effectively limited the upper age limit of eligibility for AFDC to federal standards, although there are one or two exceptions. Over the years the federal upper limit has become more liberal. In 1939, children aged sixteen and seventeen became eligible for federal matching funds (FFP) if they were attending school. The 1956 amendment dropped the school requirement, and in 1964 children aged eighteen, nineteen, and twenty could also be included in the AFDC program with federal financial participation (FFP) if they were attending high school or a community college or participated in vocational training programs. The 1965 amendment to the Social Security Act expanded the category of educational institutions so that children under the age of twenty-one could attend four-year colleges and universities while receiving AFDC with FFP.

Since 1971[14] all states which participate in the AFDC program must provide aid to all children less than eighteen years of age. But within the federal maximum the upper age limit and school requirements have been left largely to the individual states. There is considerable variation among the states within the federal limitations. Texas, for example, had an age limit of fourteen until 1963, when it was raised to sixteen (and to twenty-one by 1967), and Wisconsin provided funds to incapacitated children under twenty-one years up to 1950. Until 1965 Wisconsin did this for children aged eighteen to twenty without federal matching funds.

At the other end of the age scale, even a fetus may be defined as eligible for AFDC with FFP, even if the mother has no other children who receive AFDC, provided the fetus or its mother fulfills all other eligibility requirements. Most states, however, have not granted AFDC to mothers on behalf of their unborn children, although there has been an increasing tendency to do so.[15]

Under the original Social Security Act states were allowed to use durational residency requirements as conditions of eligibility for public assistance. For AFDC the maximum length of residence before being eligible for assistance was one year.[16] The Supreme Court decision in *Shapiro* v. *Thompson*, 1969, however, ruled that such requirements were unconstitutional interferences with interstate travel.[17] In 1950, thirty-seven of forty-eight states (77 percent) had a one-year residency requirement in the AFDC program; in 1959 that proportion had risen to 86 percent, and one state (Kentucky) had only a six-month residency requirement. In 1969, the percentage of states with a one-year residency requirement had fallen back to 78 percent. Thus certain migrant population groups were excluded from obtaining welfare in the states that had residency requirements, while similar population groups could obtain aid in the rest of the states.

Some of the most problematic of all eligibility requirements have been those that relate to family status. AFDC is aid to "dependent children." According to federal definitions, the term "dependent child" means a child who has been deprived of parental support or care by reason of death, continued absence from the home, physical or mental incapacity, or unemployment (since 1961) of a parent. All states must include in their definition of dependent children those children whose parent(s) are dead, absent, or incapacitated. Specific definitions of what constitutes continued absence and disability, however, have been left for the states to decide. Some states, but not all, may define a child as dependent only when his parents are absent or incapacitated for a certain length of time. Presumably this is to discourage people from deliberately harming themselves or their families in order to receive aid.

There are two types of such durational requirements. First, the state may impose a waiting period. This means that there must be a certain interval between the time when a particular dependency situation occurs and the time when an application for aid may be filed (for example, a child must have been deserted by his father at least three months before he becomes eligible for assistance). Second, the state may require that dependency must be expected to be of a certain duration: for example, the parent's incapacity must be expected to last for at least three months in order for a child to be defined as dependent. In this case, aid is immediately available; there is no waiting period.

Those states which make use of waiting periods most frequently impose them in cases where dependency occurs because a parent's continued absence from the home affects marital status; that is, desertion, abandonment, and separation. Requirements about expected duration are most often used to define incapacity or absence from the home owing to the imprisonment of a parent. It should be emphasized that most states have no durational requirements of any kind, although a trend toward more restrictive policies seems to have begun around 1960.

Beginning in 1961, further variation between the states became possible in the definition of dependency, since by federal standards a child also could be defined as deprived of parental support if his parent(s) (after 1967 only his father) was defined as being "unemployed." This is an optional provision, and only about half the states have at any point in time included this particular definition of deprivation of parental support. The Unemployed-Parent segment of AFDC was part of the 1961 Social Security Amendment, and the original federal outer limit on the definition of unemployment was "working less than full time," which essentially left the matter for the states to decide. In 1969, FFP was restricted to fathers working less than thirty-five hours a week, in one of the few instances where federal legislation became more restrictive. In 1971 the definition of unemployment for which FFP was available was further limited in a revision of administrative interpretations by the Secretary of HEW. This time a father was defined as unemployed only if he worked fewer than one hundred hours per month (U.S. Social and Rehabilitation Service 1971g). The limitation could be exceeded in individual cases if the work was intermittent and short-term. The specific definition of who is to be considered unemployed has been left to the states, as long as they did not exceed these federal upper limits, but this ruling still left considerable room for differences in definitions.[18]

Since AFDC is given to children who are "deprived of parental support," the definition of "parent" can also become a crucial issue, and this has been an especially controversial area in the AFDC program. The concept of who is a parent for purposes of AFDC eligibility has been left largely to the states and varies considerably from state to state. For several years children in some states, despite continual negotiations on this issue between states and the federal agency, were not considered deprived of parental support if there was any male in or around the house. Even if such a male had only the most casual relationship with the children or their mother, he was considered a "substitute parent."[19] The issue of whether there is a "substitute parent" or "man-in-the-house" has implications for whether the child is defined as deprived because of a parent's continued absence from the home. In some states only established relationships are considered, such as common-law marriages and second marriages. In these cases the man may not be legally responsible for the children, but for purposes of AFDC he is considered a substitute parent and in practice has to be dead, absent, or incapacitated to make the children eligible for AFDC.[20] The efforts of the federal agency in this respect have been to require the states to grant aid to a family if the substitute parent is incapacitated, just as they are required to do if the natural parent is incapacitated but present in the home. If the state has an unemployed father's program, the definition of unemployment must also extend to substitute fathers. In other words, the federal agency by and large accepted the states' definition of substitute fathers for a number of years, but it then forced the states to treat these "fathers" as they would natural fathers.

This situation continued until the 1968 Supreme Court ruling in *King* v. *Smith*, which required the states to grant aid to a child regardless of the status of the substitute father, if the income of the family was insufficient. However, a number of states had already abolished or severely modified their substitute parent provisions before the Supreme Court ruling took effect. The *King* v. *Smith* ruling prohibited the states from assuming that the income of such substitute fathers (including stepfathers) was available for the support of the child. This was interpreted to mean that the eligibility of a child could be conditioned by the income of a stepfather only if the state had a general law which specified that the legal responsibilities for stepchildren of *all* stepfathers in that state were the same as those of natural or adoptive fathers. Also, night raids in which welfare agencies attempted to discover the presence of a man in the house, particularly as undertaken in Washington, D.C., were declared an unconstitutional invasion of recipients' privacy.

Most of the eligibility requirements discussed so far are delimited by federal standards, although they leave great room for state interpretation and application. A second major group of eligibility requirements is characterized by few federal limitations other than that these requirements must be applied on a uniform basis to all potential recipients within each state. Two types of eligibility requirements fall in this category: those that concern the social and those that concern the economic characteristics of potential recipients. Since there are very few federal limitations for most of these requirements, the potential variation is greater than for the demographic eligibility requirements discussed above.

About twenty states had "suitable home" clauses in 1970 (twenty-two states in 1950 and twenty-four in 1960). The suitability of a home is an ill-defined condition and as such is open to widely varying interpretations. There is little information on how the concept of unsuitability is applied in the different states, but the available data suggest considerable differences. Some states, particularly the southern states, have used this requirement as a way of keeping blacks and other minority groups off welfare and as a way of punishing promiscuity and other quasi-legal unions.[21] Other states, such as Ohio, consider the home unsuitable only if the courts declare it detrimental to the child (U.S. Social and Rehabilitation Service 1971e). An important limitation on the use of the suitable home requirement, but not on its definition, was made in 1961 with the "Fleming Ruling," which says that states cannot deprive children of welfare because of the behavior of their parents. Thus states had to continue to provide AFDC payments specifically to the children in these homes or else have the children removed from their homes and provide them with benefits elsewhere, such as in foster homes. Often this put financial pressure on the state-financed foster home programs. In turn, the federal agency agreed to continue federal matching grants to children who were placed in foster homes because their own homes had been judged hazardous. However, the federal agency also ruled that in order for states to obtain federal matching funds for foster children, *all* AFDC children in the state had to receive maximum grants, that is, benefits high enough to cover 100 percent of their needs as defined by state cost standards. This was an attempt to prevent the states from shifting children to the foster care segment of the AFDC program by using the suitable home clause as a punitive measure.[22] The suitable home clause is closely related to the man-in-the-house rule or to rules concerning substitute fathers, in that both may be used to penalize a family whose members are not living up to standards of public morality. However, the latter type of rules deal with the definition of the child as being deprived of parental support, while in the case of the suitable home clause a child may be defined as deprived of parental support and fulfill all other formal rules of eligibility but still not get the aid he is entitled to because of the state's judgment on the suitability of his home.

To obtain support it is, of course, not enough for a child to be deprived of parental support and fulfill all the demographic and social requirements discussed above. The child must also be poor. In accordance with the Social Security Act each state must set a level of monthly income (the cost standard) which it considers sufficient to cover the basic needs of a family.[23] Any family that falls below this standard is eligible for public assistance in terms of income alone. Where to place this cutoff point is left totally to the determination of the state.[24]

The average income level at which a family became eligible for ADC in 1961 was $191 per month, ranging between $124 in Arkansas and $242 in Arizona (U.S. Social Security Administration 1962). By comparison, the Social Security Administration's poverty level for a nonfarm family of four headed by a female was $253 in 1961. In 1960 no state had a cost standard higher than the official poverty level, but several had cost standards that were about one-half the poverty level. In 1970 the average cost standard was at $276, while the poverty level had risen to $329. The range in 1970, however, was greater than in 1960—from $184 in North Carolina to $432 in California, or from 56 to 131 percent of the poverty level (U.S. Social and Rehabilitation Service 1971d).

As might be expected, the southern states had lower cost standards than the northern states in both 1960 and 1970. All states increased the cost standards between 1960 and 1970. However, the rate of increase during that decade varied greatly, ranging between 1.3 percent in Florida (from $220 to $223) and 111.4 percent in Pennsylvania (from $148 to $313).[25]

The states also vary considerably in the extent to which they provide public assistance recipients with what they need according to the standards of the states. There are no federal requirements about how large a proportion of the gap between a recipient's nonwelfare income and his state-determined needs the state must pay. Some states pay no benefits larger than a maximum fixed dollar amount, while others pay a certain fixed proportion of their recipients' income "gap." As a result of such limitations on welfare payments, some states provide as a maximum only about one-third of their cost standards, while others cover the complete income gap of all recipients. In general, the payment standard is the one factor the states can manipulate fairly easily. A review of month-by-month reports on changes in state welfare policies reveals that payments often are reduced as the state nears the end of the fiscal year.[26] In some cases the maximum levels of payments has actually decreased between 1960 and 1970 (Wisconsin, for example, decreased its maximum level from $226 to $217 during that decade). By lowering welfare payments the state can save money and avoid conflicts with the federal agency concerning conditions of eligibility. If the main concern of the state is to keep public assistance expenses down, providing low payments would be the simplest and least troublesome way of doing this. The fact that some states are quite willing to provide welfare recipients with fairly high payments but attempt to cut down on the number of recipients by restricting conditions of eligibility suggests that it is not just economic concerns which surface in the controversy over public assistance—particularly AFDC. It is also the problem of deciding for whom is the state willing to accept responsibility and to whom is it willing to extend a more or less decent living.

If the reader is somewhat overwhelmed by now, keep in mind that we have examined only the tip of the iceberg of state and federal welfare legislation. To get a fuller grasp of the complexity involved in determining eligibility status, consider the following additional examples of legislative developments in the AFDC program:

1. Certain types of income may be disregarded when states determine a family's financial eligibility and thus are not included as available resources to cover their financial needs. The earliest "disregard" provision concerned the conservation of income for the future identifiable needs of children—that is, savings for educational purposes. The disregarded income may be either the child's own earnings, the child's income, or family income from all sources, if the state participates in the program at all. The provision became fully effective in July of 1963, although the conservation of the child's income was possible beginning in 1957.

2. The Social Security Act Amendment of 1965 made it possible to withhold up to $5 per month of any income a family may have when determining the need of the family. This program is also voluntary and not all states participate.

3. The 1965 Social Security Act Amendment also allowed states to disregard up to $50 per month of a child's earnings, even if those earnings were not being conserved for the "future identifiable needs" of the child. This was superseded by the 1967 amendment, which made it possible for the states to disregard all the earned income of full-time students and, in addition, to exempt $30, plus one-third of

the remainder of earned income, of all other members of the assistance group. *All* states were required to exempt both these types of earned income by July 1969.[27]

4. In addition to limitations on income, states may set maximum limits on the amount of property recipients may own. In 1950, thirty-eight states had limitations on how valuable a home recipients may own. By 1970 only half that many were still considering home ownership in any way. This reduction may reflect both the realization that home ownership is an important psychological factor for the family and the fact that evaluation of the home, like evaluation of other real and personal property, is a complicated matter. Such provisions may well cost the state more to administer than they can save in denying aid to families who do not qualify for benefits,[28] especially since most AFDC families live in metropolitan areas (72.4 percent in 1969), where home ownership is less prevalent (Eppley 1970). The states that have limits on home ownership and other property[29] use widely differing standards and methods of computation.[30]

5. Some states are concerned that potential welfare recipients will attempt to circumvent property restrictions and dispose of their possessions in order to become eligible for aid. These states, therefore, have various regulations against such transactions.

6. Some states place liens, recoveries, or assignments on property owned by recipients in attempts to retrieve some of the benefits paid to recipients. These claims may be exercised when the recipient leaves the welfare rolls or dies; in the latter case, however, the state may claim the property only if the surviving spouse or dependent child is not destitute.[31]

7. Such restrictions on property and income as do exist must be seen as attempts to prevent people with assets from being parasites on state funds. A large proportion of the controversy surrounding AFDC and the other public assistance programs rests on suspicions, generally unfounded (Feagin 1972; Schiller 1973), that the poor person—or someone— is opportunistic. Similar suspicions underlie the requirements that parents and children over a certain age must register for work and accept available employment if there is "adequate" child care available. Here the suspicion is not just one of economic opportunists but also of "welfare loafers"—that is, those that are too lazy to work and thus do not share in the American cultural celebration of hard work and self-help.

As these illustrations suggest, the record of state welfare legislation is extensive and piecemeal, and it may be difficult to grasp the full intent of all the different eligibility rules in total. In their eagerness to shift the burden of welfare costs onto the federal government, the states may at times have compromised and reinterpreted their own standards to make themselves eligible for federal support. However, it should also be kept firmly in mind that the federal prerequisites for financial participation in most cases are broad and flexible and allow the states considerable leeway in interpreting their welfare mandate. In the main, however, the federal agency and some presidential administrations have attempted to expand welfare benefits to large groups of the population, while at the same time conceding to continuing strong requests for state rights and local determination. In recent years the federal courts have supported this extension of welfare by overturning some existing state regulations.

All of this points toward the need for a more comprehensive or composite measure of state welfare policies. For the response of a state to the federal guidelines may represent a more or less unified posture of either symbolic or instrumental importance—either a way of expressing collective opinions about the poor, or an instrument by which the number of those who obtain public aid or the cost of their support can be controlled.

Measure of State Restrictiveness

As the review of the various eligibility requirements illustrates, there are considerable differences, and at time similarities, in conceptions of need among the states. For this reason I have attempted to develop a summary measure of state policy toward AFDC recipients. This measure—the Total Eligibility Score, or TES—is composed entirely of formal eligibility requirements as recorded in state legislation. The TES is computed by scoring each eligibility requirement on a scale between 0 and 2, depending on how restrictive it is, and adding the scores for all eligibility requirements for each state.[32] The higher the score, the more restrictive the welfare policies.[33]

The extent to which welfare policies have become more responsive to broad social needs over time has already been illustrated by examples, but it is also evident in the decline of the TES from an average of 21 in 1950 (22 in 1960) to 13 in 1970.[34] At the same time, the lowest TES a state could possibly obtain, given federal requirements, dropped from 8 in 1950 to 0 in 1970. This indicates that the states have not uniformly moved closer to the more inclusive end of the federal requirements but have followed the overall federal changes without much change in their distribution within the federal limits. A closer examination reveals that there has been some increase in the amount of variation among the states from 1950 to 1970. In 1950 the TES ranged between 16 and 26, a difference of 10 points; in 1959, the score ranged between 14 and 31, a difference of 17 points; and in 1970 it ranged between 6 and 22, a difference of 16 points.

The above findings reveal two important points: first, there has been a continued, although not monotonic, development in federal welfare policies to allow for the extension of welfare to larger proportions of state populations. Second, federal controls of this type allow for greater potential variation between the states, and this has indeed occurred. There has been persistent, substantial, and growing variation among the states in terms of welfare policies over the last decade. In some states there have been attempts to extend welfare aspects of citizenship to large proportions of the population. Yet in other states policies have remained basically unchanged or have made benefits more exclusively available only to certain groups of the poor.

Symbolic Politics

The eligibility requirements give public and legal definitions of who may receive public assistance and who may not. These requirements, therefore, act as intermediary variables between conditions of objective needs (or demand) in a state and the resultant size and composition of the welfare population in that state. Unfortunately we do not have adequate state-by-state data on the composition of the welfare rolls.[35] We do have information on the relative number of families which receive AFDC in each state and can use this in our analysis.

As already indicated, there was considerable variation in state eligibility requirements, including variation in the TES. This suggests that there should also be at least some variation in the AFDC rolls. As we shall see, this is indeed the case. In fact, the variation in AFDC rolls is much greater than the variation in AFDC policies as measured by TES.[36]

In 1960 the percentage of families on AFDC ranged between 0.7 in New Hampshire and 4.4 in West Virginia. The mean for the forty-nine states included in this study[37] was 1.7 percent, the same as South Carolina. On the average, southern states had a higher proportion of their families on AFDC than the remainder of the nation: 2.2 percent and 1.5 percent respectively (see table 2). Regional differences, however, had diminished by 1970, when 3.1 percent of families were on AFDC in the South compared with 2.8 percent in the North. The mean for 1970 was 2.9 percent, and New Hampshire was still the state with the smallest proportion of its families on AFDC: 1.1 percent. In 1960 New York had only 1.6 percent of its families on AFDC; by 1970 it had 5.7 percent, the highest proportion of all the states. Meanwhile West Virginia, the state with the highest proportion in 1960, had increased very little: from 4.4 percent in 1960 to 4.6 percent in 1970.

In 1970 there was also considerable variation in the size of welfare rolls within the northern states. It seems useful to divide these states into two groups which may be assumed to differ in their willingness to support broader and more controversial segments of the population: one composed of those nineteen states with an Unemployed Fathers program (UF states) and one composed of the twelve states without this program (non-UF states). The pattern then becomes somewhat clearer (see table 2). In 1970 3.2 percent of all families were on AFDC in the UF states, 2.2 percent in the non-UF states. A similar pattern emerges when the same division is made among the southern states. In those with UF programs (Delaware, Maryland, Oklahoma, West Virginia), on the average 3.7 percent of the families received AFDC in 1970, compared with the remaining fourteen southern states, where 2.9 percent of the families received such assistance. Thus the major difference in AFDC rolls in 1970 was along the UF–non-UF division (3.3 percent of families on AFDC in UF states, compared with 2.5 percent in non-UF states), whereas in 1960 the major difference was between regions.

All regions, whether or not they possessed UF programs, experienced significant increases in the AFDC rolls between 1960 and 1970 (see table 2). Only two states (the Carolinas) experienced a decline in AFDC rolls during this period, but the decreases were negligible. Two other states were also virtually unchanged (West Virginia, with an increase of 1.8 percent, and Arizona, with an increase of 5.0 percent). All the remaining states experienced some increase in AFDC rolls, ranging from an increase of 12.6 percent in Alabama (from 2.7 percent in 1960 to 3.0 percent in 1970) to an increase of 267 percent in New York. These trends are perhaps unexpected, since the proportion of all families that are poor decreased an average of 41.8 percent during the same period for the forty-nine states included in this study (from 20.5 percent in 1960 to

Table 2

Average Monthly Percentage of Families Receiving AFDC, 1960 and 1970, by Region and Unemployed Father Status

| | Census Region | | |
	Total U.S.	South	Non-South
1960			
Total U.S.	1.7	2.2	1.5
UF states	1.7	2.5	1.5
Non-UF states	1.8	2.2	1.4
1970			
Total U.S.	2.9	3.1	2.8
UF states	3.3	3.7	3.2
Non-UF states	2.5	2.9	2.2
Percentage increase 1960–70			
Total U.S.	79.6	51.5	93.2
UF states	112.3	84.2	118.1
Non-UF states	50.5	40.5	59.0

Sources   *Social Security Bulletin* 1960, 1961, 1970, 1971; U.S. Bureau of the Census 1961–63, 1971–73.

Note   The division of states into UF and non-UF categories in both 1960 and 1970 is based on whether the state had an Unemployed Father program in 1970. The AFDC-U program did not become eligible for federal matching funds (FFP) until 1961.

11.7 percent in 1970). Evidently the decrease in poverty has not resulted in a decrease in dependency. It is unlikely that the decrease in poverty has been obtained only by an increase in dependency— that is, that people no longer are poor because they get public assistance. As was indicated earlier, most cost standards are substantially lower than the poverty level, as are the maximum levels of payment.

An examination of table 2 further reveals that those states which had UF programs in 1970 experienced the highest growth in AFDC rolls between 1960 and 1970. This pattern is particularly suggestive, since the states which had Unemployed Fathers programs are among the most industrialized and are most likely to be extending welfare programs on the basis of social needs more broadly conceived than objective poverty alone.

Logically, eligibility requirements should be intermediary variables between AFDC rolls and conditions of economic dependency. Therefore, they should be the most direct determinants of AFDC rolls. We would expect to find that those states which have restrictive eligibility requirements have fewer of their poor families receiving AFDC. Conversely, states with lenient or inclusive requirements would be expected to have relatively more families on AFDC.

An examination of the zero-order correlations between AFDC rolls and AFDC policies, however, reveals that such a pattern does not seem to exist. The most inclusive measure of welfare policy, the TES, seems to be almost entirely independent of AFDC rolls, particularly in 1970 $(r = .08)$.[38] Furthermore, whatever relationship does exist in 1960 is in the opposite direction from what we would expect: the more restrictive the eligibility requirements in a state, the more families received AFDC benefits $(r = .15)$.

The same pattern holds even more strongly when we look at the relationship between AFDC rolls and cost standards and maximum payments[39] in the states: the lower the cost standard and maximum level of benefit in a state, the more families receive AFDC.[40] This suggests that for 1960, at least, AFDC eligibility requirements were singularly ineffective in controlling the size of AFDC rolls. By 1970, however, all the measures of AFDC policies seem to be independent of AFDC rolls: none of the correlation coefficients between AFDC rolls and each of the three measures of welfare policies exceed an absolute value of $r = .08$.

We must conclude, then, that eligibility requirements do not have much direct influence on the size of AFDC rolls in 1960 or 1970. At best, the relationship between these two state welfare policy "outcomes" is very complex, and AFDC rolls may be determined more directly by factors other than the restrictiveness of eligibility requirements. The major importance of public assistance policies consequently may lie not so much in being able to control the size of welfare rolls (although the public seems to believe that the requirements can do this) as in reflecting public concerns about poverty and dependency in the states. As a result, state legislation on public welfare is largely a symbolic crusade (Gusfield 1963)—episodic, isolated occasions on which state legislators stand up to be counted as for "the people" and against "welfare cheaters" or for "the deserving poor" (Halper 1973), as the case may be.

The range of welfare policies for which federal funds are available has enabled state legislators to encourage the expansion of federal welfare transfers to their states, while at the same time giving vocal and written form to the declaration for home rule and fiscal caution. The consequence then, is a system of welfare legislation which is susceptible to a variety of interpretations. Considering the complexity of welfare policies, and with the advantages of hindsight, one should perhaps not have expected much relationship between legislation and welfare rolls. It is not that state welfare policies are necessarily irrelevant in determining the size of welfare rolls, but the actions of state legislators in setting these policies may be primarily symbolic statements reflecting the deeper forces of stratification and mass society.

Personal Need or State Capacity?

Approaches to Poverty

4

Stratification and Mass
Society Approaches

The results presented so far indicate that welfare policies are neither very good nor very direct predictors of the size of welfare rolls. We must look instead to other factors to explain the variation in AFDC rolls between 1960 and 1970. Several possibilities have been suggested in previous studies, although the basic ways in which states may respond to conditions of economic need seem to group themselves into two alternatives or approaches.

According to the stratification approach, welfare rolls should vary directly with economic need, since states will grant aid primarily to those most desperately poor. The more people there are in need in each state, the more families will receive AFDC benefits. The mass society approach, on the other hand, argues that poverty and need are relative conditions and that states with high mass society status will have high welfare rolls because economic needs are more broadly defined and are considered a part of citizenship. The two approaches are not always mutually exclusive, but they tend to separate themselves out in popular thought and practical action.

A number of variables were selected in chapter 2 to measure, tap, or weigh each of these approaches. In addition, measures of the fiscal capacity of the state and of the extent to which threatening groups are present in a state have also been included. Since each of these may be a parameter within which the mass society and stratification approach operates, the presence of such groups and state fiscal restraints may limit the extent to which broader conceptions of social needs can develop and persist. The threat variables and those measuring fiscal capacity, then, limit the extent to which either the mass society or the stratification approach may occur in the states. I will briefly describe each of the independent variables and further justify their inclusion and their relationship to the respective approaches: stratification and mass society.

Absolute Notions of Need:
Stratification Variables

Among the stratification variables, the proportion of families who are poor should be most clearly related to welfare rolls if poverty alone is the determinant condition. The more extensive poverty is in a state, the greater is the pressure upon welfare rolls. I have included in my analysis the percentage of families which fell below the Social

Security Administration's official poverty level[1] in 1960 and 1970.[2] For 1970, a more extreme measure of poverty was also available and has been incorporated into the 1970 analysis, since this measure may be a "truer" measure of what is considered abject or "deserving" dependency.[3]

The definition of poverty used here, of course, is not without serious shortcomings. An amount of income thought "sufficient" at one point in time may be thought insufficient at a later point, even adjusted for price changes. This tendency, in fact, is a central characteristic of the movement toward mass society. However, the SSA's low-income level is the official poverty level and seems appropriate for use in a study of public assistance programs. After all, government programs designed to deal with poverty and need should be judged against their stated objectives.

The states vary in the extent to which their levels of income eligibility (the cost standard) fall below the official SSA poverty level, and they also vary in the extent to which welfare payments improve the economic situation of their recipients. To get a more complete picture of the amount of pressure on AFDC rolls, it is necessary, then, to include additional factors that measure conditions which have periodic effects upon income and needs. The measure of unemployment used in this study takes seasonal employment and absence from the labor force into account by considering the proportion of all males or females of working age[4] who did not work the full year during 1959 and 1969 respectively. This measure thus indicates the proportion of persons of working age who either did not work at all or worked for only part of the year; that is, one to forty-nine weeks (hereafter referred to as the underemployment rate).[5] This variable is fairly closely related to conventional measures of unemployment: not working but seeking employment. Male underemployment was felt to be a particularly important variable, since it is highly correlated with economic dependency (see table 3) and has been found to be a better indicator of the extent of poverty in a state than the usual index of unemployment (Eckstein 1966, p. 207). Thus, the larger the underemployment rate, the greater the level of need in a state.

I have also included a measure of the extent to which females are excluded from the labor force; namely, the percentage of women of working age who were not employed at all during 1959 and 1969. This particular variable was thought to be more sensitive to female working experience, since females often work only part time or part

Table 3   **Incidence of Poverty by Sex and by Selected Employment Status of Household Heads, 1959 and 1969**

| | Percentage below Low-Income Level | | | |
| | 1959 | | 1969 | |
Employment Status	Males	Females	Males	Females
Worked 50–52 weeks	10.0	20.8	3.4	10.7
Worked 50–52 weeks, full time	9.1	16.6	3.0	7.7
Worked 1–49 weeks	24.0	50.9	11.9	41.8
Did not work	39.8	56.0	23.3	46.9
Unemployed	31.8	a	11.7	46.8

Source   Bureau of the Census 1971.
a   Not available.

of the year. Female employment usually is an important component of aggregate family income or may represent another form of periodic change in family income. However, most crucial is the extent to which income from public assistance may be seen as a substitute for or supplement to employment income. Absence of employment opportunities for women, then, may be particularly important in determining the pressure on AFDC rolls, since that program benefits mainly women and their children.[6]

Although family size is closely related to low income and thus to pressure on AFDC rolls,[7] it is not family size as such, but the number of people who must be supported by each worker, which is important. The family that has two earners is less likely to be poor than a family of the same size with only one earner, especially if the family with only one earner is headed by a female. The ratio of nonworkers to workers in the state was selected as the most appropriate measure here because it reflects conditions of economic need determined by the number of dependents in a state who must be supported by each worker in the state. The greater the non-worker-worker ratio, that is, the more dependents each worker must support, the more likely that state is to have families in need of outside support, all other factors being equal.

All the variables described here attempt to tap an underlying dimension of poverty or economic dependency in the state and, from a theoretical point of view, should exert a recipient-pressure on the

AFDC rolls. However, the extent of need is also closely related to family dissolution. By administrative definition the incidence of family dissolution is crucial in determining AFDC rolls. The extent to which children are deprived of parental support because one or both parents are absent from the home has been the administrative charge and a central mission of the AFDC program. In practice this has meant that one or both parents must be absent, unemployed, or incapacitated in order for a family to obtain aid. In 1969, 81 percent of all fathers of AFDC families were absent from the home. The corresponding proportion in 1961 was 75 percent.[8] Family status is therefore an overwhelming and increasingly proximate determinate of AFDC rolls.

The measure of family dissolution used here—the percentage of families which are incomplete because they are not husband-wife families—has been included with the stratification variables for several reasons. A child in such a broken home is more likely to be defined as being in need than one from an intact family. Furthermore, a number of studies have indicated that low economic status is highly correlated with marital dissatisfaction and family dissolution (Goode 1962; Scanzone 1970; Liebow 1967; Goodwin 1972). Low income often is interpreted as the inability to live up to cultural norms and expectations. This is particularly important for husbands and fathers, who are usually evaluated in terms of how well they provide for their families. The present structure of the AFDC program may itself encourage family dissolution. Often the AFDC benefits for a woman and her children are higher than a man can earn if he stays with them. A father may desert his family to provide them with better living conditions than he can offer himself, especially if welfare payments are high.[9] This particular argument has been made by several authors in their attempt to explain the growth in AFDC rolls during the 1960s (Banfield 1969; Durbin 1973; Honig 1973, 1974; Moles, forthcoming), but no adequate longitudinal or panel study supports this conclusion. In fact, Duncan and Morgan (1975, pp. 169–78) found in a six-year panel study that only 13 percent of all disrupted families ended up on welfare, and Morgan et al. (1974, pp. 264–66) found that the probability of going on welfare declines as the size of the average welfare payment increases.

The relationship between family status and economic conditions is complex, and this problem will be dealt with extensively in later chapters. For the moment it is sufficient to emphasize that the extent to which families are not intact is closely related to poverty and to the economic position of women relative to men. This latter point is illustrated by the high correlations between the proportion of families which are broken and the ratio of the industrial index for males to the industrial index for females, or the extent to which male workers in the state are better paid than female workers in the same industries ($r = -.74$ in 1960, $r = -.81$ in 1970).

The variables selected as part of the stratification model, then, measure some condition of need which the AFDC program theoretically can ameliorate. Thus all the variables discussed above are indications of the pressure on AFDC rolls or the need for this type of assistance; and in each case, the greater the value of a given variable, the greater is the potential need in the state. All the variables selected vary between the states (see Appendix C), although the variation in the female underemployment rate is relatively small, especially for 1960 (partially reflecting the high percentage figures for this variable). Nonetheless, there is sufficient variation among the states to determine the relative importance of the stratification model in explaining welfare rolls. Using these variables, then, we should be able to determine to what extent welfare rolls simply reflect poverty and need in the states, as has been suggested by the previous literature.

Relative Notions of Need:
Mass Society Variables

The mass society approach suggests that we are moving from a point where the absolute level of need in a state largely determines the size of welfare rolls to a point where, instead, the willingness of the states to consider the broader needs of citizens is important. Thus, such factors as level of education, degree of urbanization, size of professional and other "elite" occupational groups, and extent of industrialization should be positively related to more inclusive welfare policies and higher welfare rolls, because they are associated with broader definitions of need. The deciding difference between the mass society approach and the stratification approach is largely a choice of whether organizational differences among the states are seen as being important in their own right rather than because they locate people along dimensions of individual income, prestige, and honor. However, these two types of differences are often confounded.

Since voter participation is an element of citizenship, the extent to which it is granted and accepted should also be related to welfare policies and welfare rolls. The percentage of the population which is registered to vote may be considered a better measure of the extent to which political citizenship is granted in a state than voter participation in elections. A number of states, however, either do not require people to register to vote, require voter registration only in cities and counties over a certain size, or maintain no central registration records.[10] Voter participation, on the other hand, reflects both the extent to which people are allowed to participate in electoral politics (i.e., are registered to vote) and the extent to which they make use of that right. For methodological and theoretical reasons, then, voter participation was thought to be the most appropriate measure of political citizenship.

The choice of a measurement of voter participation is complicated by the four-year cycle in American electoral politics. In 1960, the percentage of the population of voting age[11] which participated in the presidential election was used. No presidential election was held in 1970, and so the percentage of the population of voting age which participated in the congresssional election was the available alternative. In all likelihood, participation in presidential elections is a more accurate and straightforward indication of the extent to which political citizenship is granted and accepted, since participation in more local elections, such as congressional elections (as well as senate and gubernatorial elections), tends to reflect particular local issues, party traditions, and so forth, which may have relatively little relationship to the mass society model. However, in actuality the pattern of participation in presidential elections and congressional elections does not seem to be drastically different.[12]

A number of additional variables have been selected because they were thought to be related to a relative interpretation of poverty and need. The level of education in a state was obviously a factor to consider. I have used as one of my measures the median number of years of schooling for the population aged twenty-five and over in the state in both 1960 and 1970.[13] This variable is a reasonably accurate measure which has been mentioned in previous literature. A more exact measure of higher education, the percentage of the population in the state aged twenty-five and over who have at least finished high school, was also included.[14] These two measures of level of education, of course, are highly intercorrelated[15] and are included mainly for methodological comparison.

Urbanization, like education, has often been seen as a condition under which people broaden their horizons and at the same time achieve a measure of citizenship not available in the more parochial or particularistic social orders of small towns and rural society. Thus Weber (1962) saw the urban center as the cradle of the concept of citizenship itself. No doubt there have been great changes in the extent to which nations, rather than cities alone, offer a fuller sense of citizenship to the members of modern societies. Yet the city is still a relatively sophisticated place where broader, more complex, and often higher standards of living are talked about and understood. Partial support for this interpretation is available in some of the cross-national studies of political development. Thus Benjamin, Blue, and Coleman (1971) found urbanization to be consistently related to political participation and support for a variety of political opinions. These authors also strongly suggest that urbanization reflects only one of several processes of modernization, separable from those of education and industrialization.

To determine the degree of urbanization, a composite index was constructed by adding the weighted proportion of the state's population residing in places of each size category. The index is weighted in favor of states with population in large places[16] and is highly correlated with other measures of urbanization such as percentage of the state's population living in Standard Metropolitan Statistical Areas (SMSAs)[17] and percentage of population living in urban places.[18] However, since some states have no SMSAs and other states have large proportions of their populations residing in small and medium-sized cities, the weighted urbanization index was considered more appropriate for this study.

A mass society is not necessarily an elite society, but it is one in which a large proportion of the population advances to a level where they are fully trusted as citizens—people assumed loyal to the nation, reasonably secure in the economic order, and bearing national cultural heritage—rather than buried in remote subcultures, parochial groups, or occupational enclaves. For the most part this means those white-collar employees who have transferable skills—skills that allow them to see the entire nation as a single labor market. No doubt there are always limits on the marketability of every skill, but this notion seems to coincide most faithfully with the relative number of people with such skills. To get a measure of this mainline occupation group, the proportion of all employed persons who are in upper white-collar occupations was computed for each state.[19]

Finally, an index of industrialization, which essentially is a measure of the presence of high-wage industries in the state, was computed for males and females for each state. This index has been developed by economists to measure the industrial structure of the state,[20] but it is also highly correlated with various measures of income or lack of income (such as poverty). The usefulness of the industrial index here is that it provides a relative measure of the competitiveness of each state. In other words, it measures the presence of a labor market which is competitive and more or less able to include or attract those with transferable skills. I would also argue, with Inkeles (1969), that the experience of industrial work itself produces values and modes of behavior associated with active citizenship. The factory therefore may be seen as a school for modernization and rationality.

I have also included a very simple measure of industrialization in my analysis; the percentage of all employed persons working in nonagricultural occupations.[21] The reason for doing so is that some approaches to modernization would emphasize simply the industrialization of a society, whether most of its participants were unskilled or had transferable skills. It is the latter element that I have attempted to single out in the industrial index, and which I would expect to be more useful in the analysis of welfare rolls. The notion that industrialization alone is important in broadening the interpretation of dependency seems to rest in part on the argument that where industrialization occurs, workers attempt to insure themselves against the dangers of industrial society by arguing for more extensive programs to protect their incomes. However, in fairly recent years it is only in very advanced societies that such arguments have been seen as legitimate and have won receptive understanding in the population at large. I would argue that industrialization alone, unless its separate components are distinguished may not be as relevant a mass society variable as the others included so far. Yet for purposes of methodological comparison I have included both types of measures in the analysis.

The variation among the states in each of the mass society variables is considerable and is sufficient to determine the relative importance of the mass society model in explaining the variation in welfare rolls for 1960 and 1970 (see Appendix C).

Earlier, no decision was made about how the per capita state revenue and per capita state taxes variables should be classified and whether they should be interpreted as stratification or mass society variables. A variation of the stratification approach argues that it is not so much the economic conditions in a state that may be important in determining welfare rolls and policies as it is the fiscal capacity of the state itself. Thus, the richer the state government is, the more people it can afford to support and therefore the more lenient can be the state's eligibility requirements and the higher the welfare rolls. However, the stratification approach gives no obvious reason why increasing state funds would be allocated to welfare programs. Still, the argument receives some support from the reports of many state policymakers who have given fiscal reasons for reducing welfare rolls and for diverting welfare costs onto the federal government by joining the AFDC program (SPCU Reports).

On the other hand, there are several reasons why both per capita revenue and per capita taxes may be considered mass society variables. Per capita taxes measures the extent to which a state is willing to tax itself in order to provide services to its residents, while per capita revenue is an indication of the extent to which the state has collected revenue from various sources, including transfer funds from local and federal revenue sources. Per capita taxes may be seen as an index of a state's willingness to provide services for its residents, while per capita revenue is an index of the state's available resources to provide such services. This should not be confused with the economic capacity of the state to undertake such responsibilities, which is most nearly measured by the per capita income.

The formula used to calculate the federal financial participation in AFDC programs suggests that the fiscal capacity of the state should be directly related to the per capita income in the state, or to the amount of individual "excess" income which might be available to the state. However, the extent to which states have been willing to tax their residents and been able to obtain funds from other sources varies greatly. The zero-order correlation between per capita revenue and per capita income was only $r = .19$ in 1960 (not significant) and $r = .27$ in 1970 ($p < .05$), while per capita taxes and per capita income were more closely related ($r = .34$ in 1960, $p < .01$; and $r = .49$, $p < .001$ in 1970).[22] Nevertheless, only about a quarter of the variation in per capita taxes can be explained by differences in per capita incomes among the states. Yet, the mass society variables do quite well in explaining the variation in per capita revenue and per capita taxes among the states (see table 21 in Appendix D). Thus, for example, the correlation between per capita revenue and percentage employed in upper white-collar occupations was $r = .54$ in 1960. The corresponding figure for 1970 was $r = .55$, and both correlations are highly significant ($p < .001$). Consequently, per capita revenue and per capita taxes will be included with the mass society variables in this study.

Convergent and Divergent
Implications of the Two Models

The zero-order correlations between the various stratification variables indicate that these are highly intercorrelated, and in about one-third of the thirty-six relationships, a stratification variable explains more than 50 percent of the variation in the others (see table 21 in Appendix D).

Among the stratification variables, almost all of the relationships are in the expected directions (the more poor families in a state, the higher are all the other indexes of economic dependency, etc.). Only the correlations between measures of female working experiences and the percentage of broken families do not follow this pattern.[23] Of the remaining thirty-two correlations, all except the correlation between nonworker-worker ratio and the percentage of broken families are significant at the .05 level, and 26 of the correlations are significant at the .001 level. The stratification variables thus seem to "hang" together as a system, with each being more closely related to one another than to most of the other variables included in the study.

Similarly, we find that most of the variables selected to tap the mass society approach are also highly intercorrelated (see table 21 in Appendix D). In about one-quarter of the relationships, one mass society variable explains at least 50 percent of the variation in another mass society variable. However, the mass society variables do not so clearly seem to form a closely related system as do the stratification variables. Several of the correlations between the mass society variables are very low; thus the correlation between urbanization and voter participation is $r = .13$ in 1960 and $r = .01$ in 1970. The correlation between the industrial index for females and the percentage with at least a high-school education in 1970 is also small ($r = .19$, but $r = .41$ in 1960). There are similar problems with the nonagricultural employment variable. Furthermore, in 1970 some of the correlations involving the nonagricultural employment variable were not in the expected direction; that is, high mass society status on one variable is not always associated with high mass society status on another variable. However, in all of the exceptions, the correlations involved are very small.

As one might expect, the variables which characterize either of these two points of departure are apt to be intercorrelated. Those states with a disproportionately high number of poor families must deal with the obvious and demanding needs of these poor. States in which there is relatively little poverty have correspondingly fewer demands from the poor and can afford to respond to less desperate needs. Thus the necessity, the ability, and the willingness to respond to broad social needs are determined partially by the economic conditions of the state.

Consequently, those states with high rates of economic dependency also tend to be those with low levels of education, small proportions of employees working in upper white-collar occupations, large proportions in farming occupations and, in general, a preponderance of relatively low-paying industries. The correlations between the mass society and the stratification variables are all in the directions indicated: the relative absence of economic dependency in a state is positively correlated with indexes of mass society, such as urbanization, industrialization, and size of occupational elite (see table 21 in Appendix D).

The situation for female employment is less clear than for other indexes of economic dependency: female underemployment is not clearly related to median level of education ($r = -.18$ in 1960 and $r = -.11$ in 1970), percentage with high school education or more ($r = -.14$ in 1960 and $r = -.10$ in 1970), percentage employed in upper white-collar occupations ($r = -.09$ in 1960 and $r = -.08$ in 1970), and voter participation ($r = .01$ in 1960 and $r = .00$ in 1970). There are similar problems with percentage of females not working and percentage of all workers employed in nonfarm occupations. This is in contrast to most of the other mass society variables, which tend to be significantly correlated with the stratification variables (see table 21 in Appendix D).

It is clear that the two sets of variables are interrelated, but not to the extent that the models they tap are identical. On the other hand, it is also possible that the two sets of variables themselves, particularly the mass society variables, may reflect more than one underlying dimension each.

Separating the Two Models in
Theory and Practice

To obtain a clearer picture of the interrelationships among the stratification variables and mass society variables, these two sets of variables were factor analyzed[24] for both 1960 and 1970.[25] The factor analyses will allow us to determine whether these variables, as expected, do indeed fall into a pattern similar to those of the mass society variables instead of reflecting mainly the economic condition of the state.

In both 1960 and 1970 four dimensions emerged from the factor analyses. Most of the mass society variables load predominantly on two factors, while the stratification variables load most heavily on two separate factors. This is the case for both 1960 and 1970. The first factor extracted in 1960, and the second extracted in 1970, contributes both to mass society and stratification variables: percentage of families poor, and percentage of broken families, male underemployment rate (only in 1960), percentage of voter participation, median level of education, and percentage with at least a high-school education. This composite factor therefore does not appear to sharply separate the two sets of variables. The overlap may be in part an artifact of regional differences between the South and the rest of the country. That is, the South is relatively poor, less well educated, and has relatively low rates of voter participation, all of which may produce high intercorrelations between these variables. To check for this possibility, a second factor analysis was carried out for both years, including the South as a dummy variable. As expected, this dummy variable loaded highest on the composite factor.

The second factor in 1960 measures primarily the dimension of urbanization and industrialization, as does the first factor in 1970: this factor includes all three industrialization indexes and the urbanization index. The third factor extracted in 1960, and the fourth in 1970, seems to be a mass society factor, reflecting the inclusion of population groups in the center: per capita revenue, per capita taxes, percentage upper white-collar employment, and to some extent the two education variables. The fourth factor extracted in 1960 is very similar to the third factor in 1970 and is clearly a stratification factor. It essentially measures conditions of female employment: female underemployment rate, percentage of females not working, nonworker-worker ratio, and male underemployment rate (only in 1970).

The fact that the mass society variables seem to fall on two separate dimensions for the American states is important, for it suggests that "modernization" or "development" may occur along several lines. Other studies of state characteristics have also found two (Hofferbert 1968; Sharkansky and Hofferbert 1969) or more (Crittenden 1967) dimensions of economic development,[26] and all seem to be quite closely related to the two dimensions we have found. I find it particularly interesting that the most traditional measures of socioeconomic development (industrialization and urbanization) fall on a different dimension than the variables most likely to measure directly the degree of mass society in Shils's sense (education, occupational elite, voter participation, and willingness to undertake government programs). Consequently, those studies which have relied primarily on urbanization-industrialization variables may have been unnecessarily limited to very narrow conclusions about the impact of development on government policies.

My findings also suggest that these state dimensions are quite stable over time, since the clustering of the variables in 1960 and 1970 is basically very similar.[27] This conclusion is also supported by the findings of Morgan and Lyons (1975) in their study of the Sharkansky and Hofferbert (1969) dimensions for 1960 and 1970. Similarly, Hofferbert (1968) found a remarkable constancy of two factors, "industrialism" and "cultural enrichment," from 1890 to 1960, which suggests that these dimensions are indeed enduring elements of the American social structure.

The major purpose of these factor analyses was to indicate the extent to which the mass society and stratification variables are separable. I do not intend to make too much of these relationships, and it would not be useful to combine the various independent variables into new factor variables according to how they cluster. To do so would likely result in variables with less variation than we now have. In addition, the particular pattern of variables which can best explain the variation in our dependent variables may not be as informative if we use only a few factor variables as when we allow a stepwise regression analysis to select from all the different independent variables to obtain the set of variables which can best predict the dependent variable.

These factor analyses show that there are more than two sets of variables. The mass society variables can be seen as measuring both urbanization-industrialization (often called modernization) and the extent to which people are included in the mainstream of society. The stratification variables can be seen as composed of both dependency and employment dimensions. The important point is to see how each set of variables bears on welfare rolls, and for this purpose no theoretical distinction seems necessary between these four sets of variables at present. Nonetheless, we are forewarned that the two major sets of variables, mass society and stratification, may be further refined as we proceed with the analysis.

What is most important, however, is that the two major models are analytically separable. The stratification approach would lead us to expect high welfare rolls in states with high rates of economic dependency, whereas the mass society approach would lead us to expect low welfare rolls in these same states. In most instances the hypotheses derived from the two models are diametrically opposed. Furthermore, over time the stratification model would lead us to expect declining welfare rolls with declining rates of poverty and other forms of economic dependency, whereas the mass society model would lead us to expect increasing welfare rolls as economic conditions improve and standards of well-being increase (i.e., reduction in economic dependency objectively defined).

Neither model is likely to be quite adequate by itself, and both are probably required. The increase in AFDC rolls between 1960 and 1970 took place in a period characterized by rising incomes and increasing employment of women. This, incidentally, lends support to the mass society model, but most important, it emphasizes the theoretical necessity of distinguishing between the two models while including both in the analysis.

Uses of Both Models for Explaining AFDC Rolls and Policies

A preliminary analysis of the zero-order correlations between each of the different sets of independent variables and AFDC rolls and selected measures of AFDC policies (TES, cost standard, maximum level of benefits) suggests that the stratification model is particularly important in explaining AFDC rolls in 1960 (see table 23 in Appendix E). The zero-order correlations between AFDC rolls and the six stratification variables are all positive in both years, indicating that the greater the need in the state, the higher the AFDC rolls. The correlations range from $r = .37$ (female underemployment rate) to $r = .70$ (male underemployment rate) for 1960, with a median value of $r = .55$. In 1970, the median value of the correlation coefficients is $r = .29$, substantially lower than for 1960, and the coefficients range from $r = .15$ (female underemployment rate) to $r = .58$ (percentage of broken families). Although clearly relevant for both years, it is obvious that the stratification model is somewhat less adequate in explaining the variation in AFDC rolls in 1970.

It is also clear that it is the poorer states, with presumably the highest pressure on the AFDC rolls, that are most restrictive with regard to overall welfare eligibility requirements. Thus the zero-order correlation between percentage of families which are poor and TES was $r = .47$ in 1960 and $r = .42$ in 1970. Similarly, considering all the stratification variables, the median correlation with TES was $r = .29$ in 1960 (ranging between $r = .03$ and $r = .47$) and $r = .28$ in 1970 (ranging between $r = .12$ and $r = .42$).

The economic eligibility requirements follow the same pattern. The correlation coefficients between the cost standard and the various stratification variables had a median value of $r = -.46$ in 1960 (ranging from $r = -.10$ to $r = -.62$) and $r = -.26$ in 1970 (ranging from $r = -.11$ to $r = -.62$). Thus the greater the need in a state, the lower was the cost standard, and the lower was the maximum benefit level as well. The zero-order correlations between maximum payment levels and the stratification variables had a median value of $r = -.44$ in 1960 (ranging between $r = -.19$ and $r = -.73$) and $r = -.37$ in 1970 (ranging between $r = -.15$ and $r = -.72$). The pattern of greater restrictiveness in the poorer states, then, is particularly clear for the economic eligibility requirements. However, in general the TES is fairly highly correlated with some of the stratification variables (percentage of families which are poor, percentage of broken families, and male underemployment rate).

At this level of analysis, then, there seem to have been some shifts in the determinants of welfare rolls, but not welfare policies, over the last decade. We shall be able to examine this in a more satisfactory manner only after other variables have been considered preparatory to a multivariate analysis. However, the stratification model is clearly important in determining both welfare rolls and welfare policies.

The mass society variables seem to be most relevant for explaining welfare policies. Almost all the relationships between the mass society variables and measures of welfare policies are in the expected direction: Higher mass society status is associated with more lenient or inclusive welfare policies, and most of these relationships are significant (see table 23 in Appendix E). Thus the correlation coefficients between the ten mass society variables and the TES have a median value of $r = -.36$ for 1960 (ranging from $r = .07$ to $r = -.48$) and $r = -.34$ in 1970 (ranging from $r = .14$ to $r = -.49$). For the cost standard, the median coefficient is $r = .41$ in 1960 (ranging between $r = .01$ and $r = .65$) and $r = .36$ in 1970 (ranging between $r = .03$ and $r = .58$). Again, the pattern for the maximum payment is very similar to that for the cost standard: the higher the mass society status, the greater the maximum payment. The median coefficient is $r = .49$ in 1960 (ranging between $r = .05$ and $r = .67$)

and $r = .38$ in 1970 (ranging between $r = -.05$ and $r = .63$). In all cases, percentage employed nonfarm has a deviant or substantially lower correlation coefficient with all the welfare policy measures compared with any of the other mass society variables.

Predicting the relative size of welfare rolls from mass society variables is clearly more complex than using the same variables to predict welfare policies. The zero-order correlations between AFDC rolls and the mass society variables for 1970 are quite small (median value of $r = .17$, ranging between $r = -.20$ and $r = .35$) and for 1960 are in a direction which suggests that for this point in time the mass society model is largely inappropriate for predicting AFDC rolls (median value is $r = -.25$, ranging between $r = .13$ and $r = -.48$).

While it is clear that the mass society approach does not provide the only or most obvious source of variation in welfare rolls among the states, neither does the stratification model. Where the mass society model attempts to measure the total integration of the state, the stratification model focuses on the relative economic placement of people in a state. Poverty in particular, but also unemployment and dependency, are well established and clearly important factors which determine the placement of people in that stratification system.

Another integral determinant of a person's status in the American society is his race. Certain groups of the population, particularly some racial groups, are consistently found at the lower levels of the social structure and are less likely to be thought of as good citizens. While the Japanese and Chinese seem to have "won" their citizenship by the end of the Second World War, a number of popular beliefs and suspicions continue to surround blacks, Indians, and Latin Americans, and these beliefs are also used to account for the persistence of poverty among these groups in an affluent society.

It is partly for these reasons that the increases in welfare rolls that took place in the 1960s became an important political issue. In the face of increasing affluence and decreasing poverty rates, it was difficult to understand why more and more people relied on public assistance. A number of explanations were presented by politicians and others to account for this anomaly. Social scientists also attempted to explain the phenomenon.[28]

One major argument, which has its foundation in the laissez-faire ideology, has been at the basis of most American public welfare policies throughout most of the history of the country (Grønbjerg, Street, and Suttles, forthcoming; Wilensky and Lebeaux 1965). The argument is essentially built on the suspicion that most of the minority poor are lazy and unwilling to exert themselves—that, in fact, this is why they are poor, and that the public welfare programs encourage them to continue unchanged in their profligate ways. Thus, the high welfare rolls are seen as reflecting the presence of large groups of such poor. This argument received a major burst of popularity with the development of the culture of poverty theory in the early to middle 1960s, and was seen (wrongly) as being a particularly accurate description of blacks, American Indians, and Latin Americans.

A variant of this argument maintained that the reason for the major increases in welfare rolls in such states as New York, California, and Illinois was the influx of southerners, particularly southern blacks, who were suspected of preferring the high public assistance payment standards in these states to the low standards in their home states. Consequently, considerable pressure was exerted to discourage migrants from obtaining public welfare.[29]

The concern with economic opportunism is evident in many of the eligibility requirements and reflects a second variant of the laissez-faire ideology argument. There have been enough scandals sprinkled throughout the history of public welfare to sustain the suspicion that some recipients were cheating the welfare system out of funds which they did not need and to which they were not entitled.[30]

As a result of the concerns over the size and composition of welfare rolls which these arguments reveal, various states have attempted to eliminate from their rolls the undeserving poor and have also been eager to cut down on welfare expenditures in general. Public reaction to rising welfare rolls and welfare scandals on a national level may influence federal legislation, although it does not necessarily lead to differences in state policies. It is clear that some reaction has taken place on the state level and has resulted in attempts to tighten eligibility requirements and in administrative crackdowns on "welfare cheaters and loafers."

Whether a state actually has a large welfare roll because it has a sizable black population or has experienced a large influx of migrants, especially from the South, has not been clearly established. There is always anecdotal evidence available to sustain such beliefs. The argument gains some support from the relatively high correlation between AFDC rolls and the percentage of the population in the state which is black ($r = .36$ in 1960, $r = .23$ in 1970; see also table 23 in Appendix E). Yet, since blacks tend to be poorer than most other racial groups, we cannot fully evaluate this pattern until we take conditions of economic need into consideration. I will attempt to do that in the following chapters.

It is clear, however, that if these beliefs about blacks and other groups exist, the presence of such "threatening" groups would likely influence a state's welfare policies. Thus the presence of blacks, the extent of net and total in-migration of nonwhites, overall population growth, and presence of southerners would be important factors in shaping a state's public assistance policies, as would continuously large or increasing welfare rolls.

In fact we find that for both 1960 and 1970 some of these "threat" factors are highly correlated with restrictive welfare policies (see table 23 in Appendix E).[31] This is particularly the case with the percentage of the population which is black and the percentage of the native population southern-born and living outside the state of birth (for both variables the correlations are significant at the .01 level or better). These two "threat" variables are also fairly closely inter-related ($r = .44$ in 1960 and $r = .54$ in 1970, $p < .001$), reflecting both the fact that most blacks reside in states with southern-born populations (mainly southern states) and the fact that most blacks are born in the South (see table 4). The variables that measure changes in minority populations (migration variables) are correlated with lenient welfare policies, as one might expect, since the northern states have experienced the highest *increase* in black population while welfare policies in these states have remained relatively lenient.

It is possible, therefore, that all of these relationships reflect regional variation, since blacks in the northern states make up a smaller proportion of the states' total population but have sharply increased in the last two or three decades. Again, these same northern states also tend to have more lenient welfare policies (see table 4).

In any event, there is little reason to think that such groups will not continue to be seen as a threat to the central value system. They will also continue to be seen as population groups which are somewhat unreliable and not deserving of any but minimal forms of public assistance. To the extent that this pattern is perpetuated in the United States, welfare policies will continue to be relatively restrictive and welfare rolls will remain relatively low.

Conclusion

In this chapter, we have examined more closely the independent variables, the relationships between them, and their zero-order correlations with welfare rolls and welfare policies. We have shown

Table 4

**Average Measures of AFDC
Policies and Selected Threat
Variables, 1960 and 1970, by
Region**

	Census Region		
Variables	Total U.S.	South	Non-South
1960			
TES	22	25	20
Cost standard	$191	$161	$206
Maximum paid	$153	$101	$178
% black	8.9	20.6	3.3
% nonwhite	11.3	21.0	6.6
% native population born in South	9.1	13.6	6.9
% population increase, 1950–60	19.1	16.5	20.3
% nonwhite in-migration, 1955–60	11.3	4.5	14.7
% nonwhite net migration, 1955–60	1.4	−3.2	3.6
1970			
TES	14	16	13
Cost standard	$276	$237	$294
Maximum paid	$213	$147	$246
% black	8.9	18.9	4.1
% nonwhite	11.5	19.5	7.5
% native population born in South	8.9	13.4	6.7
% population increase, 1960–70	13.3	12.7	13.5
% nonwhite in-migration, 1965–70	7.4	4.6	8.7
% nonwhite net migration, 1965–70	−0.2	−2.6	0.9

Sources   U.S. Bureau of the Census 1961–63,
1963, 1971–73, 1973*b*, 1973*c*; U.S.
Social and Rehabilitation Service
1971*d*, 1971*f*; U.S. Social Security
Administration 1960, 1962; SPCU
Reports.

that the variables selected to tap the stratification and mass society
approaches appear to be empirically as well as analytically distin-
guishable. However, more important, the two approaches are
separable with regard to how they can be expected to relate to AFDC
rolls: they lead to expectations in opposite directions.

In general the stratification variables seem to be fairly closely
related to AFDC rolls, and the mass society and threat variables
fairly closely related to AFDC policies. There is considerable

indication that some of these patterns have changed between 1960 and 1970 and that the mass society variables have become more important in determining AFDC rolls.

In any event, it is clear that we are likely to need a combination of independent variables taken from the several different sets to adequately explain the variation in either AFDC rolls or AFDC policies. In the following chapters I will attempt to establish just which of these independent variables are to be included in the final analysis.

Objective Poverty
and Need

5

Although state eligibility requirements have little direct influence on the size of AFDC rolls, it is clear that a series of other variables, especially those measuring the extent of need in each state, are closely related to welfare rolls. The importance of the remaining independent variables, especially the mass society ones, has not been clearly established so far. As we shall see, the mass society variables do play an increasing part in determining the magnitude and function of welfare rolls. However, the presence of need has been and continues to be a major factor in shaping welfare rolls. Yet, while the stratification variables are the source of persistent need for welfare, it is the mass society variables which account for the marginal differences in welfare rolls among the states and between 1960 and 1970.

The general aim of this chapter, then, is to assess the relative importance of the mass society and stratification approaches in 1960. For this purpose, a number of progressively more complex models for explaining the state-by-state variation in AFDC rolls for 1960 will be evaluated. Each of the models sorts through a selection of independent variables to place them in some reasonable sequence or combination by eliminating those which do not contribute significantly and independently to explaining the variation in AFDC rolls.

Responses to Economic Dependency

Public welfare is most clearly a way of responding to poverty, and we should examine the extent to which welfare is just that: a reflection of objective economic dependency in each state. One way of establishing this relationship is to examine which stratification variables best predict AFDC rolls.[1] The first part of the analysis and the construction of the first model will therefore focus only on the stratification variables and will be based on an interpretation of the correlations between these variables and AFDC rolls.[2]

In 1960 the stratification variable with the highest zero-order[3] correlation with AFDC rolls was the proportion of males over age fourteen who worked less than fifty to fifty-two weeks during 1959 ($r = -.70$). That is, the larger the proportion of males who did not work, or worked only part of the year, the more families receive AFDC. Clearly unemployment and underemployment are primary conditions contributing to high welfare rolls. The size of AFDC rolls thus is largely a reflection of the need or demand for such aid. A number of other stratification variables also have high zero-order correlations with AFDC rolls, but once we control for the percentage of males employed less than the full year, all these correlations are reduced substantially because of the intercorrelations among them.[4]

Including male underemployment as the first independent variable still leaves 51 percent of the variance in AFDC rolls unexplained. An examination of the remaining stratification variables indicates that the nonworker-worker ratio is able to reduce the unexplained variation the most, since this independent variable has a partial correlation with AFDC rolls of .41 ($p < .01$).[5] The standardized regression coefficient β[6] for this variable, if it is brought into the regression equation, is .38. This finding is hardly surprising, since the larger the number of people each worker must support the greater is likely to be the need for income to supplement thinly spread earnings. Again, the greater the need for such aid, the higher are AFDC rolls. The nonworker-worker ratio also represents a relatively new dimension in the equation, since the tolerance[7] for entering this variable is high (.60). When the nonworker-worker ratio is entered into the regression equation, the amount of unexplained variation is reduced by eight percentage points—from 51 percent, when only the underemployed rate of males was used, to 43 percent when the nonworker-worker ratio is also included.[8] An examination of the partial correlations between the remaining stratification variables and welfare rolls,[9] controlling for these two variables, indicates that the percentage of broken families has the largest partial correlation with AFDC rolls (partial $r = .32$, $p < .05$); that is, the more broken homes, the more families on AFDC. This variable also contributes a relatively new dimension to the prediction equation (tolerance .71) and has a standardized regression coefficient $\beta = .25$. When the percentage of broken families is entered into the regression equation the amount of unexplained variation in AFDC rolls is further reduced by five percentage points (from 43 percent to 38 percent).

The independent contributions of the three variables entered into the regression equation so far have all been in the expected direction: the greater the degree of objective economic dependency, the higher the AFDC rolls. In the factor analysis of the stratification and mass society variables in 1960, the three stratification variables selected in this preliminary regression analysis loaded on two separate, although somewhat correlated, factors ($r = -.16$). The first and third variables to enter into the regression equation, male underemployment rate and percentage of broken families, both received large, direct contributions from the composite factor. The second variable to enter into the regression equation, the nonworker-worker ratio, received a larger direct contribution from the female employment factor. Thus a large proportion of the variation in AFDC rolls in 1960 is determined by a combination of variables from both subsets of stratification variables.

None of the remaining stratification variables can significantly reduce the amount of unexplained variation in AFDC rolls. However, there is another variable which often is used as a summary index to economic dependency. This is the percentage of the state population which is black. Since blacks are poorer and more economically dependent than whites, it is not surprising to find that the proportion of the population which is black is positively related to most of the stratification variables; the median zero-order correlation is $r = .44$, ranging from $r = .74$ for families poor to $r = -.04$ for the female underemployment rate (see table 21 in Appendix D). We would expect, then, that if AFDC rolls are a response to economic dependency, the percentage black should be positively correlated with welfare rolls. The zero-order correlation between race and welfare rolls is $r = .36$ and thus in the expected direction.[10] However, when we control for male underemployment and non-worker-worker ratio this correlation is reduced to -.03. This indicates that the positive correlation between the percentage black and AFDC rolls may be due mainly or entirely to black residence in the poorer states, which also had high AFDC rolls in 1960.

When we control further for the percentage of broken families, the correlation between the percentage black and AFDC rolls becomes negative and significant (partial $r = -.30$, $p < .05$); that is, the larger the percentage of blacks in a state, the lower the AFDC rolls. This negative partial correlation between percentage black and AFDC rolls may reflect the fact that the states with the larger proportion of blacks have the fewest husband-wife families (zero-order correlation between percentage black and percentage of broken families is .69).[11] I will explore this relationship in the following section. If the percentage black variable is entered into the regression equation along with the three stratification variables already entered—male underemployment rate, nonworker-worker ratio, and percentage of broken families—these four independent variables explain a total of 65 percent of the variation in AFDC rolls. At this point, none of the remaining stratification variables can significantly reduce the amount of unexplained variation: none of the partial correlation coefficients are significantly different from zero.

Obviously, objective conditions of economic dependency are important determinants of AFDC rolls: three measures of economic dependency in the states jointly explain 62 percent of the total variation in AFDC rolls in 1960. Yet even including the percentage black, there is still 35 percent of the variation in AFDC rolls left unexplained. Clearly there is room for other variables to enter the regression equation.

Beyond the Stratification Model

The contribution of the percentage black variable in explaining AFDC rolls is the opposite of what we would expect if this variable were an approximate measure of poverty only. However, such a pattern fits the situation where groups who are considered a threat are also denied complete citizenship. The pattern observed for the percentage black variable must therefore be carefully evaluated.

There are three possible, although related, explanations for this pattern. The negative association between the percentage black and AFDC rolls, controlling for economic dependency, could be due to the restriction of blacks to low-level jobs such as domestic work. These jobs may be open primarily to black females, whereas white females have not been willing (or expected) to accept such jobs. Thus similar economic and family conditions may have different consequences for black and white families. Welfare is not a preferred way of life for any group, yet among whites it may be considered less degrading than accepting very low-status work.

The fact that certain jobs are seen as acceptable for blacks and not for whites does, of course, reflect underlying discrimination and prejudice against blacks. Yet it is also likely that the relationship between percentage black and AFDC rolls may be a reflection of outright discrimination against blacks: black families who are badly off may not be considered as eligible by the public assistance agencies as white families with the same objective economic conditions (Gordon 1972; Bell 1965). Both of these explanations would result in blacks' using public assistance less than whites.

However, even if there were no outright discrimination against blacks in the administration of public assistance, the mere presence of large numbers of blacks in a state may be associated with unexpectedly low welfare rolls because of underutilization by whites. The suspicions which surround blacks and their deservedness as full members in society may easily be extended to include a presumption that only, or primarily, blacks will make use of public assistance. Therefore whites may be unwilling to make use of public assistance to avoid being classed with blacks. Poor whites may also have less need for the "dole" if the larger white community at the same time is willing to provide private charity for its unfortunate but "decent" members and thus prevent their presumed degradation. Historically, however, there is little evidence for such an interpretation of my findings. Blacks generally have been discouraged or prevented from obtaining public assistance (Bell 1965; Piven and Cloward 1971). However, such restrictive actions against blacks may also have discouraged whites from applying for aid.

If there were no discrimination or concern with the status of blacks, two states with similar economic and family conditions should have similar proportions of families receiving AFDC. If blacks are prevented from obtaining public assistance, or cause whites to refrain from such aid, states with a high proportion of blacks should have fewer families on welfare. This is indeed the pattern observed, which suggests that the state public assistance rolls reflect not only objective conditions of economic dependency in the states but also the willingness—or in this case, the unwillingness—of the states to extend welfare to certain groups in the population. This argument, that public welfare may not be granted to certain groups (particularly blacks) because they are so thoroughly distrusted derives from the more general interpretation that portions of a population may be prevented from participating fully in the society on an equal basis with everyone else. In this view, the relative size of welfare rolls depends upon the extent to which public trust and assistance are extended to larger or smaller proportions of the population and thus respond to broader or narrower social needs.

The mass society variables were originally selected to reflect such extension of citizenship and degree of response to broader social needs. The interpretation of the discrimination against blacks presented above, therefore, suggests that this variable is related indirectly to the mass society model. The observed pattern, where the precentage black is negatively related to AFDC rolls, reflects the degree to which citizenship in a state is extended or limited by the presence of groups so thoroughly distrusted that they may be seen as not deserving full citizenship status. An extension of this argument would lead to the conclusion that the mass society variables may be quite important in explaining state variation in AFDC rolls, in spite of their ambiguous zero-order correlations with AFDC rolls in 1960 (see chap. 4).

The contribution of the mass society variables, however, must be examined in conjunction with that of the stratification variables, and a second, more complex, model of determinants of AFDC rolls in 1960 must be examined. This analysis will be based primarily on the top two sections of table 5, which presents a partial summary of the stepwise regression of the stratification and mass society variables on AFDC rolls in 1960. Here again the attempt is to select the variables which will best predict AFDC rolls by entering into the regression equation those independent variables which will most reduce the amount of unexplained variation at each successive step.

The first three variables to enter into the regression equation are the same variables which entered before when the importance of economic dependency in the state for AFDC rolls was examined. Conditions of objective economic dependency, as reflected in the underemployment rate for males, nonworker-worker ratio, and the percentage of broken families, are still the most important determinants of AFDC rolls in 1960. However, as each of these stratification variables is allowed to enter the regression equation, several other variables become increasingly prominent: the percentage employed in upper white-collar occupations, median level of education, and the presence of high-paying industries. The partial correlations between these variables and AFDC rolls do not become smaller as each of the three stratification variables is entered into the equation, as do the remaining stratification variables. Instead, the mass society variables become increasingly positive and six of them have significant partial correlations with AFDC rolls. Thus, the higher the mass society status, the larger are AFDC rolls.[12] In particular, the participation of voters in the presidential election in 1960 becomes an important indicator of the extent to which AFDC is granted to a large proportion of the population (partial $r = .38$, $p < .05$) and is the independent variable which can most reduce the unexplained variation in AFDC rolls (from 38 percent to 33 percent) after the three stratification variables have been entered.

When the extent of voter participation is allowed to enter the equation, the partial correlation between percentage black and AFDC rolls is reduced to $-.02$. This reinforces the foregoing interpretation that discrimination against blacks is mainly the reverse side of the extension of citizenship in general and reflects the tendency to grant public assistance first to more trusted segments of the population.

An examination of the remaining mass society and stratification variables indicates that there are still four mass society variables with significant partial correlations with AFDC rolls; percentage with a high-school education or more (partial $r = .35$, $p < .05$), percentage upper white-collar employment (partial $r = .33$, $p < .05$), per capita revenue (partial $r = .35$, $p < .05$), and per capita taxes (partial $r = .36$, $p < .05$). None of the stratification variables are significant.

When we control for the three stratification variables and the size of voter participation, per capita taxes in the state—or the extent to which the population of the state is willing to tax itself—is most highly correlated with AFDC rolls (partial $r = .36$, $p < .05$); that is, the higher the per capita taxes, the higher are AFDC rolls. The standardized regression coefficient of this variable, if it were entered into the regression equation at this point, is $\beta = .23$. If the per capita taxes variable was allowed to enter the prediction equation on the fifth step, a total of 71 percent of the variance in AFDC rolls would be explained by five variables. At this point, however, none of the remaining mass society or stratification variables could significantly reduce the amount of unexplained variation.

The variables selected up to this point have tapped three of the four factors extracted in the 1960 factor analysis of the mass society and stratification variables. Only the urbanization-industrialization factor (Factor II) is not represented. The composite factor (Factor I) is represented by three variables: two stratification variables (male underemployment rate and percentage of broken families) and one mass society variable (percentage of voter participation). The remaining two factors are represented by just one variable each: nonworker-worker ratio (female employment factor, Factor IV) and per capita taxes (Factor III, inclusion factor).

In chapter 3 I indicated that welfare policies seem to have been used to discourage certain threatening, mistrusted, or "disreputable" groups from exploiting the system of public assistance. My findings already have suggested that blacks either do not make use of the public assistance programs to the same extent as whites of similar socioeconomic status or, more likely, are prevented from doing so. There are, however, other "threatening" groups about whom policymakers have been concerned. White or black migrants from the South have been suspected of moving to northern and western states with the explicit purpose of exploiting the more lenient welfare policies of those states (Feagin 1972; Williamson 1973). It is important, then, to explore further the effect of the presence of such threatening groups on AFDC rolls.[13] For this purpose, all independent variables will be considered in my final, most complex model.

Table 5 presents a summary of the stepwise regression on AFDC rolls of all the different sets of factors: stratification, mass society, and "threat" for 1960. The first three variables to enter the regression equation are again the stratification variables of male underemployment rate, nonworker-worker ratio, and percentage of broken families. The fourth variable is also again the percentage who voted in the presidential election. However, an examination of all the variables in column 4 of table 5 reveals that the fifth variable to enter the regression equation should be the number of in-migrants between 1955 and 1960 as a percentage of the 1960 population. The percentage of in-migrants thus replaces the per capita taxes in my previous analysis.

The percentage of in-migrants has a partial correlation of .43 ($p < .01$) with AFDC rolls, indicating that the higher the in-migration, the larger are the AFDC rolls. The standardized regression coefficient, β, is .31 and the tolerance is .61. In-migration is clearly a more significant factor than fiscal capacity (partial $r = .36$, $p < .05$), and it reduces the amount of unexplained variation from 33 percent to 27 percent. The question remains, however, whether total in-migration is truly a "threat" variable or whether it indirectly measures other conditions.

There are a number of plausible explanations of why in-migration is positively related to AFDC rolls, controlling for the other variables in the prediction equation. First, a widely held view is that some people migrate from one state to another in order to obtain improved welfare benefits (Banfield 1969).[14] However, it is also possible to argue that migrants are more occupationally vulnerable, that they bring with them less adequate skills than are possessed by natives of the state (Lee 1966; Pihlblad and Gregory 1957; Gist and Clark 1938; Gist, Pihlblad, and Gregory 1941). Furthermore, migrants may face difficult periods of adjustment which cause them to use welfare (Hanson and Simmons 1969; Rieger and Beagle 1974). Finally, some have argued that migrants, because of their precarious economic position, may exhaust their resources (Brown, Schwarzweller, and Mangalam 1963; Hill, Stycos, and Back 1959) and be unable to return to their previous residences. In any event, if and when migrants receive welfare benefits in the state of destination, they may reach the point where there is no foreseeable advantage to them in further migration or return migration.

Table 5

Independent Variables, 1960

% families poor
% broken families
Male underemployment rate
Female underemployment rate
% females not working
Nonworker-worker ratio

% voter participation
Median level of education
% high-school or more education
% upper white-collar employment
Per capita revenue
Per capita taxes
Urbanization index
Industrial index, males
Industrial index, females
% employed nonfarm

% black
% nonwhite
% native population born in South
% population increase, 1950–60
% total in-migration 1955-60
% net migration 1955–60
% nonwhite in-migration 1955–60
% nonwhite net migration 1955–60

R^2
Tolerance for variable entered on this st
β of variable entered on this step

Stepwise Regression of All Independent Variables on AFDC Rolls, 1960

	Correlations with AFDC Rolls, 1960				
	Partial Correlations with AFDC Rolls, Controlling for All Variables on This and Previous Steps				
Zero-Order Correlations	Male Underemployment Rate — Step 1	Nonworker-Worker Ratio — Step 2	% Broken Families — Step 3	% Voter Participation — Step 4	% Total In-migration — Step 5
(1)	(2)	(3)	(4)	(5)	(6)
.61[a]	.19	−.01	−.19	.08	.25
.43[a]	.16	.32[c]	—	—	—
.70[a]	—	—	—	—	—
.37[b]	.14	−.29[c]	−.06	−.13	−.02
.50[a]	.29[c]	−.12	−.04	.10	.00
.67[a]	.41[b]	—	—	—	—
−.32[a]	.22	.18	.38[b]	—	—
−.48[a]	−.15	−.04	.29	.27	.08
−.47[a]	−.10	−.02	.34[c]	.35[c]	.15
−.18	.08	.12	.30[c]	.33[c]	.07
.07	.16	.16	.31[c]	.35[c]	.17
.13	.14	.28	.36[c]	.36[c]	.21
−.21	.01	.22	.16	.15	.11
−.37[b]	.03	.19	.30[c]	.18	.06
−.30[c]	−.03	.29[c]	.28	.16	.08
−.01	−.02	.20	.11	.00	−.12
.36[b]	−.04	−.03	−.30[c]	−.02	.10
.33[b]	.01	.11	−.04	.20	.19
.28[c]	−.04	.03	.05	.24	.03
−.09	−.11	.06	.18	.30[c]	−.05
.01	−.08	.06	.29[c]	.43[b]	—
−.05	−.14	.04	.12	.22	−.18
−.32[c]	−.03	.04	.16	.04	−.07
−.44[a]	−.11	.09	.14	.04	−.05
	.49	.57	.62	.67	.73
	—	.60	.71	.47	.61
	—	—	.38	.25	.34

Social Security Bulletin 1960–61, 1970–71; U.S. Bureau of the Census 1961–63, 1963, 1973*b*; *Book of the States* 1962–63.

[a]$p<.001$. [b]$p<.01$. [c]$p<.05$.

If either of these arguments is correct, it should be particularly true for those migrants who are poorest and therefore most likely to end up on welfare. However, a careful examination of the available literature suggests that none of the arguments outlined above can explain the observed relationship between in-migration and welfare rolls.

Several authors have examined the relationship between welfare payments and migration to determine whether a relatively generous welfare system attracts poor people from other states (DeJong and Donnelly 1972, 1973; Sommers and Suits 1973; Barth 1970). In each case, however, the conclusion has been reached that people do not seem to migrate especially to obtain or increase their welfare payment levels. Nor may one conclude that abolishing residency requirements for public assistance will encourage people to move to those states with high welfare payments (Chambers 1969). Economic opportunities,[15] the location of friends and relatives (Barth 1970; Brown, Schwarzweller, and Mangalam 1963), distance (Beshers 1965; Lee 1966; Startup 1971), and, for blacks at least, the size of the black population in the area of destination (DeJong and Donnelly 1973) seem to be far more important factors in motivating people to migrate than desire for welfare.

Even if people do not migrate with the purpose of exploiting the welfare system, it would still be possible to find migrants overrepresented on the public assistance rolls. This may happen if migrants are unable to compete successfully with lifetime residents in the area of destination. Migrants generally are better equipped to compete in the industrial world than are those they leave behind (Beshers 1965; Bogue, Shryock, and Hoermann 1957; Lee 1966; Pihlblad and Gregory 1957; Gist and Clark 1938; Gist, Pihlblad, and Gregory 1941; Schwarzweller 1964; Blevins 1971), especially if their origin is the South (Bacon 1971, 1973; Cutright 1974; Startup 1971). More important, however, several studies have found that migrants in particular either do as well as those they join (Featherman 1971) or are better off than nonmigrants in the area of destination (Cutright 1974; Long 1974; U.S. Bureau of the Census 1973a; Ritchey 1974; Masters 1972; Taeuber and Taeuber 1965; Lowry, DeSalvo, and Woodfill 1971).

In general, then, migrants do not seem to face particularly difficult periods of adjustment (Rieger and Beagle 1974; Hanson and Simmons 1969; Masters 1972; Taeuber and Taeuber 1965; Wertheimer 1970; Kain and Persky 1968; Freedman and Freedman 1968;

Lurie and Rayack 1966), and recent black migrants generally have been found to be less likely to receive public assistance (Masters 1972; Podell 1967; Lurie 1968; Long 1974) than native-born blacks. In fact, several authors have argued that it may even be to the benefit of low-status migrants not to be fully integrated into the local community with its available alternative lifestyles (Savitz 1960; Long 1974). This might help explain why low-status migrants especially tend to do better than their nonmigrating counterparts in the area of destination. Certainly migrants do not become so destitute that they are immobilized and unable to seek better conditions elsewhere (DeJong and Ahmad 1974; Lansing and Morgan 1967).

In my own study I have no measure of the socioeconomic standing of migrants; however, the prevalence of poverty among nonwhites is comparatively much greater than among whites. Therefore, if there is a relationship between migration and welfare rolls, we would expect to observe that pattern most clearly for measures of nonwhite in-migration. Contrary to popular expectations, but in accordance with the studies discussed above, we find that the partial correlation between nonwhite in-migration and AFDC rolls is lower than that between total in-migration and AFDC rolls: when the percentage nonwhite in-migration is included in the stepwise regression analysis, it produces a partial correlation of only $r = .04$ (partial r for nonwhite net migration is .04). It is clear that it is total in-migration which is related to welfare rolls, not measures of nonwhite migration. I must conclude with Beale (1971) that migration has little if any direct impact on welfare.

What my findings do indicate is that migrants tend to go to states where there is less poverty and, incidentally, a welfare system in which it is easier to obtain benefits. I have already indicated that available data on internal migration points to the tendency for those who migrate to go to areas where there are better employment opportunities. These areas of economic opportunity tend to be in states with high-wage industries, high levels of urbanization, a high proportion of white-collar jobs, and so forth, and we find that in-migration in fact is largest in these states (see Appendix D). Thus the correlation between in-migration and AFDC rolls most likely reflects the fact that migration indirectly measures the relative attractiveness of the state with regard to economic opportunity and perhaps even with regard to the extension of citizenship as well.

To call measures of in-migration a "threat variable," then, is rather inappropriate here. In-migration may well be perceived as a threat to which state legislators respond; however, as we have seen, this response in the form of welfare restrictions has little effect on actual welfare rolls.

When the percentage of in-migration is entered into the regression equation on the fifth step, none of the remaining variables can significantly reduce the amount of unexplained variation in AFDC rolls (see column 6 in table 5). Thus five independent variables have been selected which in combination explain 73 percent of the total variation in AFDC rolls. Four of the five variables selected have standardized regression coefficients in the hypothesized direction: high mass society status and a high degree of objective economic need are both associated with high AFDC rolls. All but one of these coefficients are significant at the .01 level or better. The first variable entered into the equation, male underemployment rate, has a standardized regression coefficient which is significant at the .05 level using a one-tailed test, but the sign of the β again is in the hypothesized direction.

The standard error for the regression coefficient b in all cases is so small (see table 6) that the sign of the regression coefficient would not change if we added or subtracted the standard error. We can therefore be reasonably certain that each variable is related to AFDC in the direction indicated by the sign of the regression coefficient ($p < .05$). That is, controlling for all other variables in the equation, the greater the underemployment rate for males (stratification variable), $\beta = .25$; the larger the nonworker-worker ratio (stratification variable), $\beta = .66$; the larger the proportion of broken families (stratification variable), $\beta = .61$; the larger the voter participation (mass society variable), $\beta = .44$; and the greater the in-migration (threat variable), $\beta = .31$; the higher are AFDC rolls.[16] Thus, both models operate in the way we had anticipated, but the stratification variables are clearly the more important in 1960.[17]

This final stepwise regression represents a considerable improvement over the two attempted earlier. It not only accounts for more of the total variance among state AFDC rolls but is able to include several variables which are of theoretical significance. Basically the set of determinants for 1960 shows a descending order in which objective economic need is most important, while measures of societal participation show a significant but secondary relationship. The only mass society variable included in the 1960 final regression equation is the one which received its highest direct contribution from the composite factor (Factor I, which contributed to both

Table 6   **Determinants of AFDC Rolls, 1960**

Variables Which Entered into the Final Prediction Equation, 1960	Regression Coefficient (b)	Standard Error of b	Standardized Regression Coefficient (β)	F-Level for β	Level of Significance[a] of β ($p \leq$)
Male underemployment rate	.041	.024	.25	2.9	.045
Nonworker-worker ratio	3.004	.563	.66	28.5	.001
% broken families	.244	.050	.61	23.5	.001
% voter participation	.023	.006	.44	13.5	.001
% total in-migration 1955–60	.042	.013	.31	9.7	.002
(Constant)	(−10.028)				

Sources   *Social Security Bulletin* 1960–61, 1970–71; U.S. Bureau of the Census 1961–63, 1963, 1973*b*; *Book of the States* 1962–63.

[a]Using a one-tailed test; d.f.=43

stratification and mass society variables). This, together with the magnitude of the βs for two of the three stratification variables included in the prediction equation, emphasizes the extent to which it is the stratification variables which primarily explain the variation in AFDC rolls. Put differently, in 1960 the response to deprivation and need in the various states was primarily in the form of the stratification approach, reflecting objective conditions of need.

Conclusion

In sum, we have been able to settle two main issues in this chapter. First we have established that the stratification and the mass society variables operate differently with regard to AFDC rolls, although the two sets are quite highly intercorrelated in 1960. Second, we have established which mix of factors is associated with AFDC rolls in 1960 and have been able to explain a total of 73 percent of the state-by-state variance in AFDC rolls. Not surprisingly, measures of economic dependency were found to be the most important factors in determining the relative size of AFDC rolls. However, it was also apparent that economic dependency was not a sole or sufficient factor. Once we have controlled for the most important measure of poverty we find that AFDC rolls clearly reflect the extent to which welfare responds to broader social needs.

This extension of social citizenship in some states may have two sources: on the one hand, some states have more potential AFDC recipients because their eligibility requirements are more lenient. On the other hand, some states may have a larger proportion of their potential AFDC recipients actually receiving benefits than other states. It is difficult to establish whether potential recipients in some states do not receive AFDC because they are discriminated against or because these potential recipients find the welfare option more stigmatizing than other options so that they fail to collect benefits to which they may be entitled. The net result, however, is that AFDC rolls are not just a reflection of the relative degree of economic dependency in the state, although poverty certainly is the most important element. AFDC rolls are also a reflection of the relative standard of well-being in the state: the higher the standards, the higher the AFDC rolls.

In 1960 AFDC rolls were thus determined foremost by incidence of poverty and secondarily by extension of citizenship in the state. As we shall see in the next chapter, the mix of variables determining AFDC rolls is considerably different in 1970: the extension of citizenship has become more important, while conditions of economic dependency have lost ground in determining AFDC rolls.

Relative Poverty and
Collective Response

6

In 1960 measures of economic dependency were the primary factors in determining AFDC rolls. In 1970 the situation was considerably more complex. Poverty and economic dependency are no longer the sole or primary factors in determining AFDC rolls, and by 1970 the proportion of families in a state that received AFDC benefits had come to reflect more nearly the state's willingness to undertake responsibility for its more unfortunate members.

Between 1960 and 1970 welfare benefits in the United States expanded to include diverse populations, some of whom are persistently poor, but an increasing number of whom come from different stations of life. One clear indication of this trend is the extent to which poverty in a state has come to be less related to the size of welfare rolls. In 1960 the correlation between the percentage of families that were poor in a state and the proportion of families that were receiving AFDC was $r = .61$. By 1970, this correlation had been reduced to $r = .28$. During the same decade the zero-order correlations between welfare rolls and various measures of economic dependency (that is, the proportion of males and females working less than fifty to fifty-two weeks a year and the ratio between nonworkers and workers) had been reduced to about one-half the size of the correlations in 1960 (see columns 1 and 2 of table 7). The maximum amount of variation in welfare rolls explained by any measure of economic dependency was reduced from 49 percent in 1960 to 15 percent in 1970. Clearly considerations other than poverty alone had become prevalent by 1970.

It is evident that between 1960 and 1970 at least some states moved in the direction of extending welfare according to broader social needs. The degree of urbanization was correlated negatively with AFDC rolls in 1960 ($r = -.21$) but positively in 1970 ($r = .17$). There are similar changes from a negative to a positive correlation between welfare rolls and other indexes of relative well-being: the proportion of all workers employed in upper white-collar occupations, the prevalence of high-wage industries for males and females, and percentage employed in nonfarm occupations (see columns 1 and 2 in table 7). For two of the indexes of mass society—level of education and extent of voter participation—the correlations did not actually reverse signs between 1960 and 1970, but they were nevertheless substantially reduced in size respectively from a correlation of $r = -.48$ to $r = -.20$ (median level of education) and from $r = -.32$ to $r = -.16$ (voter participation).

In order to determine whether these changes in the zero-order correlations may be considered substantial, the null hypothesis that $\rho_1 = \rho_2$ for each set of correlations in 1960 and 1970 was tested.[1] In other words, we are examining whether the correlation between AFDC rolls and a given independent variable, for example, percentage of families poor, is substantially different in 1970 and 1960. It would of course be most interesting to find that the two correlation coefficients are significantly different from one another, since this would support my argument that the 1960s saw a shift in the approach to welfare in the American states.

Since we are dealing with forty-nine of the fifty states at two different points in time, these two sets of cases are neither samples nor independent of one another. Consequently, the results of testing such a series of hypotheses cannot be considered solely in terms of statistical significance but will mainly allow us to indicate whether the changes are "substantial."

Column 3 in table 7 shows the significance levels for the null hypotheses involving AFDC rolls and all the independent variables. There were no significant changes in the correlations between AFDC rolls and any of the threat variables included in both the 1960 and 1970 analyses except for the correlation with nonwhite net migration. However, in agreement with the discussion above, there were substantial reductions in most of the zero-order correlations between AFDC rolls and the stratification variables. Only the correlations involving female underemployment ($r = .37$ in 1960, $r = .15$ in 1970) and the percentage of broken families ($r = .43$ in 1960 and $r = .58$ in 1970) were not significantly different in 1970 compared with 1960. The change in the correlation coefficient between the percentage of females not working and AFDC rolls from $r = .50$ in 1960 to $r = .23$ in 1970 was significant only at the .076 level.

The shift in the correlations between AFDC rolls and mass society variables from 1960 to 1970 is fairly substantial. However, the correlations involving per capita revenue ($r = .07$ in 1960, $r = .30$ in 1970), per capita taxes ($r = .13$ in 1960, $r = .35$ in 1970), and voter participation ($r = -.32$ in 1960, $r = -.16$ in 1970) do not differ much over the decade. Furthermore, the change in the correlation involving median level of education was barely significant ($p < .061$), from $r = -.48$ in 1960 to $r = -.20$ in 1970.

Overall, the results in table 7 support the argument that there were substantial changes in most of the determinants of AFDC rolls between 1960 and 1970. Most stratification variables were significantly less related to AFDC rolls in 1970 than in 1960. Most

Table 7

Independent Variables

% families poor
% broken families
Male underemployment rate
Female underemployment rate
% females not working
Nonworker-worker ratio

% voter participation
Median level of education
% high-school or more education
% upper white-collar employment
Per capita revenue
Per capita taxes
Urbanization index
Industrial index, males
Industrial index, females
% employed nonfarm

% black
% nonwhite
% born in South
% population increase
% total in-migration
% total net migration
% nonwhite in-migration
% nonwhite net migration

Changes in Zero-Order Correlations between AFDC Rolls and Independent Variables, 1960–70

Zero-Order Correlations with AFDC Rolls		Significance of Changes in Correlations between 1960 and 1970
1960	1970	
(1)	(2)	(3)
.61[a]	.28[c]	$p \le .025$
.43[a]	.58[a]	Not significant
.70[a]	.39[b]	$p \le .015$
.37[b]	.15	Not significant
.50[a]	.23	$p \le .076$
.67[a]	.31[c]	$p \le .069$
−.32[c]	−.16	Not significant
−.48[a]	−.20	$p \le .061$
−.47[a]	−.16	$p \le .025$
−.18	.17	$p \le .041$
.07	.30[c]	Not significant
.13	.35[b]	Not significant
−.21	.17	$p \le .031$
−.37[b]	.05	$p \le .019$
−.30[c]	.28[c]	$p \le .002$
−.01	.33[b]	$p \le .047$
.36[b]	.23	Not significant
.33[b]	.25[c]	Not significant
.28[c]	.14	Not significant
−.09	−.05	Not significant
.01	−.20	Not significant
−.05	−.08	Not significant
−.32[c]	−.24	Not significant
−.44[a]	−.07	$p \le .020$

s U.S. Bureau of the Census 1961–63, 1971–73, 1973b,c; *Social Security Bulletin* 1960, 1961, 1970, 1971; *Book of the States* 1962–63.

[a]$p < .001$.   [b]$p < .01$.   [c]$p < .05$.

mass society variables had changed significantly from a point in 1960 where high mass society status was inversely related to AFDC rolls to 1970 where high mass society status tended to be directly related to high AFDC rolls even in these zero-order correlations.

None of these changes in the zero-order determinants of AFDC rolls can be attributed confidently to changes in the interrelationships among the independent variables, at least as far as the mass society and stratification variables are concerned. It has already been shown in the factor analyses of the mass society and stratification variables that very similar results were obtained in 1960 and 1970. Of the few significant changes in zero-order correlations between the mass society and stratification variables, almost all occurred among pairs of variables that included measures of the economic standing of women in some way.[2] There were also several changes between correlations involving threat variables and other independent variables between 1960 and 1970. This pattern is to be expected, since there were changes in how mass society and stratification variables relate to AFDC rolls, but with one exception (nonwhite net migration) not in how the threat variables related to AFDC rolls (see table 7).

Clearly, then, AFDC rolls seem to be related differently to most of the independent variables in 1970 than they were in 1960. The stratification variables have lost ground, but from an examination of the zero-order correlations alone it is uncertain whether any of the mass society variables have gained much influence on AFDC rolls. The stepwise regression of all the independent variables on AFDC rolls in 1970 will make it possible to evaluate the contribution of each set of variables in 1970, which then can be compared with the determinants of AFDC rolls in 1960. This will also make it possible to establish whether the independent variables can explain as much of the variation in AFDC rolls in 1970 as in 1960.

Responding to Relative Needs

Column 1 of table 8 shows all the zero-order correlations between AFDC rolls and the stratification, mass society, and threat variables for 1970. The highest correlation is between AFDC rolls and the percentage of broken families ($r = .58$), the only correlation that is significant at the .001 level. This variable was one of only three variables which had higher correlations with AFDC rolls in 1970 than in 1960 (increasing from $r = .43$ in 1960).[3] In other words, the extent to which families in a state are broken is more clearly related to the proportion of all families receiving AFDC by 1970.

When the percentage of broken families is entered into the regression equation for predicting AFDC rolls in 1970, all of the mass society variables become positively correlated with AFDC rolls, in several cases significantly so.[4] Some of the stratification variables also have high partial correlations with AFDC rolls, particularly the various measures of employment.[5] Yet the variable with the highest partial correlation is the state per capita revenue (partial $r = .47$), which would have a standardized regression coefficient of $\beta = .39$ if it was brought into the regression equation on step 2 (tolerance = .98). Thus the higher the per capita revenue, the higher are the AFDC rolls, a pattern also found in the 1960 analysis.[6] When the per capita revenue is entered on step 2 (see column 3 of table 8), the total amount of explained variation is increased to 48 percent from 34 percent.

Entering this second variable into the regression equation reduces all the partial correlations between the mass society variables and AFDC rolls but increases all the partial correlations for the stratification variables. Controlling for the percentage of broken families and the per capita revenue, all the stratification variables dealing with underemployment now have significant partial correlations with AFDC rolls ($p < .01$ or less). The variable with the highest standardized regression coefficient is the underemployment rate for women.

When the underemployment rate for females is entered into the regression equation on step 3, the amount of unexplained variation is reduced to 38 percent. Thus the first three variables to enter in 1970 explain about as much of the variation in AFDC rolls as the first three variables did in the 1960 analysis, in spite of the fact that almost all the zero-order correlations with AFDC rolls were smaller in 1970 than in 1960. The main difference is that in 1960 the first three variables to enter the regression equation were stratification variables. In 1970, only two of the three are stratification variables.

The fourth variable to enter the regression equation is the percentage of the population aged twenty-five and over who have finished high school (partial $r = .41$, $p < .01$; see column 4 in table 8). The standardized regression coefficient $\beta = .44$ indicates that the better educated the population of a state is, the higher are the AFDC rolls. The tolerance for this variable is fairly low (.32), partly because of the relatively high zero-order correlation with the

Table 8

Independent Variables, 1970

% families poor
% families very poor
% broken families
Male underemployment rate
Female underemployment rate
% females not working
Nonworker-worker ratio

% voter participation
Median level of education
% high-school or more education
% upper white-collar employment
Per capita revenue
Per capita taxes
Urbanization index
Industrial index, males
Industrial index, females
% employed nonfarm

% black
% nonwhite
% native population born in South
% population increase 1960–70
% total in-migration 1965–70
% total net migration 1965–70
% nonwhite in-migration 1965–70
% nonwhite net migration 1965–70

R^2
Tolerance for variable entered on this st•
β for variable entered on this step

Stepwise Regression of All Independent Variables on AFDC Rolls, 1970

	Correlations with AFDC Rolls, 1970				
	Partial Correlations with AFDC Rolls, Controlling for All Variables on This and Previous Steps				
Zero-Order Correlations	% Broken Families Step 1	Per Capita Revenue Step 2	Female Underemployment Rate Step 3	% High-School or More Education Step 4	% Total In-migration 1965–70 Step 5
(1)	(2)	(3)	(4)	(5)	(6)
.28[c]	.01	.14	−.15	.12	.29
.32[c]	.02	.14	−.14	.12	.28
.58[a]	—	—	—	—	—
.39[b]	.31[c]	.42[b]	−.02	.01	.12
.15	.36[c]	.51[a]	—	—	—
.23	.35[c]	.45[b]	−.06	.15	.17
.31[c]	.30[c]	.38[b]	−.11	.12	.15
−.16	.31[c]	.17	.28	.15	−.03
−.20	.24	.08	.28	−.12	−.20
−.16	.39[b]	.16	.41[b]	—	—
.17	.40[b]	.20	.27	−.01	.10
.30[c]	.47[a]	—	—	—	—
.35[b]	.35[b]	−.07	.16	.14	.11
.17	.17	.14	.27	.07	.07
.05	.17	.02	.19	−.06	−.19
.28[c]	.09	−.08	.20	−.01	−.05
.33[b]	.02	−.06	.03	−.19	−.17
.23	−.41[b]	−.26	−.31[c]	−.22	−.16
.25	−.17	−.33[c]	−.19	−.06	.01
.14	−.12	−.07	−.10	−.16	.06
−.05	−.09	−.22	−.05	−.29	−.08
−.20	−.06	−.30[c]	−.22	−.33[c]	—
−.08	−.19	−.19	−.07	−.27	−.10
−.24	−.03	.00	.18	.03	.02
−.07	.11	.12	.34[c]	.17	.10
	.34	.48	.62	.68	.72
	—	.98	.91	.32	.73
	—	.39	.39	.44	−.22

U.S. Bureau of the Census 1971–73, 1973b,c; Social Security Bulletin 1970, 1971.

[a]$p<.001$.   [b]$p<.01$.   [c]$p<.05$.

percentage of broken families ($r = -.68$). As is indicated in column 4 of table 8, most of the other mass society variables are also positively correlated with AFDC rolls, although not significantly so. Still, the percentage of the adult population with at least a high-school education can contribute most to reducing the variation in AFDC rolls and, if entered into the equation on step 4, increases the total amount of explained variation in AFDC rolls to 68 percent.

Only one of the remaining variables has a partial correlation which is large enough to be included in the regression equation: percentage of total in-migration 1965–70 (partial $r = -.33$, $p < .05$; see column 5, table 8). When total in-migration is allowed to enter the regression equation, none of the remaining variables can significantly reduce the amount of unexplained variation in AFDC rolls (see column 6, table 8). The negative partial correlation between total in-migration 1965–70 and AFDC rolls in 1970 is in sharp contrast to the analysis for 1960, where the percentage of total in-migrants was *positively* related to AFDC rolls, controlling for other variables in the equation. The reversal of the relationship between AFDC rolls and measures of migration between 1960 and 1970 will be discussed below.

When this fifth and final variable is entered into the regression equation for 1970, the total explained variation in AFDC rolls is increased by four percentage points to a total of 72 percent. This is very near the proportion of the variation in AFDC rolls, as was explained by the five variables selected in 1960 (73 percent). By any criterion, further regression analysis seems unjustified, and by 1970 it appears that the larger the proportion of broken families, $\beta = 1.02$, $p < .001$ (stratification variable); the greater the per capita revenue, $\beta = .33$, $p < .01$ (mass society variable); the greater the proportion of females underemployed, $\beta = .45$, $p < .001$ (stratification variable); the higher the proportion of the adult population with at least a high-school education, $\beta = .51$, $p < .001$ (mass society variable); and the smaller the total in-migration between 1965 and 1970, $\beta = -.22$, $p < .05$ ("threat" variable), the higher are AFDC rolls.[7] Furthermore, all of these standardized regression coefficients are significantly different from zero at least at the .05 level (see table 9). In the final regression equation the percentage of broken families is still the most important variable (the β is highest for this variable), but a mass society variable is the second most important (percentage with at least a high-school education). In 1960 the two most important variables were both stratification variables (nonworker-worker ratio and percentage of broken families). The underemployment rate for females (a stratification variable) is the third most important variable in the 1970 equation, followed by a mass society variable (per capita revenue). Least important is the "threat" variable (percentage of total in-migration between 1965 and 1970).

Table 9 **Determinants of AFDC Rolls, 1970**

Variables Which Entered into the Final Prediction Equation, 1970	Regression Coefficient (b)	Standard Error of b	Standardized Regression Coefficient (β)	F-Level for β	Level of Significance[a] of β (p ≤)
% broken families	.538	.068	1.02	63.1	.001
Per capita revenue	.004	.001	.33	10.3	.01
Female underemployment rate	.192	.039	.45	24.0	.001
% high-school or more education	.071	.020	.51	12.3	.001
% total in-migration	−.050	.021	−.22	5.4	.013
(Constant)	(−24.023)				

Sources	U.S. Bureau of the Census 1971–73, 1973b, c; *Social Security Bulletin* 1970, 1971.
[a]	For a two-tailed test; d.f.=43.

The situation in 1970 differs from that in 1960 not only with regard to the relative number of stratification and mass society variables included, but also in how the four mass society and stratification factors extracted in chapter 4 are represented in the final prediction equations. In 1960 the composite factor (Factor I) was represented by three variables: two stratification variables (male underemployment rate and percentage of broken families) and one mass society variable (percentage of voter participation). In 1970 the composite factor (Factor II) is represented by two variables, a stratification variable (percentage of broken families) and a mass society variable (percentage with at least a high-school education).

The inclusion factor was not represented by any variable in 1960, but in 1970 that factor is represented by one variable, per capita revenue. The female employment factor is represented by one variable in both 1960 and 1970 (nonworker-worker ratio in 1960, female underemployment rate in 1970). At the end of either decade no variable from the modernization factor (urbanization and industrialization) entered the regression equation.

Mass society variables, then, are clearly more prominent in 1970 than in 1960, both in the number and type of mass society variables included in 1970 compared with 1960 and in terms of their relative importance in the final prediction equations (size of the βs). Thus AFDC rolls in 1970 are less a reflection of the extent of objective need in the states. The prominence of the mass society variables suggests instead that relative as well as absolute notions of need have become prevalent. Thus states with better-educated populations and greater willingness to undertake collective responsibilities (as measured by per capita revenue) by 1970 were extending AFDC to a greater proportion of their families than would have been the case in 1960, or than we would expect on the basis of objective need for welfare alone. The intervening decade, then, seems to have been a genuine watershed, and the states seem to have moved sharply toward the mass society approach, although that movement was still incomplete by 1970.[8]

Migration: Push or Pull

The first four of the variables which entered the regression equation in 1970 seem to be operating in much the same way as the same or similar variables operated in 1960; that is, the higher the mass society status and the greater the extent of economic dependency in the state, the higher are the AFDC rolls. However, controlling for other variables in the regression equation, total in-migration between 1965 and 1970 is negatively correlated with AFDC rolls in 1970, whereas the corresponding measure in 1960 was positively correlated with AFDC rolls. Obviously, these relationships should be further examined.

One possibility is that the negative partial correlation between AFDC rolls and population increase in 1970 reflects the type of variables included on the first four steps of the regression analysis. In 1970, these variables are either clearly mass society variables (percentage with at least high-school education and per capita revenue) or stratification variables which are more ambiguous measures of economic dependency (percentage of broken families and female underemployment) than the variables included in 1960 (male underemployment and nonworker-worker ratio). In other words, in 1960 we may have controlled for direct economic dependency when we looked at the partial correlation between AFDC rolls and in-migration, whereas in 1970 we have controlled more for mass society variables.

Migration in the United States is generally believed to be the joint result of a push out of an area owing to inadequate economic opportunities and the pull into another area which has attractive economic conditions such as high wages and job opportunities (Lee 1966). This interpretation is supported in this study by the zero-order correlations between the percentage of total in-migration and the corresponding mass society and stratification variables in 1960 and 1970.[9] Several points should be emphasized about these relationships. Percentage of total in-migration is positive related to the major mass society (inclusion) variables[10] in both 1960 and 1970: the median correlation was $r = .50$ in 1960 and $r = .40$ in 1970. None of the modernization variables[11] are significantly related to the amount of in-migration in either of those years: the median correlation was $r = .21$ in 1960 and $r = .11$ in 1970. Also, a few of the stratification variables are related in both years to the percentage of in-migration in the expected direction: the greater the need, the smaller is the in-migration. However, all these relationships are quite weak: the median correlation was $r = -.20$ in 1960 and $r = -.21$ in 1970.

The relationships between the amount of in-migration and some of the "threat" variables suggest a possible regional complication: in-migration was greatest to those states with large southern-born populations ($r = .51$ in 1960, $r = .35$ in 1970). However, the relative size of the black (and nonwhite) population is not significantly related to total in-migration ($r = -.18$ in 1960, $r = -.23$ in 1970). Nor does the average rate of in-migration differ between the southern (11.1 percent) and non-southern states (11.9 percent). For both regions, the correlation between AFDC rolls and total in-migration is negative ($r = -.32$ in the South and $r = -.15$ outside the South), but not significantly so. The observed relationship between AFDC rolls and total in-migration, therefore, cannot be attributed to regional factors alone.

Instead, the relationships reported above suggest that in-migration is determined by both mass society and stratification conditions, but particularly the former. In 1970, however, total in-migration enters the regression equation more as a measure of poverty in the state, since we have controlled for mass society status. This interpretation is also supported by an examination of the successive partial correlation coefficients between AFDC rolls and percentage of total in-migration as each independent variable is selected into the final prediction equation. In 1970 the percentage of total in-migration variable behaves very much like the stratification variables: the partial correlation coefficient increases each time a mass society variable is entered and decreases each time a stratification variable is entered into the equation (see table 8). In 1960, on the other hand, conditions of poverty were controlled and in-migration reflects less the push out of the state owing to economic dependency (which I argue is the case in 1970) than the attractiveness of the state as a destination. In 1960 the percentage of total in-migration followed the general pattern of the mass society variables in the stepwise regression analysis; that is, the partial correlation coefficient increased when a stratification variable was entered and decreased when a mass society variable was included in the analysis (see table 5). In 1960, therefore, migration may operate more as a mass society variable than in 1970, when it is primarily a stratification variable.

The Cycle of Family
Disorganization and
Economic Opportunity

In both the 1960 and the 1970 analysis the percentage of broken families was a major factor in determining the size of AFDC rolls. The specific ways in which this variable operates as a stratification variable deserves close examination, for the relationship between the extent of family dissolution and the character of economic conditions is highly complex and surrounded by considerable controversy. On the one hand, a state with a relatively small proportion of all families intact is likely to have greater economic dependency because female-headed families, which constitute the majority (77.4 percent in 1970) of families which are not husband-wife families, have lower incomes and are employed less than male-headed families.[12] However, it is also likely that low-income and unemployment may be one of the factors contributing to family dissolution. In other words, not only does the existence of broken families influence measures of economic dependency, but for various reasons marital status itself may be altered by economic conditions.

A common assumption is that the availability of public assistance itself causes the breakup of low-income families. This would of course directly explain the high positive correlation between AFDC rolls and percentage of broken families. According to this approach, low-income males often decide to leave their families in order to make their dependents eligible for public assistance (Banfield 1969; Honig 1973, 1974; Durbin 1973; Moles, forthcoming). In many ways abandonment for such reasons appears to be rational economic behavior, since welfare payments often provide greater financial assistance to a family than an unskilled or semiskilled male could earn even if he were working full time.

It is presumably this touch of rational opportunism, often so admired in the American culture, that has made the argument that welfare causes family dissolution so appealing to so many people. The general public, as well as politicians, public administrators, and social scientists, seems to have endorsed it, especially when attempting to explain the growth in public assistance during the 1960s. However, there is considerable reason to doubt that the welfare system ought to take the major blame for the breakdown of low-income families. Most writers subscribing to the argument have concentrated mainly on elaborating the ways in which welfare *may* encourage fathers to desert, with only a hint of supporting data (Banfield 1969). Where data are presented, they are usually of such a nature as to provide only indirect, and often ambiguous or superficial, support for the argument (Honig 1973, 1974; Moles, forthcoming; Durbin 1973). In other words, there is much casual empiricism, some bias, and very little hard data supporting the interpretation that welfare causes family dissolution (Shiller 1973; Rein and Heclo 1973; Glazer 1969).

Careful analysis of the available data suggests that poverty itself, not dependency, is the cause of family dissolution (Shiller 1973). There are reasons to think that the strain of low income and unemployment may significantly diminish conjugal cohesion directly (Scanzone 1970; Goode 1962; Monahan 1955; Udry 1966, 1967), especially during periods of generally improving economic conditions such as the 1960s. A number of observers have also emphasized the economic performance of wives relative to that of their husbands. Both these arguments imply that it is very important to most families that the husband maintain, at least symbolically, superiority in the area of family income (Liebow 1967; Suttles 1968; Komarovsky 1964; Gans 1962). If a wife's earnings are high compared with those of her husband or if the husband's income is comparatively low, this may strain the marriage, since it runs counter to the cultural ideal where the husband is the provider and the wife no serious threat to his position as head of the household. Furthermore, if high earnings are available to women, females are less dependent on actual or prospective mates. There may be fewer reasons for a married woman to save the marriage at any cost and less reason for a woman to marry in the first place (Goode 1962; Havens 1973).

To examine whether the relative position of women in the economy is an important factor in determining the proportion of families which are broken, I computed the ratio between the industrial index for males and the industrial index for females. The higher this ratio, the more males are employed in high-wage industries compared with females. The data suggest that there are strong reasons for emphasizing the importance of the relative position of women in the economy, since the ratio between the industrial index for males and the industrial index for females is the single most important predictor of the extent to which families are broken in a state in both 1960 ($r = -.74$) and 1970 ($r = -.81$): the more males are paid relative to females, the fewer families are broken.

Overall economic conditions, however, are also important: the more families which are poor and the more males who are under-employed, the larger is the percentage of broken families in both 1960 and 1970.[13] In states where females have relatively high earnings compared with males[14] and where more females are employed, especially full year, there are more broken families. It is difficult to know the exact direction of the causal relationship between these variables. Possibly it runs both ways: a relatively independent economic position of women in a state may increase family dissolution, while family dissolution from other causes may itself increase the relative economic standing of females, since female heads of households tend to work more and earn more than married females.

The major point needing emphasis is that in 1970 the percentage of broken families was the most important determinant of AFDC rolls, whereas in 1960 that variable entered only on the third step of the stepwise regression analysis. The relative economic position of females seems to have become a more important factor for AFDC rolls in 1970 than in 1960. Furthermore, the strength of the relationship between the ratio of industrial indexes and percentage of broken families was greater in 1970 ($r = -.81$) than in 1960 ($r = -.74$). We can add that it is the percentage of females who are underemployed which enters into the regression analysis in 1970, whereas it was the percentage of males underemployed that entered in the 1960 analysis.

The increasing importance of the economic position of women is further illustrated when we examine changes in employment conditions during the decade. There was no change between 1960 and 1970 in the extent to which females were employed only part of the year, but there were decreases in the extent to which females were not working at all (-6.8 percentage points) or were under-employed (-6.6 percentage points), while male underemployment decreased -7.2 percentage points.[15] Thus females became more integrated into the economy as active participants between 1960 and 1970, and AFDC rolls seems to have become more directly related to the economic position of women rather than to the total amount of economic dependency in the state.[16] This conclusion is also supported by the results of the factor analysis in chapter 4. In 1960 variables relating to female employment separate out on one factor. In 1970 there seems to be no distinction between male employment and female employment variables. Both fall on the same factor.

The Uneven Growth in AFDC Rolls: 1960-70

These results suggest that a more comprehensive examination should be undertaken of state variation in the growth of AFDC rolls between 1960 and 1970. AFDC rolls increased substantially in most states and not at all in a few others. Overall the change was very great, with the proportion of families on AFDC increasing an average of 79.6 percent in the forty-nine states, ranging from an increase of 267 percent in New York to a decrease of 7.5 percent in North Carolina. This uneven growth in welfare rolls is also indicated by the relatively low zero-order correlation between the time series variables of welfare rolls—1960 AFDC rolls and 1970 AFDC rolls—($r = .64$).[17]

Using the AFDC rolls in 1960 to predict the 1970 AFDC rolls explains only 41 percent of the 1970 AFDC rolls variation. Obviously considerable changes took place during the 1960s in the pattern of factors which determine AFDC rolls. The residual in 1970, that is, the differences between the actual 1970 rolls and the AFDC rolls predicted in 1970 on the basis of the 1960 rolls, also varies considerably from state to state. The range of the residual, or error (4.2 percentage points), is almost as great as the range of the actual 1970 AFDC rolls (4.6 percentage points) and greater than the range of the 1960 AFDC rolls (3.7 percentage points).

Once again the changing position of women in the economic structure seems to have had an impact on AFDC rolls. The results in table 10, column 1, show that one of the best predictors of growth in AFDC rolls is the increase in male underemployment, followed closely by the increase in female underemployment. In other words, the larger the number of men and women employed full year, the less AFDC rolls grew ($r = .65$). These particular findings should be carefully examined, for they seemingly lend support to the argument that many people, poor and otherwise, have come to prefer the leisure of welfare to the unpleasantness of work. This premise has gained particular currency in recent years because it both explains the recent growth in public assistance rolls and links it directly to increasing welfare payments. More important, perhaps, it caters to the traditional American belief that public welfare endangers private enterprise and the work ethic (Piven and Cloward 1971; Wilensky and Lebeaux 1965; Grønbjerg, Street, and Suttles, forthcoming). More generous welfare payments, then, are seen not only as encouraging males to abandon their families, but also as providing poor people with less incentive to work (Banfield 1968, 1969; Garfinkel and Orr 1974; Durbin 1973; Kasper 1968; Spall and McGoughran 1972; U.S. Congress, House Committee on Ways and Means 1969; Hausman 1970; Winegarden 1973).

Some of these concerns have their origin in the culture of poverty theory and emphasize the presumed special aversion of poor people to hard work and self-discipline. However, most of the supporting data have been developed by economists, who generally seem to assume that only economic motives drive people to work (further economic enrichment in the case of the already rich, economic necessity in the case of the poor). Therefore, if welfare payments are "generous" there is less need to work and the price of leisure may become so low that people will prefer welfare to work. If welfare payments increase (as they generally did during the 1960s), more people will, according to this argument, find leisure available at a sufficiently low cost and cease work and obtain welfare instead.

I have already discussed the shortcomings of the culture of poverty theory in chapter 1, but there are also several problems with the "price of leisure" explanations provided by the economists. Not only is it often extremely difficult to determine whether there is in fact a disincentive for welfare recipients to work because of the highly variable and complex "tax rates" applied to nonwelfare income (Heffernan 1973; Lurie 1974), but the lack of jobs for which welfare recipients would qualify, considering their low levels

Table 10
                  Zero-Order Correlations between Selected Variables and Percentage Increases in Independent Variables, 1960-70

Variables Measuring the Percentage Increase in Independent Variables	Percentage Increase in AFDC Rolls (1)	Corresponding 1960 Independent Variables (2)
% increase in poverty	.38[b]	−.36[b]
% increase in broken families	.16	−.50[a]
% increase in male underemployment rate	.48[a]	−.48[a]
% increase in female underemployment rate	.45[a]	−.00
% increase in females not working	−.03	.33[b]
% increase in nonworker-worker ratio	.39[b]	−.24
% increase in voter participation	−.01	−.32[c]
% increase in median level of education	−.31[c]	−.92[a]
% increase in high-school or more graduates	−.15	−.66[a]
% increase in upper white-collar employment	.06	−.41[a]
% increase in per capita revenue	.50[a]	−.48[a]
% increase in per capita taxes	.42[a]	−.35[b]
% increase in urbanization index	−.54[a]	−.39[b]
% increase in industrial index, males	−.26[c]	−.73[a]
% increase in industrial index, females	−.37[b]	−.60[a]
% increase in nonfarm employment	−.43[a]	−.92[a]
% increase in black population	.19	−.40[b]
% increase in nonwhite population	.49[a]	−.67[a]
% increase in native population born in South	.20	−.64[a]
% increase in restrictiveness of TES	−.26[c]	−.05

Sources   U.S. Bureau of the Census 1961–63, 1971–73, 1973b; *Social Security Bulletin* 1960, 1961, 1970, 1971; *Book of the States* 1962–63; U.S. Social Security Administration 1960, 1962; U.S. Social and Rehabilitation Service 1971d, f; SPCU Reports.

[a]$p<.001.$ [b]$p<.01.$ [c]$p<.05.$

of education and job skills, as well as their frequent ill health and lack of adequate child-care arrangements (Hausman 1970; Garfinkel and Orr 1974; Winegarden 1973), are more likely to influence the work participation of welfare mothers than is the level of welfare payments (Shea 1973; Burnside 1971; Reid and Smith 1972; Hausman 1969; Goodwin 1972). As Schiller (1973) and Rein and Wishnov (1971) conclude, there is considerable mobility between work and welfare, and often people occupy both statuses at the same time, using welfare to supplement inadequate earnings. Welfare recipients, in fact, are strongly motivated to work and have considerable work experience in spite of the low quality of jobs available to them (Shiller 1973; Goodwin 1972; Reid and Smith 1972; Burnside 1971; Davidson and Gaitz 1974; Burch 1974).

It is partly for these reasons that I am hesitant to make the obvious interpretation of the high positive correlations between the increase in male and female underemployment and increase in AFDC rolls between 1960 and 1970 (see table 10). It is important to note that male and female full-year employment increased in *all* states. The growth in AFDC rolls thus cannot be blamed on a presumed rejection of work by recipients. What may be argued instead is that in those states where economic opportunities for women (and men) improved relatively little, more families obtained welfare than in the states which saw great increases in employment opportunities. In other words, I argue that lack of adequate employment influences welfare rolls, rather than the other way around. A similar explanation may account for the finding that AFDC rolls increased most in those states which made the least progress in industrialization and urbanization.

A further examination of table 10 reveals the not surprising finding that large increases in welfare rolls were associated with large increases in per capita revenue ($r = .50$) and per capita state taxes ($r = .42$). It is of course difficult in either of these cases to know the direction of the causal relationship: whether AFDC rolls increased because more revenue was available to finance the programs[18] or whether the state government collected more revenue in order to finance a growing welfare program.

Most of the correlation coefficients reported in table 10, column 1, however, should be interpreted with some caution, since the change between 1960 and 1970 in many of the measured conditions is relatively small. More important, the states which changed most in terms of mass society status were the states which had lagged furthest behind in the previous decade. Almost all the zero-order correlations between the 1960 base variables and the increase in the corresponding variables between 1960 and 1970 indicate fairly strong negative relationships (see table 10, column 2). This is particularly important since the correlation between a variable in

1960 and the corresponding variable in 1970 generally is positive and very high for most of the mass society, stratification, and threat variables (see table 11, column 1). Correlating growth in AFDC rolls with changes in mass society, stratification, and threat conditions is quite problematic because of this "ceiling effect." It would therefore be more appropriate to examine which conditions in 1960 best predicted the subsequent increase in AFDC rolls. However, these findings do indicate that the states became more similar in their social and economic conditions during the 1960s. This is in itself a strong indication of an overall movement toward higher mass society status in the United States.

It was previously demonstrated that there were significant changes in the factors which determined AFDC rolls in 1970 compared with 1960. Specifically, it was argued that during that decade there was a shift toward higher mass society status among the states. Mass society variables gained ground, while conditions of poverty and need—that is, stratification variables—lost in being able to explain the state-by-state variation in AFDC rolls. This interpretation is strongly supported by the results in table 11, columns 2 and 3, which show the zero-order correlations between two measures of 1960–70 changes in AFDC rolls and mass society, stratification, and threat variables in 1960.

The results in table 11, column 2, indicate that AFDC rolls increased most in those states with high mass society status and least in the poor states: thirteen of the sixteen zero-order correlations between the percentage increase in AFDC rolls and mass society and stratification variables in 1960 are significant in the expected direction. Only per capita revenue, per capita state taxes, and percentage of broken families were not related to the increase in AFDC rolls. A similar pattern emerges when the zero-order correlations between the 1960 variables and the residual AFDC rolls in 1970 are examined, controlling for the 1960 AFDC rolls (see column 3 of table 11).

In contrast to these findings for the mass society and stratification variables, very few of the "threat" variables are related to increases in AFDC rolls. In most cases, with one important exception, AFDC rolls increased least in those states with large proportions of "threatening" groups (blacks, nonwhites, migrants), but few of these correlations were significant.

The important exception to this pattern is the correlation between the percentage increase in AFDC rolls and the percentage of nonwhite net migration in 1965–70. For these two variables $r = .52$

Table 11   **Zero-Order Correlations between 1960 Independent Variables and 1970 Independent Variables, and Selected Measures of Growth in AFDC Rolls, 1960-70**

	Zero-Order Correlations		
Independent Variables 1960	Corresponding 1970 Independent Variables	% Increase in AFDC Rolls 1960–70	Residual of 1970 AFDC, Controlling for 1960 AFDC
	(1)	(2)	(3)
% poor	.97[a]	−.58[a]	−.33[b]
% broken families	.95[a]	.03	.24
Male underemployment rate	.71[a]	−.60[a]	−.27[c]
Female underemployment rate	.87[a]	−.52[a]	−.40[b]
% females not working	.93[a]	−.40[b]	−.22
Nonworker-worker ratio	.95[a]	−.54[a]	−.28[c]
% voter participation	.82[a]	.28[c]	.11
Median level of education	.90[a]	.38[b]	.21
% high-school or more education	.98[a]	.33[b]	.17
% upper white-collar employment	.93[a]	.39[b]	.38[b]
Per capita revenue	.84[a]	−.09	.06
Per capita taxes	.84[a]	.07	.30[c]
Urbanization index	.91[a]	.52[a]	.49[a]
Industrial index, males	.94[a]	.57[a]	.44[a]
Industrial index, females	.92[a]	.59[a]	.50[a]
% employed nonfarm	.96[a]	.36[b]	.39[b]
% black	.99[a]	−.21	−.04
% nonwhite	.99[a]	−.20	−.01
% native population born in South	.99[a]	−.20	−.04
% population increase, 1960–70	——	.12	.09
% total in-migration 1965–70	——	−.20	−.20
% total net migration 1965–70	——	.07	.03
% nonwhite in-migration 1965–70	——	.19	−.00
% nonwhite net migration 1965–70	——	.52[a]	.34[b]
Total eligibility score, 1960	.70[a]	−.19	−.13
Total eligibility score, 1970	——	−.35[b]	−.28[b]

Sources   U.S. Bureau of the Census 1961–63, 1971–73, 1973*b*; *Social Security Bulletin* 1960, 1961, 1970, 1971; *Book of the States* 1962–63; U.S. Social Security Administration 1960, 1962; U.S. Social and Rehabilitation Service 1971*d*, *f*; SPCU Reports.

[a]$p<.001.$ [b]$p<.01.$ [c]$p<.05.$

$(p < .001)$, indicating that the greater the nonwhite net migration during the second half of the 1960s,[19] the greater the increase in AFDC rolls. This finding might by itself lend support to the Piven and Cloward argument that welfare rolls increased mainly in those cities which had seen a large influx of southern blacks (1971, p. 189). However, Piven and Cloward maintain that it was black migration during the 1950s which caused the growth in AFDC rolls in the 1960s by creating political pressures in the areas of destination. That argument is not supported by my data: nonwhite net migration 1955-60 has a lower correlation with growth in AFDC rolls $(r = .38)$ than does nonwhite net migration 1965-70 $(r = .52)$.

The positive relationship between nonwhite net migration during the 1960s and the growth in AFDC rolls during the same period could of course also be interpreted as lending support to the usual argument that welfare rolls in the large industrial northern states increased because southern blacks flocked to these areas during the 1950s and 1960s. However, as was discussed in chapter 5, available data suggest that nonwhite migration cannot be blamed for the growth in AFDC rolls. The allegation that welfare rolls have increased mainly, or at least in part, because of the migration of poor blacks from the South to the northern industrial states, where they could obtain welfare because eligibility requirements for AFDC are more lenient, will be discussed in greater detail in the following chapter. At this point it should be emphasized that there is only circumstantial evidence in support of such an argument. Other factors, such as mass society status, seem to be more important.

This interpretation is also supported by the very strong negative correlations between nonwhite net migration 1965-70 and the stratification variables in both 1960 (median $r = -.46$, ranging between $r = -.33$ and $r = -.69$; see table 22 in Appendix D) and 1970 (median $r = -.41$, ranging between $r = -.21$ and $r = -.68$; see table 21 in Appendix D). Similarly, nonwhite net migration 1965-70 is positively related to most mass society variables in both 1960 and 1970. The median correlation was $r = .48$ in 1960 (ranging between $r = -.03$ and $r = .68$; see table 22 in Appendix D) and median $r = .46$ in 1970 (ranging between $r = .04$ and $r = .72$; see table 21 in Appendix D). Thus the amount of nonwhite net migration may simply measure the relative attractiveness of the state, and the positive correlation between growth in AFDC rolls and nonwhite net migration is probably spurious.

A final point which should be mentioned here is the negative correlation between growth in AFDC rolls and changes in the Total Eligibility Score (see table 10), indicating that welfare rolls grew more in those states which liberalized their eligibility requirements the most. As will be shown in chapter 7, this is the first and only indication in this study that eligibility requirements may in fact have some impact on AFDC rolls. These findings suggest that at any given time conditions such as poverty, need, and mass society status may be more important in determining the relative size of AFDC rolls. However, over time, liberalizing these requirements may affect the growth of AFDC rolls (Spall and McGoughran 1972).

Conceptions of Mass Society and Their Impact

The differences in the determinants of AFDC rolls in 1960 and 1970 may be expectable in view of the political and social events of the 1960s. The meaning of citizenship and all the rights and duties associated with it was widely debated during the decade. The civil rights movement helped focus attention on areas where the political, economic, and social aspects of citizenship had been partially denied to some members of the population. During this time there was an increasing tendency to question whether the right to vote, to obtain quality education, and to enter occupations on the basis of qualification alone was extended fully to blacks, Puerto Ricans, Indians, females, and diverse ethnic groups.

This concern with whether all members of society were allowed to receive valued goods on an equitable basis also focused attention on the distribution of income and welfare. Although welfare may not be considered to be of unqualified positive value, it is nevertheless a form of benefit. It became increasingly clear in the 1960s that this "good," as well as poverty, was unevenly distributed and it became a source of controversy. The 1960s saw the greatest volume of direct antipoverty legislation since the Great Depression. And for the first time the Supreme Court entered the field of public assistance politics by requiring that the states and the federal government extend public assistance uniformly to all. Thus public assistance moved in the direction of being a right which could not be arbitrarily denied. People had always had the right to apply, but the interpretation of welfare legislation became the issue, and the problem of whether an individual could sue to obtain welfare benefits became an even sharper issue.

It has been argued here and elsewhere (Marshall 1964; Shils 1975) that concern with citizenship and the rights of the lower-status members of society is likely to be associated with such factors as urbanization, education, and industrialization. It is to be expected, then, that these factors will come to be important in determining the size of welfare rolls. By 1970 this pattern had become evident even for the AFDC program, which is generally regarded as the stepchild and the most stigmatizing of all public assistance programs.

Conclusion

In 1960, indexes of economic dependency were primary factors in determining the relative size of AFDC rolls. By 1970 such indexes had declined in importance and had to some extent been replaced by mass society variables. This reflects trends toward both the extension of citizenship and the continuity of economic dependency. In both years, indexes of mass society status were important, and in both 1960 and 1970 a mix of complex factors determined AFDC rolls. The net change between 1960 and 1970 was in the direction of increasing emphasis on mass society in the determination of AFDC rolls. Also important is the extent to which measures of economic dependency included in the 1970 analysis refer more to the economic dependency of women rather than to overall indexes of poverty in the states.

Between 1960 and 1970, then, there was a shift in the relative importance of the two sets of social conditions which determine AFDC rolls: the willingness and the necessity to care for the poor. AFDC rolls have come to reflect more the degree to which states are willing to undertake broad social responsibilities and less the degree to which there are desperate economic needs in the states. This is not meant to imply that there are no longer any very poor Americans. But the number of poor has probably declined and the contribution of the various public assistance programs to this decline should not be neglected.[20]

Changing Concepts
of Deservedness

7

Public concern with the rights and duties of citizenship was present to a high degree in the political life of the 1960s and seems to have had its effect on the public assistance rolls. The impact of the civil rights movement on AFDC rolls may have occurred in three different, although related, areas and can be seen as a response to clearly demonstrated effects of discrimination in education, employment, and housing.

As was indicated earlier, AFDC eligibility requirements became considerably less restrictive during the 1960s owing to the prodding of the federal government, the enactment of specific Social Security Act amendments, and individual state actions. The result has been a well-documented expanding pool of formally eligible recipients (Durman 1973; Chambers 1969; Durbin 1973; Greenston and MacRae 1974; Honig 1974; Lynch 1967; Spall and McGoughran 1972). Second, there is some reason to think that court decisions, welfare rights organizations, and various other antipoverty organizations have succeeded in preventing arbitrary or illegal denials of aid to eligible recipients (Martin 1972; Bailis 1972; Piven and Cloward 1971; Helfgot 1974; Van Til 1973; Tripi 1974; Steiner 1974). Thus more of the potential recipients may have been added to the rolls by reducing or eliminating some of the informal restrictions that operate within each welfare office. Rules concerning eligibility for public assistance under the Social Security Act had rarely before been subject to court interpretation. Most of these recent legal developments restricted state options in welfare policies, at times quite severely. These efforts to broaden both formal and informal rules of eligibility seem to have been most successful in states with large urban centers and in those which are highly industrialized. Consequently, AFDC rolls have increased most in these states, although there may have been smaller increases for similar reasons in other states.

Finally, and perhaps most important, making welfare legally available and widely known to larger groups in the population, increasingly considering welfare as the right of any citizen in need, and emphasizing structural causes of poverty have necessarily reduced the stigma of welfare. There are no easy ways of documenting such a decrease in stigma. Although public opinion polls often include questions about welfare and welfare recipients, most of these concern whether welfare is an important political issue and whether more public funds should be allocated to it. Where questions about the character of welfare recipients have been asked, survey locations, sampling procedures, and the wording of questions have been so variable as to make any but the most superficial

comparisons difficult (Schiltz 1970). The issues are further complicated when we recognize that many may see the recent expansion in
welfare rolls as resulting in the inclusion of many nondeserving
people. There is considerable evidence that welfare recipients,
especially in the AFDC program, continue to be popularly thought
of as lazy, immoral opportunists (Alston and Dean 1972; Bell 1965;
Elman 1966; Feagin 1972; Kallen and Miller 1971; Perry and
Snyder 1971; Schiltz 1970; Williamson 1973, 1974a).

However, such popular opinions may have only limited impact on
applications for welfare. There are reasons to think that welfare
recipients themselves not only are aware of such popular stereotypes
(which generally are false, see Feagin 1972) but often endorse them
as being applicable to most recipients, although not to themselves.
The result of course is that many recipients consider welfare very
stigmatizing (Meyers and McIntyre 1969; Horan and Austin 1974;
Kerbo, Silberstein, and Snizek 1974; Goodwin 1972; Stuart 1975;
Williamson 1974b). However, the fact that welfare is stigmatizing
does not mean that people are unwilling to use it if they think it
necessary to support their families. In fact, it is entirely possible that
the more people think welfare recipients in general are undeserving,
the more they may be willing to go on welfare themselves, because by
comparison they may think they are more deserving.

The development of the Welfare Rights Organization (WRO) and
increasing rates of application strongly suggest that for some, at
least, going on welfare may be unpleasant because of what other
people think, but it is no longer something to be terribly ashamed
of (Goodwin 1972; Meyers and McIntyre 1969; Kerbo, Silberstein,
and Snizek 1974). By 1970, then, people may have become more
willing to apply for public assistance while they still had some
resources left, rather than to wait and try to get by until they had
absolutely no other alternative, in part because they thought themselves no worse than others taking welfare and in part because the
stigma itself had lessened.[1]

It is likely that both the decrease in informal discrimination and
the lessening of the stigma of welfare have occurred most fully in the
highly industrialized, well-educated, and civic-minded states. Both
of these factors represent some of the intervening variables between
formal AFDC eligibility requirements and the AFDC rolls. They
reflect a series of decisions made by potential recipients (whether or
not to apply for public assistance), applicants (whether or not to
fulfill agency requirements in order to obtain approval of application), and public welfare officials (whether or not to approve
applications and whether or not to continue assistance to a re-

cipient). This is not to say that these decisions are the only elements involved in how welfare policies become translated into welfare rolls, but they are crossroads in obtaining an adequate understanding of that process.

The striking thing about formal welfare policies is that they do not seem to have a straightforward and direct relationship to AFDC welfare rolls. In spite of the frequent public demands for tightening up the eligibility requirements, the correlation between the Total Eligibility Score (TES)[2] and AFDC rolls was $r = .15$ in 1960, a slight indication that the more restrictive the state was, the higher was the proportion of families receiving AFDC. At best, this would indicate that formal requirements of eligibility were largely ineffective in controlling the number of families who became eligible for AFDC or that poor and reluctant states have poor and reluctant welfare systems. By 1970 the correlation between the AFDC rolls and the TES was $r = -.08$, which indicates that these restrictions were hardly related to welfare rolls at all.

The lack of an obvious relationship between formal eligibility

Table 12

Independent Variables, 1960

Male underemployment rate
Nonworker-worker ratio
% broken families
% voter participation
% total in-migration, 1955–60
Total eligibility score

requirements and AFDC rolls could simply reflect the fact that two states may have similar eligibility requirements (as, for example, do West Virginia and California) but very different economic conditions. Thus identical eligibility requirements may produce great differences in the potential number of recipients who fulfill these requirements, if one state has a high degree of economic dependency and the other does not. If there are differences in the potential number of eligible recipients, there may also be differences in the number of people who actually get admitted to the rolls.

In order to examine whether there might be a relationship between AFDC rolls and AFDC policies, once various measures of dependency have been controlled, the TES was entered into the stepwise regressions on AFDC rolls in both 1960 and 1970. In neither year do welfare policies enter into the regression analysis, although the partial correlations are always negative: the higher the AFDC rolls, the more lenient are eligibility requirements (see tables 12 and 13 for a summary of the stepwise regression on AFDC rolls, including the TES as one of the independent variables, for 1960 and

Stepwise Regression on AFDC Rolls, Including AFDC Policies, 1960

	Correlations with AFDC Rolls, 1960				
	Partial Correlations with AFDC Rolls Controlling for All Variables on This and Previous Steps				
Zero-order Correlations	Male Under-employment Rate	Nonworker-Worker Ratio	% Broken Families	% Voter Partici-pation	% Total In-migra-tion
	Step 1	Step 2	Step 3	Step 4	Step 5
(1)	(2)	(3)	(4)	(5)	(6)
.70[a]	—	—	—	—	—
.67[a]	.41[b]	—	—	—	—
.43[a]	.16	.32[c]	—	—	—
.32[c]	.22	.18	.38[c]	—	—
.01	−.03	.06	.29[c]	.43[b]	—
.15	−.14	−.16	−.25	−.16	−.10

s *Social Security Bulletin* 1960, 1961;
U.S. Bureau of the Census 1961–63,
1963, 1973*b*; U.S. Social Security
Administration 1960, 1962; SPCU
Reports.

[a]$p<.001$.   [b]$p<.01$.   [c]$p<.05$.

Table 13

Independent Variables, 1970

% broken families
Per capita revenue
Female underemployment rate
% high-school or more education
% total in-migration, 1965–70
Total eligibility score

1970). Although this indicates that the relationship between AFDC rolls and state policies is in the expected direction, it is nevertheless clear that the composite measure of AFDC eligibility requirements, TES, cannot contribute much to the variation in AFDC rolls, even when conditions of need are taken into account.

**Mass Society and
Conceptions of
Deservedness**

In spite of these findings it is quite possible that some relationship does not exist between welfare policies and welfare rolls. The basis for this expectation is that mass society and stratification conditions may determine both welfare rolls and welfare policies, although not necessarily in similar ways. For example, eligibility requirements would be expected to be most lenient in those states with high standards of living, well-educated populations, and high degrees of industrialization. The higher the mass society status of a state the

Stepwise Regression on AFDC Rolls, Including AFDC Policies, 1970

	Correlations with AFDC Rolls, 1970				
	Partial Correlations with AFDC Rolls, Controlling for All Variables on This and Previous Steps				
Zero-order correlations	% Broken Families — Step 1	Per Capita Revenue — Step 2	Female Underemployment Rate — Step 3	% High-School or More Education — Step 4	% Total In-migration 1965–70 — Step 5
(1)	(2)	(3)	(4)	(5)	(6)
.58[a]	—	—	—	—	—
.30[c]	.47[a]	—	—	—	—
.15	.36[c]	.51[a]	—	—	—
.16	.39[c]	.16	.41[b]	—	—
.20	−.06	−.30[c]	−.22	−.33[c]	—
.08	−.31[c]	−.15	−.28	−.22	−.16

Social Security Bulletin 1970, 1971; U.S. Bureau of the Census 1971–73, 1973*b,c*; U.S. Social and Rehabilitation Service 1971*d,f*; SPCU Reports.
[a]$p<.001$.   [b]$p<.01$.   [c]$p<.05$.

more lenient the state should be, and therefore the lower the TES. This argument is thus the same as the one presented when the influence of mass society factors on the size of AFDC rolls was discussed: the higher the mass society status, the more welfare is seen as a means of extending social citizenship and the greater is the percentage of families on AFDC.

Conditions of high economic dependency, on the other hand, would increase the need for public assistance among residents of the state. Since this high level of dependency would impose severe financial burdens on the state's limited resources, there might also be a tendency to make eligibility requirements as restrictive as possible in the poorer states. However, perhaps more important, poor states also generally have low mass society status. Following my argument above, the extension of the various forms of citizenship would be least developed in these states. Instead, the system of welfare is likely to operate to maintain existing distinctions between different status groups (see also Piven and Cloward 1971, chap. 7). Thus high rates of poverty should be associated with high welfare rolls but strict welfare policies. In other words, welfare policies would attempt to diminish the impact of economic dependency on state finances as well as to maintain a substantial distance between the center and the periphery. The presence of a positive zero-order correlation between AFDC rolls and the TES in 1960 indicates that conditions of economic dependency determined both high welfare rolls and restrictive welfare policies at that time. The negative zero-order correlation between AFDC rolls and TES in 1970, then, may indicate that poverty and economic dependency have lost ground in determining welfare rolls and welfare policies in the states.

In both 1960 and 1970, indexes of mass society and economic dependency were analytically distinct in how they influenced AFDC rolls: high mass society status would be expected to lead to high AFDC rolls, but so would high rates of economic dependency. In terms of welfare policies, however, no clear distinction can be made between measures of these two different social conditions: low mass society status would be expected to lead to restrictive eligibility requirements, as would high rates of economic dependency. And high rates of economic dependency tend to occur in the states with low mass society status. The two approaches cannot be separated in their effects upon welfare policies.

An examination of the correlations between the TES and indexes of mass society and economic dependency also shows how difficult it is to make distinctions between the two approaches in their effects on welfare polices. The zero-order correlations between the TES and the mass society variables are almost all negative and large in both 1960 and 1970.[3] Thus the median correlation was $r = -.36$ in 1960 (ranging between $r = .07$ and $r = -.48$) and median $r = -.35$ in 1970 (ranging between $r = .14$ and $r = -.49$; see table 21 in Appendix D). This suggests that the higher the mass society status, the more lenient the state is in its welfare policies.[4] At the same time, the greater the economic dependency in the state, the more restrictive are the AFDC eligibility requirements[5] (Gary 1973). The median correlation between the TES and the stratification variables was $r = .29$ in 1960 (ranging between $r = .03$ and $r = .47$), and median $r = .28$ in 1970 (ranging between $r = .12$ and $r = .42$; see table 21 in Appendix D). The correlations between indexes of mass society and economic dependency and the measures of welfare polices are of similar magnitudes and directions in 1960 and 1970. None of the zero-order correlations between TES and any of the independent variables were substantially different in 1970 compared with 1960, indicating that there has been little change in the factors which

determine the leniency or restrictiveness of AFDC eligibility requirements during the 1960s.

Examining all the mass society and stratification variables, we
find that in both 1960 and 1970 a mass society variable has the
highest zero-order correlations with the TES: percentage of voter
participation in 1960 ($r = -.48$, $p < .001$) and percentage with at
least a high-school education in 1970 ($r = -.49$, $p < .001$). Both of
these variables received high direct contributions from the composite factor as determined by the factor analyses in chapter 4.

This slight tendency for high mass society conditions to be the
more important determinants of lenient welfare policy is further
supported by the results of stepwise regression analyses of mass
society and stratification variables on the TES in 1960 and 1970. In
both years only mass society variables enter the equations, and in
each case high mass society status is associated with lenient welfare
policies. More than one-third (35 percent) of the total variation in
the TES in 1960 was explained by two mass society variables:
percentage of voter participation ($\beta = -.46$, $p < .001$) and per capita
taxes ($\beta = -.34$, $p < .01$).[6] In 1970, only the percentage with at least a
high-school education entered the equation ($\beta = -.49$, $p < .001$),
explaining 24 percent of the variation in the TES. However,
controlling for this variable, the partial correlation coefficient for
per capita taxes and per capita revenue are $r = -.22$ and $r = -.23$
respectively ($p < .15$), too small to significantly reduce the amount of
unexplained variation in the TES in 1970. But it should be noted
that the per capita taxes in both 1960 and 1970 operate in the same
direction: the greater the fiscal capacity of the state, the more lenient
are the AFDC eligibility requirements. Thus states may be as lenient
as they think they can afford. Or, as was argued before, states which
are more willing to tax themselves and undertake greater responsibilities for their citizens also seem to be extending these responsibilities to the poor by making more people eligible for AFDC. My
more general finding that eligibility requirements are most lenient in
high mass society states is supported by Gary (1973), who found that
high socioeconomic development, low level of need for welfare, and
high level of taxes all tend to be associated with lenient eligibility
requirements and high welfare payments.

Citizens of
Questionable Status

The total amount of variance explained in the two regression
analyses attempting to explain AFDC policies is small (24 to 35

percent) compared with the amount of variation explained in the AFDC rolls. It is likely, therefore, that factors other than measures of mass society and economic dependency may be important in determining how restrictive or lenient a state is with regard to its AFDC policies. One likely source of variation is the extent to which there are present in the state groups which are threatening because they are not considered wholly reliable in their devotion either to the state or to overall goals and values shared by members of the American society.

Migrants have been singled out in this manner by a number of states (for example, New York). The basic underlying issue here is really one of citizenship. Migrants are not fully citizens of the state into which they are moving. Their very migration is often taken to indicate that they have already rejected their attachments to one state and consequently may do so again. There are doubts, also, whether such individuals may be willing to shoulder the full duties of citizenship: working and paying taxes. Yet generally they are assumed to be eager for the rights of citizenship: voting, holding office, obtaining welfare, and so forth.[7] It is significant in this respect that there have been established legally defined waiting periods (durational residency requirements) before migrants could exercise these rights.[8] Some assurance of long-term commitments to take on the duties of citizenship, particularly paying taxes, seems to be needed before migrants are granted full status along with long-term residents of the state.

Similarly, some racial and ethnic groups have also been seen as exploiters or marginal members of the society at different points in time. However, these groups usually face a somewhat different problem than migrants do. The issue of citizenship here has usually been loyalty not to a particular state but to American ideals. Groups at the bottom of the stratification system (particularly blacks) have for this very reason been considered "national" citizens of questionable standing (see also Grønbjerg, Street, and Suttles, forthcoming). The United States is a society which has traditionally maintained an ideology celebrating free enterprise and the self-made man. Any person or group who fails to make at least token approximations to these goals can easily be suspected of not sharing fully in the public belief in the "American way." At the very least people must share a belief in the value of work and the possibility of self-improvement. Those who are thought not to share these beliefs are seen as being clearly outside the mainstream of the American society: they are thought to have a culture of poverty or some other individual or group deficiency which explains their low standing in society. And since each group does not seem to share in the overall cultural orientation, they tend not to be considered full citizens with the same rights and duties as all other members of society (Shils 1956).

Thus one way of proving one's worthiness to obtain full standing in American society is to work hard and to demonstrate it by having something to show for the hard work: that is, income or property. The importance of this avenue of obtaining social and economic citizenship in the United States is particularly important, since so many Americans have maintained vestiges of their previous national loyalties.[9]

To rank low in the status hierarchy, then, leaves some room for doubt about how dedicated that person is to the work ethic and thus how deserving he is of full membership in American society. Only people who work are considered willing and capable of sharing in the burdens of maintaining the society—are considered "to pull their weight," as Archie Bunker emphasizes each week to millions of Americans. The myth of the self-made poor dies hard in America, especially when the myth is confounded by racial and ethnic prejudices (see also Alston and Dean 1972; Feagin 1972; Kallen and Miller 1971; Williamson 1973, 1974a; Schiltz 1970).

It is not surprising, then, that when the percentage black, the percentage nonwhite, and various measures of migration are allowed to enter into the regression analysis of AFDC policies, the percentage black is the most important determinant of the TES in both 1960 and 1970 ($r = .51$ in 1960, $r = .49$ in 1970).[10] The more blacks there are in a state, the more restrictive are the AFDC policies. Tables 14 and 15 present the stepwise regression analysis of the mass society, stratification, and "threat" variables on the TES in 1960 and 1970 respectively.

Both these analyses indicate that the greater the presence in the state of a group whose deservedness of full citizenship is questionable, the less likely the state is to be lenient in its welfare policies. The percentage black is the first variable to enter the regression equations in both years, and its standardized regression coefficients are $\beta = .33$, $p < .05$ in 1960 and $\beta = .46$, $p < .001$ in 1970. However, the state's willingness to undertake broad social responsibilities for its residents continues to be extended into welfare policies themselves. In both years the second variable to enter the prediction equations for the TES is the per capita taxes, and in the final equations the standardized regression coefficients for this variable

Table 14

Stepwise Regression of All Independent Variables on TES, 1960

	Correlations with TES, 1960			
		Partial Correlations		
	Zero-Order Correlations	% Black	Per Capita Taxes	% Born in South
		Step 1	Step 2	Step 3
Independent Variables, 1960	(1)	(2)	(3)	(4)
% families poor	.47[a]	.16	.09	.10
% broken families	.34[b]	−.01	.02	.09
Male underemployment rate	.35[b]	.11	.17	.11
Female underemployment rate	.03	.05	−.04	−.09
% females not working	.07	.07	.00	−.05
Nonworker-worker ratio	.24[c]	.09	.04	.02
% voter participation	−.48[a]	−.09	−.16	−.09
Median level of education	−.40[b]	−.09	.04	−.02
% high-school or more education	−.45[a]	−.16	−.03	−.08
% upper white-collar employment	−.33[b]	−.11	.07	−.10
Per capita revenue	−.40[b]	−.32[c]	−.09	−.07
Per capita taxes	−.36[b]	−.34[b]	—	—
Urbanization index	−.14	−.05	.01	−.05
Industrial index, males	−.36[b]	−.12	−.01	−.08
Industrial index, females	−.22	−.06	.06	.00
% employed nonfarm	.07	.08	.18	.11
% black	.51[a]	—	—	—
% nonwhite	.25[c]	−.16	.04	.09
% native population born in South	.35[b]	.17	.30[c]	—
% population increase, 1950–60	−.09	−.07	.11	−.09
% total in-migration, 1955–60	−.14	−.06	.12	−.09
% total net migration, 1955–60	.03	.03	.19	.02
% nonwhite in-migration, 1955–60	−.23	.09	.05	.11
% nonwhite net migration, 1955–60	−.25[c]	−.01	−.04	−.05
R²		−.26	.34	.40
Tolerance for variable entered on this step		—	.98	.74
β for variable entered on this step		—	−.30	.28

Sources U.S. Bureau of the Census 1961–63, 1963, 1973b; *Book of the States* 1962–63; U.S. Social Security Administration 1960, 1962; SPCU Reports.

[a]$p < .001$. [b]$p < .01$. [c]$p < .05$.

Table 15 | **Stepwise Regression of All Independent Variables on TES, 1970**

	Correlations with TES, 1970		
		Partial Correlations	
Independent Variables, 1970	Zero-Order Correlations	% Black Step 1	Per Capita Taxes Step 2
	(1)	(2)	(3)
% families poor	.42[a]	.15	.06
% families very poor	.44[a]	.16	.08
% broken families	.29[c]	−.16	−.05
Male underemployment rate	.33[b]	.25	.19
Female underemployment rate	.13	.23	.11
% females not working	.12	.13	.03
Nonworker-worker ratio	.27[c]	.20	.13
% voter participation	−.39[b]	−.03	.00
Median level of education	−.41[a]	−.11	−.03
% high-school or more education	−.49[a]	−.22	−.12
% upper white-collar employment	−.35[b]	−.19	−.06
Per capita revenue	−.42[a]	−.29[c]	−.05
Per capita taxes	−.34[b]	−.33[b]	—
Urbanization index	−.07	−.04	.05
Industrial index, males	−.30[c]	−.15	.00
Industrial index, females	−.15	−.20	−.03
% employed nonfarm	.14	.01	.13
% black	.49[a]	—	—
% nonwhite	.15	−.28	−.12
% native population born in South	.38[b]	.15	.19
% population increase, 1960–70	−.01	−.01	.12
% Total in-migration, 1965–70	−.13	−.02	.07
% Total net migration, 1965–70	.14	.08	.15
% nonwhite in-migration, 1965–70	−.25[c]	−.02	−.10
% nonwhite net migration, 1965–70	−.22	−.09	−.02
R^2		.24	.32
Tolerance for variable entered on step		—	.98
β for variable entered on step		—	−.29

Sources   U.S. Bureau of the Census 1971–73, 1973*b, c*; U.S. Social and Rehabilitation Service 1971*d, f*; SPCU Reports.

[a]$p<.001.$ [b]$p<.01.$ [c]$p<.05.$

are $\beta = -.37$, $p < .01$ in 1960 and $\beta = -.29$, $p < .05$ in 1970. Thus the greater the per capita taxes of the state, the more lenient are AFDC policies.

The percentage of the native population which is born in the South also contributes to explaining the restrictiveness of AFDC policies in 1960: partial $r = .28$, $p < .05$, with a standardized regression coefficient of $\beta = .28$, $p < .05$ in the final equation. However, this variable does not enter into the regression equation at all in 1970, although the direction of the relationship continues to be the same (partial $r = .19$). Whether southern-born individuals (e.g., "hillbillies") may also be considered to have questionable loyalty to the state of residence or to the overall cultural orientation is unclear. At least it is unclear whether people believe this is the case. These southern-born individuals are migrants, although not necessarily recent migrants, and thus could be suspected of having limited loyalties in non-southern states. The southern-born may also on the one hand carry their political convictions with them and on the other hand be able to influence welfare policies in the states to which they migrate in large numbers. It is more likely, however, that this variable simply indicates that AFDC policies are more restrictive in the South, since the states with the highest proportion of southern in-migrants are southern or southwestern states.

Because characteristics of southern states (the percentage black and, to a limited extent, the percentage born outside the state but in the South) seem to be prominent in determining the TES in both 1960 and 1970, we should look separately at which factors determine AFDC policies in the southern and non-southern states. When the data are analyzed separately by region, only one variable enters the equation in all cases. The results for 1970 indicate quite clearly that at least some of the overall variation in the TES reflects regional differences: per capita revenue is the only important factor in the southern states ($\beta = -.69$, $p < .001$), while level of education, as measured by the percentage with at least a high-school education, is the prominent factor in the non-southern states ($\beta = -.34$, $p < .05$). In other words, the higher the mass society status, the more lenient are the AFDC eligibility requirements in both regions.

The results for 1960 appear to be somewhat different. Here per capita taxes is the most important factor in the southern states ($\beta = -.52$, $p < .05$), but in the non-southern states the presence of blacks is the crucial factor ($\beta = .38$, $p < .05$). It should be emphasized, however, that the percentage black also was important in 1970 in the non-southern states ($r = .33$)—almost as important as the percentage with at least a high-school education $(r = -.34)$, which was the variable actually selected.

On balance then, the presence of blacks seems to be an important determinant of AFDC eligibility requirements in the non-southern states as well as in the total United States. This suggests that the presence of such a suspect group is indeed important in determining how restrictive all states are with regard to the AFDC program. But, as we have seen, fiscal limitations are also important in determining how far the state can and will go in undertaking reponsibilities for its citizens.

The mass society, stratification, and "threat" variables leave a substantial amount of variation in the TES unexplained in both 1960 and 1970 (60 and 68 percent respectively). Here it is possible only to speculate on some of the additional factors which may be important in determining the restrictiveness of AFDC policies. Political traditions and composition of state legislative bodies (especially in terms of rural and urban residence) are perhaps obvious possibilities, but certain institutional features of the state public assistance systems seem likely additions. Whether the director of a state public assistance program is a political appointee or a civil servant may be important, as might be the ease or difficulty of instituting new public assistance policies. In some states, for example, new policies can be instituted by executive directives; in other states, formal legislation must be passed to accomplish even minor changes in public assistance policies. In still other states, for example Texas until very recently, most welfare policies can be changed only through amendments to the state constitution (SPCU Reports). Such institutional characteristics may of course be seen as reflecting the relative modernization and professionalization of different state governmental structures,[11] and thus related to mass society status. This interpretation is supported and may well be one of the major findings in Walker's study (1969) of the diffusion of innovative state politics: larger, wealthier, industrial (i.e., mass society) states adopt policy innovations more quickly than other states.[12] However, the importance of any of these factors for welfare policies (eligibility requirements) remains relatively unexplored.

**Limitations of Previous
Measures of Welfare Policy**

The analysis of AFDC policies so far has used the Total Eligibility Score as the dependent variable. This variable is a composite index of all the different eligibility requirements a state may have. However, in reviewing the literature on state welfare policies a quite different measure is generally used, especially by political scientists. The public assistance policy of a state is generally operationalized in terms of the average benefits paid to different recipient groups.[13] Consequently, the meaning of this particular variable should be examined, along with its relationship to other measures of welfare policies. In particular these include the TES, the cost standard (the income level below which a family is economically eligible for AFDC), and the maximum level of benefits available to recipients in the state.

It is important to note that the TES, which is an inclusive measure of eligibility requirements, has consistently lower correlations with indexes of mass society and economic dependency than do the economic eligibility requirements—that is, the cost standard, the maximum amount of benefits a state will pay, and the average payments to AFDC recipients in the state.[14] Particularly, the correlations with urbanization-industrialization variables are lower. These patterns hold for both 1960 and 1970 (see table 16). The maximum benefits the state may pay, as well as the average size of benefits, have very little to do with eligibility requirements, but mainly say something about how generous the state is in monetary terms once a person or a family has been found eligible for public assistance. These measures, then, might be considered fairly good indicators of how liberal the states are in their welfare payments. Yet the fact remains that such measures are invariably closely related to economic conditions in the state, as the political scientists have well demonstrated. The cost of food, housing, clothing, and public utilities are integral parts of the formula which determines the cost standard and thus the maximum level of benefits. Since these costs can be established with a fairly high degree of accuracy in each state, the cost standards and levels of payment may therefore not be very negotiable in terms of state policies. After all, it is rather difficult to argue that a family of four in New York should be able to live for exactly the same amount of money as a family of similar size and composition in Mississippi or Indiana. It is for these reasons that we would expect the cost standard, as well as the level of payments, to be highly correlated with measures of economic well-being in the state. This is the case, as is evident from table 16 and as many previous studies have concluded. However, the actual dollar differences in state cost standards are far too great to be explained solely in terms of differences in levels of income or cost of living standards. The correlations between cost standards and measures of economic conditions should be interpreted as relationships of rank.

There is, of course, considerably more to public assistance than how poor people must be to obtain aid and how large are the benefits they are paid. As was indicated in the discussion of eligibility requirements in chapter 3, states have a large arsenal of rules they can use to control who gets onto the public assistance rolls and how recipients may be treated once they are on the rolls. How recipients are treated may be determined as much by the notorious understaffing of public assistance offices and the high turnover rates among public welfare caseworkers as by official decrees. However, there are a number of different formal criteria that people must fulfill to be eligible for AFDC. These criteria may have little or no relationship to the income of the individual or the standard of living in the state: the recipient must be of a certain age, have certain family characteristics, be willing to discuss his personal history in detail, have a "suitable home," be willing to sign up for employment even when no jobs are available, and so forth.

There is, in other words, a lot more to welfare policies than economics. We find, in fact, that some of the states which traditionally have been proclaimed liberal are liberal only when it comes to how poor people have to be before they may become eligible for AFDC and how much money these states are willing to provide their recipients. New York, for example, has one of the highest cost standards and payment standards in the nation, but it also employs a number of other methods of controlling who gets onto the welfare rolls which other states with less liberal payment standards may not employ—for example, employment requirements, restriction on property, and restriction on home ownership. In fact, the two large industrial states of New York and California are very near the United States average for the TES in both 1960 and 1970,[15] and Illinois is considerably more restrictive than the average for the United States.[16] This does not seem to justify classifying these states as liberal in any overall sense of the term, although they certainly appear so if one is looking only at average levels of payments, as most observers have done so far.[17] Not surprisingly, the average payment seems little more than a reflection of the maximum level of benefits the state provides its recipients,[18] in spite of considerable state differences in how payments are limited and which income disregards are available.

The factors which determine the average AFDC benefits and the

Table 16

Independent Variables,
1960 and 1970

% families poor
% broken families
Male underemployment rate
Female underemployment rate
% females not working
Nonworker-worker ratio

% voter participation
Median level of education
% high-school or more education
% upper white-collar employment
Per capita revenue
Per capita taxes
Urbanization index
Industrial index, males
Industrial index, females
% employed nonfarm

% black
% nonwhite
% native population born in South
% population increase
% total in-migration
% total net migration
% nonwhite in-migration
% nonwhite net migration

Zero-Order Correlations between Alternative Measures of AFDC Policies and Independent Variables, 1960 and 1970

1960 Correlations			1970 Correlations			
TES	Cost Standard	Maximum Paid	TES	Cost Standard	Maximum Paid	Average Payments
(1)	(2)	(3)	(4)	(5)	(6)	(7)
.47[a]	−.62[a]	−.73[a]	.42[a]	−.62[a]	−.72[a]	−.78[a]
.34[b]	−.50[a]	−.44[a]	.29[c]	−.25[c]	−.33[b]	−.35[b]
.35[b]	−.49[a]	−.65[a]	.33[b]	−.26[c]	−.41[b]	−.43[a]
.03	−.10	−.19	.13	−.11	−.15	−.21
.07	−.25[c]	−.21	.12	−.19	−.30[c]	−.38[b]
.24[c]	−.44[a]	−.45[a]	.27[c]	−.38[b]	−.47[a]	−.52[a]
−.48[a]	.47[a]	.67[a]	−.39[b]	.51[a]	.63[a]	.68[a]
−.40[b]	.64[a]	.57[a]	−.41[a]	.53[a]	.60[a]	.63[a]
−.45[a]	.65[a]	.59[a]	−.49[a]	.51[a]	.52[a]	.57[a]
−.33[b]	.42[a]	.48[a]	−.35[b]	.32[c]	.44[a]	.40[b]
−.40[b]	.19	.22	−.42[a]	.18	.27[c]	.31[c]
−.36[b]	.16	.17	−.34[b]	.18	.24[c]	.33[b]
−.14	.30[c]	.37[b]	−.07	.17	.15	.24[c]
−.36[b]	.55[a]	.63[a]	−.30[b]	.58[a]	.58[a]	.63[a]
−.22	.40[b]	.50[a]	−.15	.40[b]	.32[c]	.37[b]
.07	.01	.05	.14	.03	−.05	−.02
.51[a]	−.54[a]	−.68[a]	.49[a]	−.45[a]	−.59[a]	−.63[a]
.25[c]	−.38[b]	−.43[a]	.15	−.40[b]	−.40[b]	−.38[b]
.35[b]	−.27[c]	−.43[a]	.38[b]	−.40[b]	−.55[a]	−.59[a]
−.09	.40[b]	−.01	−.01	.13	−.05	−.04
−.14	.29[c]	−.03	−.13	−.09	−.09	−.15
.03	.32[c]	−.03	.14	.01	−.08	−.09
−.23	.41[a]	.30[c]	−.25[c]	.40[b]	.34[b]	.39[b]
−.25[c]	.49[a]	.43[a]	−.22	.29[c]	.48[a]	.55[a]

ces U.S. Bureau of the Census 1961–63, 1963, 1971–73, 1973*b,c; Book of the States* 1962–63; U.S. Social Security Administration 1960, 1962; U.S. Social and Rehabilitation Service 1971*d,f*; SPCU Reports.

[a]$p<.001$.   [b]$p<.01$.   [c]$p<.05$.

maximum level of benefits available to AFDC recipients are, foremost, measures of general economic well-being (see table 16). It is therefore hardly surprising that few of the studies on welfare policies by political scientists have revealed any significant relationship between average public assistance payments (and thus also maximum level of benefits) and a wide range of indexes of political culture,[19] once economic conditions and industrialization have been controlled (Dye 1966). The Total Eligibility Score is a more inclusive measure of welfare policies and is less tied to particular economic conditions. It is possible therefore that such a measure would be more useful to political scientists in assessing the relationship between political structure and policy outcomes, if such a relationship indeed exists apart from the conditions of economic dependency and industrialization.

The Translation of Welfare Policies into Welfare Rolls

The major conclusions that can be made at present about AFDC policies are as follows. First, the presence of groups seen as threatening, most notably blacks, seems to be important in determining restrictiveness of the policies. Second, it is difficult to make any clear distinctions between the mass society and the stratification models with regard to welfare policies. The two models seem almost indistinguishable and appear to operate parallel to one another. Third, there have been few if any changes between 1960 and 1970 in how these factors determine the restrictiveness of AFDC policies. In part this may be because both mass society and stratification variables tend to make welfare policies lenient in the same states. The variation in welfare policies, then, seems not to reflect the shifting pattern from concern with economic dependency to concern with responsibility for broader social needs. It is at this point that the relationship (or lack of relationship) between welfare policies and welfare rolls becomes decisive.

It was demonstrated in chapters 5 and 6 that a mixture of mass society and economic dependency variables determined AFDC rolls in 1960 and 1970. But it was also indicated that measures of mass society were more important in determining AFDC rolls in 1970 than they had been in 1960. The absence of such shifts in the determinants of welfare policies during the same period raises the question of the exact relationship between formal eligibility requirements and AFDC rolls. Why, in short, have indexes of mass society become more important in determining the variation in AFDC rolls without a similar shift in the state-by-state variation in AFDC policies?

One possible explanation of this paradox is evident from a closer analysis of the changes in welfare policies between 1960 and 1970. The broadening of the AFDC program to include larger proportions of the population is evidenced by the drop in the average TES from 21.8 in 1960 to 13.5 in 1970. Furthermore, when the changes in the TES for each state during this period are examined it becomes clear that all but one state (Wisconsin) were more lenient in 1970 than in 1960. The average decrease in the TES was 9 points, ranging from no change in Wisconsin and a decrease of 4 points in Arizona to a decrease of 15 points in Massachusetts and of 14 in Vermont and Arkansas. In terms of relative change, the average decrease was 37.8 percent. In short, there was a substantial movement toward more lenient AFDC policies in the 1960s. More important, there does not seem to have been a major change in the internal distribution of the states on the TES between 1960 and 1970. The zero-order correlation between the TES in 1960 and in 1970 is $r = .70$.[20] Those states which were most restrictive in 1960 continued to be so in 1970; those which were most lenient in 1960 were also most lenient in 1970.

These findings on AFDC policies suggest that *all* the states, except Wisconsin, moved toward liberalization of AFDC requirements to about the same extent. It is this fact that hides the overall movement toward mass society among all the states in terms of AFDC policies. It is apparent, then, that at least part of the increase in the AFDC rolls between 1960 and 1970 is due to a greater leniency of AFDC policies across the board (see also Greenston and MacRae 1974; Lynch 1967). One of the reasons mass society indexes have become increasingly important in determining AFDC rolls may be exactly this movement of the welfare policies toward mass society.

A number of other factors may be important in explaining how welfare policies are realized in welfare rolls. We have already touched on two possible answers to this problem: the extent to which more people are willing to apply for public assistance for which they are eligible and the extent to which public welfare officials may let those who apply onto the public assistance rolls. These factors interact to produce rates of utilization for public assistance.

By attempting to farm out welfare expenditures to the federal government, while also trying to be responsible to popular concerns about welfare, the states have found themselves in a legal swamp in which it is almost impossible to determine deservedness completely by

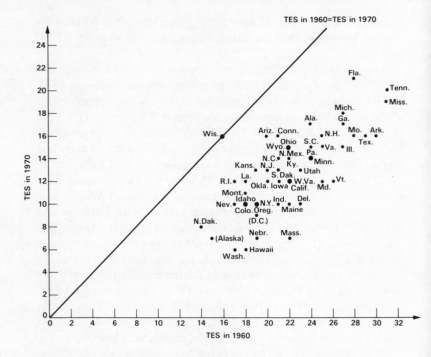

Fig. 1.   Scatter diagram of TES in 1960 versus TES in 1970

legal criteria. Welfare manuals used by case workers are literally inches thick and are filled with errata, notes to update rule changes, warning tracers that current rules are to be updated, and cross references between rules that often seem to have little to do with one another if they are not contradictory. No wonder these manuals until recently were defined as confidential information. The public right to read such manuals, however, is of questionable value, since they are largely an inclusive list of numerous piecemeal legislative directives. The result may be, in Street's terms (Grønbjerg, Street, and Suttles, forthcoming), an elephantine bureaucracy which is so inarticulate that it leaves vast room for sheer arbitrariness. For every rule there is an exception, or if not an exception then an alternative interpretation, or if not an alternative interpretation then a possible rule change or appeal. But even if a given rule were clear, it might not be possible to determine whether a potential recipient is in conformity with it because of difficulties in verifying that conformity (Gordon 1972). Under such circumstances, the major guidelines available to caseworkers or eligibility technicians (those who determine an applicant's eligibility status) may well be their own interpretation of what is or should be the overall character, or "intent," of the public assistance program (Cloward and Piven 1966, 1968). The discretionary powers available to public welfare administrators may of course also make them more subject to more or less constant political pressure to limit welfare expenditures and keep people off welfare (Albin and Stein 1968; Piven and Cloward 1971).

The number of persons eligible for welfare must be established before rates of participation can be determined. But because it is so difficult to determine who is eligible for public assistance, the few studies which have attempted to deal with the issue of participation must be examined with some caution. It is clear, however, that lack of knowledge about available aid is an important factor in preventing complete utilization of public assistance (Greenston and MacRae 1974; Moles, Hess, and Fascione 1968; Piven and Cloward 1971). Similarly, the lower the level of need, the less likely people are to be recipients (Anderson and D'Amico 1969; Moles, Hess, and Fascione 1968; Moles 1971). Consequently, not all eligible persons will receive public assistance because of their ignorance or their preference for less troublesome sources of income. Nevertheless, there are indications that rates of participation have increased during the 1960s, especially during the latter part of that period (Boland 1973; Greenston and MacRae 1974; Durman 1973; Rein and Heclo 1973; Steiner 1974; Schwartz and Tabb 1972).[21]

Piven and Cloward (1971) have argued that it is an increased acceptance of claims for welfare that explains the increase in AFDC rolls, particularly after 1965. They also argue that public officials ran scared because of the riots in the 1960s and consequently attempted to constrain the unrest by letting blacks and other potential troublemakers onto the public assistance rolls (see also Betz 1974). The data which Piven and Cloward, and Betz as well, use to support their arguments is at best ambiguous. Durman (1973) and Seufert (1974) have persuasively argued that the data presented by Piven and Cloward do not support the hypothesis that civil unrest leads to growth in welfare rolls. Both Durman and Seufert indicate that neither the presence of blacks nor the incidence of riots bears any determinate relationship to increases in AFDC rolls. However, for whatever reasons, there were substantial increases in both the rate of applications and the rate of approvals of applications on a national basis between the early 1960s and the late 1960s[22] (see also Schwartz and Tabb 1972).

The question, then, is whether these increases in rates of applications and approvals have actually been greatest in the states characterized by high mass society status, as one might expect. If that is the case it would help explain why welfare rolls have become more related to indexes of mass society as opposed to measures of economic dependency. Since welfare rolls increased mainly in the states characterized by high mass society status, this is indirect evidence that rates of applications and approvals increased most in these states. Unfortunately, there is not much direct evidence available on this. Much of the anecdotal evidence presented by Piven and Cloward suggests that various poverty organizations and community action programs in the larger industrial cities were able to get a number of people on welfare both by encouraging people to apply and by helping them get their applications approved. At least one study reports that welfare rights organizations are more frequently found in urban than in rural areas (Meyers and McIntyre 1969, p. 109). While there is very little adequate comparative data on how successful these organizations and agencies were in different states, the problem might be approached by assuming that such groups are most active in the more urbanized states. It is also likely that public assistance caseworkers are more willing to work with welfare rights groups, and in general show greater sympathy with the poor, in the larger urban centers, and thus by extension in the urban states (Meyers and McIntyre 1969).[23]

There is some evidence from a limited number of states that by

1970 high mass society states did approve a larger proportion of applications than other states (see table 17, columns 1 and 2). Correspondingly, the incidence of poverty is negatively correlated with the percentage of applications which are approved ($r = -.44$, $p < .001$). In those states where economic needs supposedly are less severe, not only are the eligibility requirements more lenient, but a larger proportion of those who apply have their applications approved by public welfare officials. Furthermore, it does not appear that the degree of objective dependency is very important in determining the number of people who apply for aid. In fact, the proportion of families which apply for AFDC is highest in those states with high mass society status,[24] while the correlation between the rate of application and indexes of economic dependency are *all* close to zero. The presence of poor families seems to bear almost no relationship to application rates ($r = -.04$, see table 17, columns 3 and 4). These findings make a strong argument for the need to analytically distinguish between the mass society and stratification approaches.

In a further attempt to separate the two approaches, the correlations between the number of applications per 1,000 poor families and indexes of mass society and economic dependency were also examined. By looking at applications in relation to poverty I have essentially attempted to control for the economic necessity of applying for public assistance. As one might expect in these circumstances, the rate of application is more highly related to high mass society status and low incidence of economic dependency (see table 17, columns 3 and 4). The two measures of application rates are highly intercorrelated ($r = .83$), which again suggests that the magnitude of application for public assistance is determined not so much by economic necessity as by the conditions under which people have come to consider public assistance a right due to them as citizens.

There is reason to think, then, that four factors may be important in explaining the shift in AFDC rolls from reflecting primarily conditions of economic dependency toward reflecting conditions of mass society. First, almost all states have moved toward higher mass society status in terms of liberalizing formal eligibility requirements. This alone might produce a change in the determinants of AFDC rolls. Second, it has also been shown that by 1970, at least, the states with high mass society status had the highest rates of application and the highest rates of approval of applications. It is likely, then, that the overall national increase in these rates between

Table 17

Independent Variables, 1970

% families poor
% families very poor
% broken families
Male underemployment rate
Female underemployment rate
% females not working
Nonworker-worker ratio

% voter participation
Median level of education
% high-school or more education
% upper white-collar employment
Per capita revenue
Per capita taxes
Urbanization index
Industrial index, males
Industrial index, females
% employed nonfarm

% black
% nonwhite
% native population born in South
% population increase, 1960–70
% total in-migration, 1965–70
% total net migration, 1965–70
% nonwhite in-migration, 1965–70
% nonwhite net migration, 1965–70

Total eligibility score, 1970
AFDC rolls, 1970

Sources U.S. Bureau of the Census 1971–73, 1973*b,c; Social Security Bulletin* 1970, 1971; U.S. Social and Rehabilitation Service 1970, 1971*a, b,c,d,f*; SPCU Reports.

Note Rates of applications and rates of approvals are based on averages for

**Zero-Order Correlations
between Rates of Approval for
AFDC Applications and Rates
of Application for AFDC and
Independent Variables, 1970**

	Zero-Order Correlations, 1970		
% Applications Approved of All Applications	% Applications Approved of All Approved & Denied Applications	Number of Applications per 1,000 Families	Number of Applications per 1,000 Poor Families
(1)	(2)	(3)	(4)
−.44[a]	−.51[a]	−.04	−.53[a]
−.47[a]	−.54[a]	−.01	−.51[a]
−.40[b]	−.49[a]	.01	−.23
−.14	−.26	.14	−.12
.04	−.07	.12	−.06
−.07	−.14	.12	−.18
−.19	−.25	.08	−.31[c]
.52[a]	.57[a]	.10	.38[b]
.36[b]	.46[a]	.14	.47[a]
.48[a]	.53[a]	.26[c]	.55[a]
.18	.22	.37[b]	.46[a]
.24	.41[b]	.40[b]	.45[a]
.08	.30[a]	.32[c]	.42[a]
−.16	−.12	.17	.22
.21	.28[c]	.22	.59[a]
−.05	−.01	.15	.39[b]
−.21	−.25	.22	.25
−.54[a]	−.51[a]	−.08	−.33[c]
−.39[b]	−.25	.08	−.09
−.57[a]	−.56[a]	−.07	−.27[c]
−.10	−.13	.02	.18
.01	.02	.08	.15
−.15	−.17	.12	.26[c]
.48[a]	.38[b]	−.06	.23
.16	.22	.22	.46[a]
−.52[a]	−.46[a]	−.37[b]	−.47[a]
.00	−.03	.48[a]	.21

the four three-month periods covered by each of the A-9 NCSS Reports. The data was available for forty-seven states for the correlations presented in column 1, for forty-one states for the correlations presented in column 2, and for forty-three states for the correlations presented in columns 3 and 4.

Column 2 excludes from the base applications that were withdrawn and cases where the client could not be located.

[a]$p<.001.$ [b]$p<.01.$ [c]$p<.05.$

the early and later part of the 1960s, calculated by Durman (1973), primarily reflected increases in approval and application rates in the mass society states.

Third, the extent to which people find public assistance less stigmatizing and more nearly their right as citizens is likely to have increased particularly in the states where eligibility requirements have become more lenient and where higher expectations about the rights and duties of citizens have become established. Finally, it is most likely to be in these states that public welfare officials have come to share such orientations, whether through changing ideological commitments[25] or through the increasing prodding of welfare rights organizations.

Conclusion

Because of the close correspondence between the mass society and the stratification models, most of the states which have low rates of economic dependency have high mass society status, and vice versa. The situations faced by states at the two extremes are fundamentally different. States with a high incidence of economic dependency have a high demand for public assistance owing to economic needs in the populations. There is great pressure on these states to provide at least minimum benefits for a fairly large proportion of their populations. To provide for a larger proportion of the population through public assistance involves a strain on state finances, especially when the population of the state is poor and can pay taxes only to a limited extent. There is need, then, from the point of view of the state, to limit expenditures as much as possible. The poor states may do this either by reducing the maximum amount of money paid to any recipient (Florida and Mississippi in particular use this avenue) or by using a number of restrictive eligibility requirements to limit public assistance to the most deserving and least suspect residents of the states—that is, those with the least questionable citizenship status (Texas and Tennessee have some of the most restrictive eligibility requirements).

In the poor states, then, welfare policies tend to counteract the economic pressures on the welfare rolls. Since welfare policies tend to be so restrictive in these states, and since each state is primarily concerned with restricting welfare to the most respectable and deserving poor, public assistance recipients are surrounded by suspicions about whether they really are good enough citizens to justifiably receive benefits. Because of these suspicions, state public assistance programs may become only the last resort for people who have no other way of living. In these circumstances, public assistance is more a duty grudgingly accepted by the state than the right of the residents. The poor states seem to operate as if they would prefer not to grant any public assistance, but since there are such obvious needs, they must do so. However, because they want to make sure that their funds only go to those who "deserve" it, those in need may see it as more "stigmatizing" (see also Tropman 1973; Tropman and Gordon 1974; Piven and Cloward 1971).

In those states characterized by high incomes, high industrialization, high voter participation, large occupational elites, and high urbanization, the situation seems to be quite different—almost the reverse. Here the people's economic need for public assistance is less desperate; however, because of the high industrialization and urbanization, the fallibility of the laissez-faire model for economic actions by individuals and collectivities is more obvious and more widely accepted. Thus, notions of public or collective responsibility tend to be further developed, and these outlooks may be shared by both public welfare officials (Frederickson 1974; Hart 1974) and residents (Almond and Powell 1966; Briggs 1961; Dahrendorf 1974; Elazar 1972; Marshall 1964).

The overall liberalization of eligibility requirements suggests that all states have moved in this direction in their formal welfare policies. If welfare is considered more stigmatizing in some states than in others, fewer people can be expected to apply for public assistance there (all other factors equal), especially since the stigma so often is expressed in very low grants, paternalism, and lack of consideration for human dignity. However, several studies have suggested that only a moderate proportion of those who are eligible for welfare actually receive any benefits,[26] and this gap between potential and actual recipients may be subject to a great deal of variation between the states (Greenston and MacRae 1974). In those states where welfare is most stigmatizing we might expect public welfare officials not only to share in the low public regard for welfare recipients, but also to be anxious to guard themselves against accusations of "mollycoddling." Such officials would presumably be more reluctant to approve applications. Somewhat the same conclusion has been drawn by Meyers and McIntyre (1969, p. 109):

[In] certain types of communities, as indicated by level of affluence, where grant levels are high, welfare rights groups are more likely to be found, caseworkers tend to be more client oriented and the clients themselves are more conscious of the stigma attached to welfare but also more confident of their ability to influence welfare department decisions which affect their lives.

This interpretation is also supported by the findings of the present study; namely, that rates of applications are highest in states with high mass society status and low poverty rates. Similarly, we also find that once a person has applied for welfare he or she is more likely to get the application approved in states with high mass society status and low rates of economic dependency.

Obviously there is continuing concern in the United States with proving that one deserves full citizenship status as well as a persistence of discrimination against "threatening" groups (Schwartz and Tabb 1972). To the extent that these patterns persist, the transformation of the United States' system of welfare into that of the welfare state remains incomplete and partial.[27]

The 1960s

A Watershed in the Extension of Citizenship

8

Any society must be concerned with the well-being of its members. To insure an "adequate" standard of living for all has become increasingly important, however, as standards of living in general have improved, as government has become increasingly involved in a variety of activities, and as more people have come to desire full participation and to accept the belief that such participation by all is in fact possible and desirable. The purpose of this study has been to place the significant growth of public assistance in the American states into this broader perspective of sociological theory about mass society.

In recent years, particularly during the 1960s, both the number of welfare recipients and the amount of welfare expenditures have increased dramatically, despite a general rise in personal income. The growth has been particularly great in the largest, most industrialized, and wealthiest states. It is this increasing separation of poverty and dependency and the correspondingly closer association between affluence and dependency which is responsible for the crisis in our understanding of welfare.

Most of the attempts to explain this paradox have tried to account for dependency by focusing on the characteristics and presumed desires of the poor. The growth in welfare has thus been seen as reflecting (1) a growing instability of the family, especially the black family; (2) an increasing preference for welfare over work; (3) growing immorality (illegitimacy, cheating) and irresponsibility (child abandonment, desire to have "something for nothing"); and (4) migration to exploit high welfare payments in some states. Others have blamed the welfare system itself or the society in general. Thus some have explained the growth in welfare in terms of (1) an increasing tendency for the welfare system and its specific rules and regulations to encourage and reward dependency; (2) an increasingly overgrown and inept bureaucracy stifled by red tape; (3) political competition between parties and between different levels of government for the votes and support of the poor; (4) manipulation of the poor by a power-hungry elite to insure political stability; and (5) increasingly important effects of discrimination in education, housing, and employment as credentials are becoming more important.

There can be no doubt that the causes and consequences of poverty and dependency have occupied center stage during the last decade and a half. I consider this an important fact in itself, for it reflects a growing public awareness and an effort to come to grips with a central problem of modern society: What is the role of the individual in the complex social structures which have developed? This question concerns not only what factors are responsible for the location of the individual in the social structure, but what kinds of obligations he ought to have, to whom he is obligated, to what kinds of services and benefits he is entitled, and who is responsible for providing him with these rights. As American society has become increasingly differentiated and complex so has this system of rights and obligations. The general tendency increasingly has been to make the collectivity, or government, not only the arbitrator between individuals but also the guarantor and granter of the individual's rights.

The pattern of welfare rolls and welfare policies, as it exists in the states, has been interpreted as being part of this general process of "modernization" and its association with broadening of citizens' rights and increasing popular participation. The basic hypothesis of the study is that the United States has been gradually and haltingly moving toward a mass society in which the definition of citizenship is being extended to include economic rights and duties as well as universal suffrage, freedom of speech, thought, and religion, the right to own property and to enter into contracts, and the right to equal justice under the law. At the same time, the United States has been moving away from a pattern where poverty alone was the occasion for the distribution of public aid—what I have called the stratification model of public assistance. The 1960s seems to have been a period of intensive development in this direction. This is not to say that the United States is on a long, continuous, and unbroken path that inevitably will push the nation further toward mass society. There are reasons to think that this movement toward mass society is limited ultimately by the continuing belief that certain groups in American society do not deserve full citizenship status. It is also limited by the internal inconsistencies of the American system of categorical welfare programs which lead to such disparities in benefits that the system is easily subject to criticism.

In a modern nation like the United States, with its constitutionally mandated and culturally endorsed decentralization of government functions, not all political subdivisions move equally fast in the direction of mass society or modernization. Although the United States as a nation generally is ranked as one of the most "modern" nations of the world, there is considerable variation in "modernity" among the fifty states. The differences between the states in this respect are probably quite small compared with the differences among the nations of the world. Nonetheless, these state-by-state differences are sufficient to analyze the movement from a stratification to a mass society approach to public assistance.

The "modern" states—that is, those with high degrees of industrialization, urbanization, and mass organization—are characterized by well-educated populations who spend much of their time and effort as members of different organizations, for example, institutions of higher education and various economic and governmental bureaucracies. Thus, the populations of these political units tend to be organizationally skilled and sophisticated, with relatively clear notions of their rights and, perhaps to a lesser extent, their duties as citizens of the state or collectivity. In these states, then, we would expect to find the greatest belief in and collective support for the economic, political, and social rights of citizens. Correspondingly, this type of collective responsibility should be greatest in those subunits of the United States which are most "modernized" and most likely to have a "moralist" state culture (Elazar 1972, pp. 93–102).

This notion of extensive collective responsibilities toward the individual is, however, only one of two extreme considerations which may influence different states in their approach to the distribution of welfare. In some cases government responsibility for its citizens is still sharply limited by overriding ideological convictions. Such notions of limited government are integral elements of the laissez-faire system, which has served as the model and ideological foundation for the American society in many years. That is, although the laissez-faire system has not been a very accurate description of the American society for some time, its ideological components—that is, the beliefs that hard work and ability will be rewarded with success, that success is the reward also of virtue, and that government must not interfere with this "natural" process—are still strongly present in the American culture (Wilensky and Lebeaux 1965, pp. 34–35; Fine 1964; Rischin 1968; Arieli 1964; Sutton et al. 1956) and are important ingredients of the "welfare crisis." The frequently observed inefficiency of government intervention in many areas has lent further support to the argument that government should have only limited responsibility for its citizens.

The emphasis in this study, therefore, has been on these two distinct but overlapping approaches to public assistance in the United States: a stratification appoach, which is related to the concept of limited government, and a mass society approach, related to expanding definitions of democracy and citizenship. If the stratification approach were prevalent there would be no cultural or social differences between the states in how they responded to poverty and need; only economic differences in available resources and the extent of poverty would be important in explaining why some states had higher welfare rolls than other states. States with a high incidence of economic dependency would have a correspondingly high pressure on their public assistance rolls, and these states would be most likely to adopt restrictive eligibility requirements to limit their sparse resources to those judged most in need.

If the mass society approach were prevalent, factors other than income and economic dependency would be important in explaining the relative size of welfare rolls and restrictiveness of welfare policies in the states. Urbanized and industrialized states with well-educated populations, high degrees of citizen participation in politics (voter participation), large upper white-collar occupational groups, and a willingness to tax themselves would also be the most willing to extend public assistance to a larger proportion of the population than could be expected on the basis of personal need alone. Such states, then, would have more liberal interpretations of economic need and would thus assume the responsibility for broader social needs.

**The Mass Society and
Stratification Approaches
in the American States
1960–70**

This study has attempted to evaluate the relative importance of the mass society and stratification approaches to public assistance in the American states. Briefly, we have found that in both 1960 and 1970 a mix of the two approaches operated in the expected directions to determine the size of AFDC rolls. Controlling for other variables selected into the final prediction equations, high levels of economic need and high mass society status are both associated with high welfare rolls. There was a shift during the decade, however, in the relative importance of the factors associated with each approach. In 1960 the stratification approach was clearly the most dominant, but by 1970 the states had moved sharply in the direction of the mass society approach. This finding was further supported by the 1960–70 time series analysis, which demonstrated that welfare rolls rose predominantly in the states with high mass society status.

When AFDC eligibility requirements were examined with regard to the two approaches, the mass society model was clearly the more significant in explaining the variation in my measure of welfare policies—that is, Total Eligibility Score (TES)—in both 1960 and 1970: the higher the mass society status, the more lenient were the policies. Furthermore, there was no change in determinants of the TES between 1960 and 1970, as there had been in the determinants of the AFDC rolls. Nevertheless, the overall liberalization of state eligibility requirements suggests a movement toward the mass society approach in the area of welfare policies as well.

A state's mass society status and the selective extension of citizenship associated with it are thus important in accounting for the variation in AFDC eligibility requirements: who is granted fuller citizenship and under what conditions. The importance of these concerns is also apparent from the nature of the eligibility requirements themselves (residency requirements, suitable-home rules, etc.). However, the presence of blacks in a state bears a significant relationship to the restrictiveness of eligibility requirements: the larger the proportion of blacks, the more restrictive are the eligibility requirements. This might be interpreted as just another documentation of the discrimination and racism which pervades the American society. However, it must also be understood as the broader tendency to qualify the extension of citizenship. To this extent, diminishing racism is a mode of extending citizenship. Conversely, the persistent suspicions surrounding numerous minority groups, especially racial groups, may retard the extension of welfare in the states. This points to the importance of understanding the more general problem of how citizenship is granted rather than dealing with racial discrimination alone.

**AFDC Policies and
Their Outcomes**

The eagerness with which the states originally decided to participate in some form of the AFDC program, as well as their lack of enthusiasm for other parts of the program, indicates that *state* fiscal considerations are appreciably important in determining welfare policies. The importance of the per capita revenue and per capita taxes variables in the regression equations to predict both AFDC rolls and AFDC policies in 1960 and 1970 argues for a similar conclusion. Furthermore, as Schwartz and Tabb (1972) have suggested, there are good reasons to think that the strain on state (and federal) fiscal capacities brought about by the growth in welfare rolls and welfare payments is at least partly responsible for the various attempts to clamp down on welfare during the late 1960s and early 1970s (in contrast to Piven and Cloward 1971). However, it is not just public assistance expenditures which have been of focal concern at the state level. At least as much emphasis has been placed on *who* receives assistance. The problems of "how much" and "who" may, of course, be related, but the two alternatives point to different ways of spending a given sum of money. My emphasis in looking at eligibility requirements has been on dealing with the problem of who gets onto the AFDC rolls and how many families consequently received AFDC benefits.

It is clear from my findings that formal requirements of AFDC eligibility have very little, if any direct relationship to AFDC rolls. There is an indirect relationship in that welfare policies and welfare rolls are both determined by mass society status and measures of economic dependency in the states, but welfare policies seem to play no direct role in determining welfare rolls. Notwithstanding the controversy surrounding AFDC rolls and various eligibility requirements, welfare policies still may play the latent but important function of maintaining a public fiction of who is "deserving" in American society. Since eligibility requirements are widely accepted as direct ways of determining who may receive public assistance, these policies have great symbolic value. They express a public view of welfare, and they allow a local politician to show his constituents how concerned he is over the use of taxpayers' money. The problem of who should receive welfare is fundamental in American society because of the national ideologies which surround work and achievement. The variations in formal eligibility requirements for public assistance, then, help reveal the public character attributed to AFDC recipients in different states. It is in the eligibility requirements that we can read indirectly the reciprocal expectations between citizen and state. As the eligibility requirements have become more lenient, the individual's claims on the state have increased.

Social Movements and the Definition of Citizenship

It is clear that important changes in the American system of welfare took place between 1960 and 1970. In trying to understand how these changes have come about, I have emphasized the transition (albeit incomplete) toward mass society for most of the states, and the associated extension of social citizenship rights. Because of the importance of mass society conditions, however, it becomes necessary to examine as well the social movements which help create and change the definition of citizenship, especially during the 1960s. The civil rights movement focused national attention on the abridgment of the citizenship rights of black Americans. This took place at the same time that the nation turned toward its domestic affairs after the preoccupation with foreign policy and the Cold War during the 1950s. In several ways, however, the Cold War raised the issue of how the United States treated its poor and its minority groups, especially as the United States intensified its attempts to obtain the allegiance of the new nations. Domestic racial discrimination and widespread poverty did not enhance the image of the United States as the third world nations became increasingly important in world politics.

The rediscovery of poverty during the late 1950s and early 1960s was partly an outgrowth of this renewed focus on domestic affairs (Steiner 1966), but equally important is the fact that the President's Council of Economic Advisors and the Bureau of the Census had begun to collect and analyze statistical data on employment and income. This demonstrated the existence of poverty and discrimination, and neither could be easily ignored any longer. As a result, nonindividual, or structural, causes of poverty (especially discrimination and regional depressions) received considerable publicity during the early part of this period.

Several other factors were also important. Thus a social-welfare constituency (in the phrasing of Schwartz and Tabb 1972) including social scientists, professional social workers, and welfare bureaucrats had come into existence and power with the Kennedy administration. It was a constituency with vested interests in sustaining and increasing social welfare expenditures and programs. This group has generally been credited with the 1962 Social Security Amendment, which emphasized social services to welfare recipients, and with the formulation of the War on Poverty programs (Steiner 1966, Schwartz and Tabb 1972; Moynihan 1969). There are many reasons why most of these policies failed to reduce dependency (Steiner 1974; Lowi 1969), but the important point is that they and a long series of other social welfare programs were instituted in the first place.

These programs and policies were the manifestations of greater government commitment to the general welfare of its citizens. The link between the individual and the nation-state was strengthened.[1] Not only was the federal government becoming more involved in a variety of welfare concerns (housing, health, community, unemployment, etc.), but the War on Poverty explicitly included the principle of citizen participation in the very design and administration of government programs. For a time the individual was called upon to give service to the nation (Peace Corps, Vista, etc.),[2] and politicians and public officials elaborated at length on the need to make all groups integral members of society.

Although one might be tempted to ignore such public statements as pure rhetoric with no necessary relationship to actual policies, they nevertheless create public obligations to which lip service, at the very least, must be given. More important, such public statements suggest to those in need, especially those who are not represented by lobbies or interest groups, how receptive to their demands public officials should be. In other words, I am suggesting that a climate of rising expectations was created during the Kennedy and Johnson administrations, whether intended or not. Furthermore, actions taken by the courts and the federal government reinforced those expectations, especially the use of federal troops to enforce school desegregation, the Twenty-fourth Amendment to the Constitution (1964), and the Voting Rights Act of 1965.

The civil rights movement originally emphasized the need to extend civil rights to all members of society, especially blacks, who for so long had been shortchanged. However, the focus on civil rights quickly spilled over into political and later social rights. It became clear that a person's civil rights were not fully guaranteed until they were backed by political rights and the power of the vote. This is one of the main reasons the civil rights movement quickly came to emphasize voter registration as a way to enforce the civil rights guaranteed by the Constitution. However, it also became clear that granting blacks political rights would not be adequate if they did not have the economic security and power to stand up to political pressure. Consequently, the civil rights movement found itself in the business of supporting strikes and battling discrimination in employment, housing, and so forth. The experiences of the civil rights movement thus clearly indicate the interconnections between Marshall's (1964) three forms of citizenship rights.

During the 1960s the civil rights movement for blacks served as an inspiration for a large number of other minority groups who also increased their demands for full rights. Thus American Indians, Mexican-Americans, homosexuals, women, welfare recipients, and migrant workers organized to obtain the rights to which they felt entitled. Most of these demands focused on social rights, and many were endorsed and supported both by politicians and by middle-class establishments: churches, social workers, and so on (Jenkins 1975). All the groups made essentially the same argument: they emphasized that they were only asking for the rights and privileges that other groups already had. Consequently, it could be said that their demands were for inclusion in the center on an equal basis with those already there.

The massive amount of social welfare legislation which came into existence during the 1960s may be seen as a response to these social movements, and it legitimized many of their claims. Administrative actions by the federal government and the courts were also important, for they reinforced the notion that public assistance was a right and that those receiving it were to be granted full citizenship rights along with everyone else. Thus, for example, the so-called night raids were declared an unconstitutional invasion of privacy by the Supreme Court, as was the man-in-the-house rule (*King* v. *Smith* 1968). Residency requirements were declared unconstitutional (*Shapiro* v. *Thompson* 1969) because they were judged to interfere with the constitutional rights of interstate travel.

The changing political climate of the early 1960s and the hopes raised by the civil rights movement were probably partially responsible not only for the major social welfare legislation but for the urban riots as well, although there are no good explanations of what caused the riots, except that they seemed to occur most where there was a large population with limited rights of citizenship (Danzger 1968; Spilerman 1970). A good deal of the social welfare legislation was enacted before the riots, and the rest during the urban unrest of the middle-to-late 1960s. The riots probably reinforced the belief, shared by some minority groups, that the federal government would deliver goods and services if pushed enough. However, Piven and Cloward (1971) have probably overstated their case when they claim that the riots alone gave rise to the concern with social welfare and the growth in public assistance rolls. Those processes were well under way several years before the major riots occurred.

The riots may have had a direct impact on welfare rolls because the resultant destruction of housing and businesses increased the need for public assistance (Seufert 1974). However, since federal money seemed to flow relatively freely into the riot cities, this may also have threatened the position of those who considered themselves citizens in better standing than blacks (see Howell 1973, pp. 31-32). The popular support George Wallace received during his presidential campaigns of 1968 and 1972 may well have represented strong resentment on account of invidious comparisons among different racial and ethnic groups. Although the results of these comparisons have probably contributed to the continuing controversy surrounding public antipoverty programs, it is also likely that a number of poorer white persons decided that they also deserved some form of public welfare. In fact, the proportion of public assistance recipients who are white increased slightly between 1960 and 1970 (Durman 1973; Eppley 1970).

The picture of changes in public assistance which emerges between 1960 and 1970 in the American states is, of course, part of a larger historical movement toward mass society. A more national scale of organization, high demand for well-educated employees, higher incomes, and increasing urbanization and industrialization have led to increasing government responsibilities and demands for public services. The history of the United States, as well as of most other modern nations, has shown an uneven trend in this direction. Along with these changes there has been a movement toward the extension of citizenship in several different areas. It is nevertheless certain that few past decades of American history saw such massive changes in the distribution of welfare and the extension of citizenship as did the 1960s. Possibly only the Progressive Era and the Great Depression saw changes of similar magnitude. It is unlikely that many future decades will see similar momentous changes, for the American experience in the extension of welfare and citizenship has been one of great unevenness.

Politically, citizenship in the United States was granted to a larger proportion of the total population between 1960 and 1970. It was a period in which enfranchisement (votes for eighteen-year-olds, the Voting Rights Act) was extended, civil rights were clarified, and broad initiatives were taken to identify and expand the center relative to the periphery. The initiative arose with such leaders as Martin Luther King and presidents Kennedy and Johnson, and it declined as the disorders of the late 1960s threatened the notion that full citizenship could be extended to every American.

Of course, neither political nor civil rights have been completely extended to all members of American society. There are still individuals who find themselves faced with substantial barriers to voting, just as there are those who are obviously restricted in their civil rights. The granting of "social citizenship" (Marshall 1964, p. 72), the right to economic welfare and security, is even less realized in the United States than the first two forms. The civil rights movement, with its emphasis on civil, political, *and* social rights both preceded and overlapped the extension of public assistance. The growth in the AFDC program must be seen as the result of the confluence of all these factors: the civil rights movement, a focus on domestic affairs, the rediscovery of poverty, changing political alliances, and attention to citizenship rights in general—a combination of historical circumstances which is not likely to be repeated in the near future (see also Schwartz and Tabb 1972). During the 1960s, then, AFDC came to be granted less on the basis of economic dependency alone and more nearly to reflect how willing the states are to consider the broader needs of their citizens.

Social Policy and Limits to the Mass Society

The persistent and increasing regional unevenness in the extension of public assistance is likely to limit the legitimacy of the welfare system itself. The disparities which exist in coverage and benefits within the United States can only raise the issue of whether such a system is fair and fulfills its purpose of providing aid to all those in need. Clearly it does not. The same questions of legitimacy emerge when the welfare system in its totality is examined. The categorical nature of welfare programs in the United States and the resultant attempts to classify recipients into different piles with different eligibility requirements, different provisions, and different benefits, with little regard for economic needs, maintains and sharpens the invidious comparisons between different groups in the American society, for some groups may benefit far more from one program than other groups do from other programs.

These two factors are part of the underlying structure of American society which, at least in the short run, may limit the movement toward mass society. However, welfare programs by their very nature must benefit some groups more than others, if only because of demographic differences between recipients. After a certain point, then, welfare programs may increase inequality (Janowitz 1976) along some dimensions, although they may appear to diminish inequality in other areas. The system of welfare in the United States is a case in point. Each "reform" of the welfare programs has brought with it new inequities while alleviating old ones. One may note here that the strong selling point of Nixon's Family Assistance Plan (FAP) was that it would primarily aid the working poor. Perhaps the persistence of such inequities is less noticeable during periods of affluence, such as the early 1960s, when everyone may benefit from the larger pie (Rein and Heclo 1973; Marshall 1961). But the inequities persist and may in some sense even have increased during the 1960s, with the expansion of welfare programs occurring primarily in the states that already had the highest mass society status.

These may be some of the reasons why controversy continues to surround the deservedness of public assistance recipients in the United States. Furthermore, the controversy does not seem to be diminishing in intensity, and the riots of the 1960s may have prompted a relatively strong reaction to any further liberalization of welfare policies and administrative practices. Since the percentage of the population of a state which is black is the major determinant of how restrictive are the state's eligibilty requirements for AFDC, this also indicates that there is continuing ambivalence about deservedness. It is particularly significant that those groups whose citizenship is most contestable remain prominent factors in explaining and shaping public policies. This continued ambivalence about the deservedness of full citizenship status for the poor, blacks, and migrants has been an integral part of the American cultural tradition throughout the country's history. It has been a potent factor in explaining the type and extent of policies of social change this society experienced (Grønbjerg, Street, and Suttles, forthcoming), and it emphasizes the extent to which such continued cultural fragmentation also limits the further movement toward mass society in the United States.

In societies like the United States, with its strong ideology emphasizing limited government and its extensive cultural and political fragmentation, social reforms thus generally have taken such forms as to create not only new inequities, but reactions against reform. Periods of reform in the United States, therefore, have tended to be followed by what Suttles calls periods of witch-hunting (Gronbjerg, Street, and Suttles, forthcoming, chap. 1). Or, as Steiner (1974) puts it, since reform follows reality, it is therefore largely ineffective in obtaining its stated goals, and consequently is denounced and rejected.

My selection of the AFDC program for study is important here because it is the largest and most rapidly growing of all the public assistance programs and, as such, a source of controversy. It is also the program where there has been the greatest ambivalence about who deserves this form of aid. Part of the controversy has centered on the deserting father, who was seen as attempting to avoid his familial and social responsibilities. But at least as important is the fact that AFDC involves families whose adult members cannot convincingly use the acceptable excuse of involuntary unemployment to explain their low incomes. These are the individuals, then, who most clearly fall short of both the American dream and responsible citizenship. The suspicion persists that it is because of their own shortcomings that they are not more successful. Their worthiness as citizens is the most questionable of any group, since so many of them belong to racial and ethnic groups who in any case are thought to have reasons for diminished loyalty to the country.

It has been emphasized throughout this study that the movement from the early situation in American history, where socioeconomic status almost fully determined one's status as a citizen, toward a condition where citizenship in all its different forms is more uniformly available, is incomplete and is likely to continue to be so. This latter conclusion seems to lend support to a series of hypotheses recently developed by Harold Wilensky in his cross-national study of welfare systems (Wilensky 1975). He singles out several structural characteristics of nations which, he argues, are likely to retard social welfare development. Some of these characteristics are very prominent in American society and are among the factors I have emphasized in this study: extensive and continuing private welfare programs, high visibility of middle-class tax burdens relative to that of upper-income groups, the tradition of self-employment and especially its association with the laissez-faire ideology, and great social distance between groups at the lower end of the stratification system and those at the upper end, such as the social distance between blacks and whites. I might add that the United States is characterized by a high degree of social heterogeneity, along with extensive political and administrative decentralization.[3]

In the event of a severe economic crisis, new political coalitions, or a popular war, it is likely that the United states could make still another halting step toward the mass society.[4] It is probable that such a movement would primarily entail a nationalization of welfare programs. Specifically, the federal government would likely take over the financing and administration of public assistance, public works, and unemployment programs. If the recent nationalization of the so-called adult public assistance programs (OAA, AB, APTD, ABD) into the Supplemental Security Income (SSI) program is any guideline, conditions of eligibility may not become more lenient because of such a takeover by the federal government—only more uniform across the United States. Once permanent national programs are established, however, further developments toward mass society are possible, because it is very difficult to retrench on programs once they are established and benefit a broad cross-section of the population. More important, a national program would abolish many of the inequities inherent in the present programs, relieving welfare of some its susceptibility to critical attacks.

In a "true" mass society, where the center approaches the periphery (Shils 1975) and full citizenship is extended to all (Marshall 1964), conditions of eligibility for all welfare programs would be designed to remove the effects of disability (social, physical, and economic) on the social position of the individual. Every eligible person would have the right to obtain such assistance and would in fact be expected to make use of the available system of aid. The stigma of welfare then would be insignificant, almost everyone who is eligible would be willing to apply for aid, and most applications would be likely to be approved. Ironically, under such circumstances, local variations in welfare caseloads and expenditures would once again reflect stratification conditions—that is, regional variations in poverty, family conditions, and employment opportunities. It is only in the transition stages, and in societies with strong regional political control, that the transition from stratification conditions to mass society can be identified by using the type of state-by-state comparison employed in this study.

The extension of citizenship is part of the process of modernity and, as Dahrendorf (1974) emphasizes, is the institutional counterpart to rationality crystallized into a social role: man can make rational decisions only if he is a full member of society. Citizenship has come to include not only equality of opportunity, a chance to participate in the community, but also a generalized right vis-à-vis the political community (Dahrendorf 1974).

Whether a "true" mass society can in fact come into existence hinges on this latter process, the growth of citizenship into more differentiated social roles. As Marshall indicates (1964), social rights must be accepted and extended to all if citizenship is to have its fullest meaning. The major problem then becomes exactly what social rights are to encompass. Does it mean the equal right to unequal opportunities, in which case one could argue that inequalities are no longer class distinctions, but socially acceptable (Marshall 1964)? Or will the full extension of social rights inevitably mean the right to equal status, in which case social policies must be compensatory programs to make up for the initial handicaps of the poor and make them equal with the nonpoor (Dahrendorf 1974)? In short, the ultimate limitation on the development of the mass society may be how much equality social structures can survive. Some (e.g., Marx and his followers) have argued that complete equality is possible, but most writers seem to believe that modern complex societies need some amount of inequality to maintain self-regulation and continue operation.[5]

A whole different set of problems concerns whether any society can financially afford the major investments in social policies which would be necessary to reduce the social impact of inequalities to a minimum. There are reasons to think that these factors are crucial. The inherent and ultimate limits to the development of the welfare state may well be determined by how much of the society's economic product can be invested in maintaining and improving the standard of living, especially during conditions of high inflation (Janowitz 1976). It is also likely that these economic factors of limitation will come into operation before complete equality of outcome is anywhere near realization, as the recent experiences of the Scandinavian countries suggest. If in fact the complete transition to the mass society is impossible, when such a transition has been expected and perhaps even promised, the result is likely to be considerable political instability, or at least dissatisfaction.

Some have argued that there is no danger that any society, especially a capitalist one, would ever approach a true mass society—that the welfare state, as it has developed, has benefited the well-to-do at least as much as the poor and thus has brought no basic change in the social structure (Offe 1972; Piven and Cloward 1971, for example). Thus welfare in this perspective is seen at best as a meager compensation for the price of industrial development without dealing directly with human needs.

Although conditions for the poor did improve during the 1960s, the process was painful, halting, controversial, and at times difficult to notice. Furthermore, as indicated above, it is unlikely that the United States will face the prospects of a "true" mass society in the near future, if ever. Nevertheless, the history of the United States is marked by a movement toward the expansion of citizenship and increasing federal responsibility. Progress in this direction has been uneven in the past, and it is likely to continue to be so in the future. The 1960s help us to understand the underlying process, and that understanding is an important part of the process itself. The movement toward mass society is not a self-regulated, "natural," or automatic process, but one which demands leadership, knowledge, and commitment to solving the problems of social integration and of determining the place and role of the individual in the complex, modern social structure. The solution chosen must be one involving the expansion of citizenship rights rather than their abridgment, as has been the case in totalitarian societies. It is not an easy path, and certainly it is one that demands understanding of the consequences of social policy.

In conclusion, I wish to emphasize the two most important implications of this study for social welfare policies in general. First, I have demonstrated that welfare policies have little direct effect on welfare rolls. Conditions of need and mass society status seem to be more important than eligibility requirements. Furthermore, administrative practices may have a more direct relationship to the actual number of people receiving AFDC than formal policies. Administrative practices may be especially important, since implementations of legislative changes may nullify the intentions of the law. One might also argue that the social and political "climate" of the state—its movement toward mass society, or the extent of economic dependency within it—may influence public assistance agencies and officials in their treatment of applications and recipients.

The evidence on this issue is, of course, indirect and incomplete. It is not known that the political climate of a state has such a direct influence on the administration of welfare. However, the findings that eligibility requirements have little relationship to AFDC rolls and that the mass society and stratification variables bear a close relationship to both AFDC rolls and policies support such an interpretation. Similarly, it seems likely that the stigma of welfare, both its extent and its degree, is likely to be inversely related to conditions of mass society.

One of the reasons it is not possible to be more affirmative in these statements is that very little is known about the gap between the actual number of recipients and the number who are eligible for assistance in each state, given all eligibility requirements. It is difficult, then, to judge how each eligibility requirement might affect the potential number of recipients in each state. How many, for example, were excluded by residency requirements in Illinois compared with Georgia? Some eligibility requirements may be functional alternatives to one another in terms of the number of people they include or exclude as potential recipients. For example, it is uncertain how the number of families excluded in Minnesota because their property holdings are too high compares with the number included because their children are in a certain age group. Without such estimates of the specific effects of each degree of severity of all eligibility requirements for all states it is difficult to make any confident statement about how welfare policies become translated into welfare rolls. It seems that obtaining such information about the specific effects of different eligibility requirements, given different economic conditions, would be essential to cast some light on the crisis of understanding which surrounds the welfare system in the United States. Only then can the nation hope to move beyond polemical debate to effective social action.

It is clear that court decisions, leadership by national figures, and social movements have had a great effect on both welfare rolls and welfare policies. Furthermore, welfare policies, in the form of eligibility requirements, should not be discounted, for they constitute a part of the general social statement of people's right to citizenship. This, I argue, is in fact one of the most important functions of formal eligibility requirements. The policies have considerable reality in this sense, along with the social structures of the separate states.

Furthermore, the results of this study clearly point to the need for a universal and standaradized national welfare system. I feel that such a program is one of the few ways to prevent cultural fragmentations and invidious comparisons from standing in the way of further expansion of citizenship in the United States. I am assuming that expansion of citizenship is not only desirable but necessary if the United States is to maintain an integrated society, and the nation has a long way to go before the process of mass society development reaches its ultimate limits (Dahrendorf 1974; Janowitz 1976).

To be most effective in promoting the further extension of citizenship, a national welfare program would have to diminish not only regional and ecological inequities but characterological and cultural distinctions between recipient groups. This would most easily be accomplished by some form of guaranteed annual income or universal flat grant system. However, this study has also pointed to the many ideological and structural obstacles such program proposals would likely face in the United States. I doubt that either of those two proposals is in any danger of being implemented in the near future.

Acknowledgments

My special appreciation and gratitude go to Morris Janowitz; it was in my conversations with him that the major theoretical thrust of this study was developed. I also want to thank him for his very careful readings of the entire manuscript, his suggestions for revisions, and his continuing encouragement. Very special appreciation also goes to my husband, Gerald Suttles. Not only did he take a lively interest in the study and help me in developing and sharpening many of the ideas, he also suffered through at least four drafts at very close range—and rarely complained. His encouragement, comments, time, and patience—particularly with my sentence structure—have not only made this a better study, but have helped me survive deadlocks and frustrations. He has been a true friend and colleague, and I thank him for it.

David Street read the manuscript closely and made numerous valuable suggestions. Edward Shils, Philip M. Hauser and Leo A. Goodman provided critical commentary and helpful guidance. I also want to thank David McFarland, Edward O. Laumann, and Robert W. Hodge for their comments on earlier drafts. Many other people have on occasion commented on the study, and in the process my own thinking has been clarified. I want to thank all of them.

My deep gratitude also goes to Mrs. Catherine Miller, chief of the State Plan and Program Characteristics Branch, Division of Program Implementation and Review of the Assistance Payments Administration, under the Social and Rehabiliation Service, United States Department of Health, Education, and Welfare. Not only did she provide important data and information, but her willingness to share her extensive knowledge and experience vastly deepened my own understanding of public assistance in the United States. I want to thank her for the time, energy, and interest she was willing to give me and this study. She also read the manuscript closely and can take most of the credit for a more or less technically accurate account of the AFDC program.

As is usually the case, however, I have not always followed the advice of others, and I accept full responsibility for the results and interpretations reported in this study.

Last, I want to thank various institutions and organizations which made this study possible. Hofstra University Computing Service provided me with complete research assistance and free computer time, and Clair Gittelson, acting director of the Computing Service, was especially patient in helping me survive my first serious encounter with a computer. The State University of New York at

Stony Brook has also provided me with considerable computer time and programming assistance. The research project on the Human Side of Poverty, funded by the Rockefeller Foundation, provided support for part of this study. The Ford Foundation made it possible for me to finish this study in a shorter time than would have been possible otherwise by making funds available to me for typing services, while the Albion Small Fund of the University of Chicago has been generous in making available a loan to aid in the publication of this manuscript. Finally, Veronica Abjornson, Barbara Consorte, Carole Roland, Wanda Olivera, and Michele Caplette competently and carefully typed several versions of the manuscript. I thank all of them.

Appendix A

Construction of the
Total Eligibility Score

The index constructed to measure the overall restrictiveness of eligibility requirements is based on twenty eligibility factors. Although the maximum level of benefit paid to recipients in a state is not an eligibility factor, it is nevertheless a strong indication of welfare policies. Consequently, this measure was also included in the Total Eligibility Score (TES). A basic objective was to make the index comparable across time so that trends could be discerned. Thus the index was designed to reflect both changes in federal standards and changes in state policies within federal limitations. For example, it includes measures on whether the states have AFDC-U programs, although such programs could not have received FFP until after 1961. Using the guidelines given by Meyers and McIntyre (1969, pp. 11-13) the index was constructed as follows:

Eligibility Factors	**Score**
1. *Age limit of dependent child*	
under 21	0
under 18	1
under 16	2
2. *Aid to unborn children*	
available	0
not available	2
3. *Durational residency requirements*[1]	
none	0
6 months	1
more than 6 months (1 year)	2
4. *Duration of waiting period in cases of desertion, abandonment, or separation*	
no requirement	0
less than 6 months	1
6 months or more	2
5. *Duration of period of expected imprisonment of parent(s)*	
no requirement	0
less than 6 months	1
6 months or more	2
6. *Duration of period of expected incapacity of parent(s)*	
no requirement	0
less than 6 months	1
6 months or more	2

7. *AFDC-U program*

    yes, unemployed if working less than "full time"
        (federal definition)   0

    yes, unemployed if working less than 34 hours/
        week (less than federal definition)   1

    no program   2

8. *"Man-in-the-house" rule (substitute parent)*[2]

    no requirement   0

    lenient, will consider man's contribution to
        family income   1

    strict, automatic ineligibility   2

9. *Suitable home requirement*

    no requirement   0
    only if court order   1
    has requirement   2

10. *Cost standard used in determining an
applicant's need for assistance*

    90 percent or more of SSA poverty level   0
    67–89 percent of SSA poverty level   1
    less than 67 percent of SSA poverty level   2

11. *Reservations of income for future identifiable
needs of child*

    a portion of family income may be reserved   0
    child's earnings or income may be reserved   1
    no reservation of income is allowed   2

12. *Disregarding $5 per month from family income
in determining needs*

    per recipient   0
    per family   1
    no provision   2

13. *Disregarding student's earnings in
determining need*[3]

    yes, full amount may be disregarded (1967
        amendment)   0

    yes, up to $50 per month may be disregarded
        (1965 amendment)   1

    no provision   2

14. *Disregarding $30 plus one-third of remaining
earnings of nonstudent recipients*[3]

    yes (1967 amendment)   0

    yes, but less than provided for in 1967
        amendment   1

    no provision   2

175   Construction of the Total
Eligibility Score

15. *Limit on value of home*
    no limit   0
    value of home "considered"   1
    maximum value   2

16. *Limit on value of other property (personal) per standard family*[4]
    $941 and over (1959), $1,251 and over (1970)   0
    $470–$940 (1959), $626–$1,250 (1970)   1
    less than $470 (1959), less than $626 (1970)   2

17. *Provisions concerning transfer of property*
    no provision   0
    yes, including recipient ineligible for 1
       year or less   1
    yes, recipient ineligible for 2 years or more   2

18. *Provisions concerning recoveries, liens, and assignments of property*
    no provision   0
    claim on estate   1
    secured claim   2

19. *Employment requirements*
    none   0
    employable parent must accept suitable work   1
    employable parent and child must accept
       suitable work   2

20. *Requirement that mother must file suit against deserting father*
    no provision   0
    provision   2

21. *Maximum level of benefits paid as percentage of poverty*
    85 percent or more of SSA poverty level paid
       as maximum   0
    60–68 percent of SSA poverty level paid
       as maximum   1
    less than 60 percent of SSA poverty level paid
       as maximum   2

---

1. No state allowed to have such requirements after 1969.
2. No states allowed such requirements after 1968.
3. All states required to have these provisions by July 1969.
4. Adjusted for changes in the price index (CPI).

The minimum restrictiveness score on the TES (assuming FFP) was 9 in 1959, since some programs did not receive FFP before the 1960s, and 0 in 1970. The maximum restrictiveness score was 42 in 1959, but only 34 in 1970, because certain provisions were declared unconstitutional ("man-in-the-house" rules and durational residency requirements) and others were made mandatory for all states (earnings exemptions) during the 1960s. There is clear evidence of a massive movement toward more lenient welfare policies, especially in the latter part of the 1960s.

Appendix B

Results of Factor
Analyses,
1960 and 1970

The general procedure used in the factor analyses, summarized in chapter 4, was a principle factoring method with oblique rotations. There were two reasons for using oblique rotations. First, the mass society variables and the stratification variables could be expected to be somewhat intercorrelated. The basic purpose of the factor analysis was to see if there was a closer set of intercorrelations among each set of variables than between the sets. An oblique rotation allows us to do this. Second, an oblique rotation makes it possible to determine better the grouping or clustering of the variables, since this particular method of rotation allows us to obtain the direct contribution of a factor to each variable.[1]

Two of the matrices produced by this particular type of factor analysis are important for our purposes. The structure matrix (see tables 18 and 19, figures in parentheses) presents the correlations between the variables and the factors. The square of the *structure* coefficients measures the *total* contribution of each factor to the variation in the different variables. The square of the *pattern* coefficients (see tables 18 and 19), on the other hand, represents the *direct* contribution of a given factor to the variance of a variable. The difference between the square of a structure coefficient and the square of a pattern coefficient reflects the indirect contribution of the remaining factors on that variable (due to the correlations between the different factors). The pattern matrix, because it reflects the direct contribution of each factor to the different variables, delineates the grouping or clustering of variables more clearly than the structure matrix. Consequently, most of the discussion of the interrelationships between the independent variables in chapter 4 was based on the coefficients of the factor pattern matrices.

The factor structure coefficients do not present as clear a clustering as the pattern coefficients, because some variables may not cluster on a factor but nevertheless may have high correlations with that factor owing to indirect contributions of other factors. An examination of the factor correlations (correlations between the factors themselves) shows that some of the factors are indeed fairly highly intercorrelated, particularly the female employment factor and the urbanization-industrialization factor ($r = .44$ in 1960, $r = .34$ in 1970). The urbanization-industrialization factor was also correlated with the inclusion factor in 1970 ($r = -.31$), but not in 1960 ($r = -.17$).

1. The total contribution of a factor (i.e., the correlation between a factor and a variable) thus can be separated into two parts: the direct contribution and the indirect contribution through correlated factors.

Table 18

Stratification and Mass Society
Variables, 1960

% voter participation
Median level of education
% high-school or more education
% families poor
% broken families
Male underemployment rate

Female underemployment rate
% females not working
Nonworker-worker ratio

% upper white-collar employment
Per capita revenue
Per capita taxes

Urbanization index
Industrial index, males
Industrial index, females
% employed nonfarm

Factor Pattern Coefficients and Factor Structure Coefficients from Factor Analysis of Stratification and Mass Society Variables, 1960

Factor Coefficients, 1960							
Composite Factor I		Urbanization–Industrialization Factor II		Inclusion Factor III		Female Employment Factor IV	
Pattern	Structure	Pattern	Structure	Pattern	Structure	Pattern	Structure
(1)	(2)	(3)	(4)	(5)	(6)	(7)	(8)
.777	(.764)	−.114	(−.228)	−.122	(.077)	.051	(−.116)
.731	(.849)	−.129	(−.380)	.314	(.512)	−.113	(−.296)
.760	(.872)	−.030	(−.302)	.367	(.555)	−.129	(−.275)
−.700	(−.820)	.418	(.659)	.001	(−.243)	.228	(.521)
−.920	(−.855)	−.255	(−.153)	−.093	(−.256)	−.226	(−.191)
−.711	(−.726)	−.062	(.244)	.174	(.001)	.438	(.515)
.216	(.019)	.255	(.595)	−.048	(−.075)	.853	(.934)
.046	(−.118)	−.053	(.387)	−.089	(−.108)	.987	(.960)
−.285	(−.429)	.098	(.512)	.016	(−.100)	.817	(.904)
.426	(.589)	−.350	(−.454)	.497	(.650)	.151	(−.089)
.095	(.264)	.246	(.058)	.915	(.897)	−.028	(.029)
−.164	(.086)	−.162	(−.315)	.870	(.862)	−.086	(−.166)
.047	(.198)	−.727	(−.777)	−.055	(.084)	−.113	(−.438)
.519	(.677)	−.718	(−.819)	.083	(.325)	.042	(−.358)
.143	(.343)	−.819	(−.934)	.021	(.201)	−.187	(−.570)
−.232	(−.051)	−.854	(−.823)	.016	(.108)	−.030	(−.370)

s U.S. Bureau of the Census 1961–63, 1973b; *Book of the States* 1962–63.

e Oblique rotations; iterations = 9; delta = 0. Figures in parentheses represent the factor structure coefficients.

Table 19

Stratification and Mass Society
Variables, 1970

% voter participation
Median level of education
% high-school or more education
% families poor
% broken families

Male underemployment rate
Female underemployment rate
% females not working
Nonworker-worker ratio

% upper white-collar employment
Per capita revenue
Per capita taxes

Urbanization index
Industrial index, males
Industrial index, females
% employed nonfarm

Factor Pattern Coefficients and Factor Structure Coefficients from Factor Analysis of Stratification and Mass Society Variables, 1970

Factor Coefficients, 1970							
Composite Factor II		Urbanization–Industrialization Factor I		Inclusion Factor IV		Female Employment Factor III	
Pattern	Structure	Pattern	Structure	Pattern	Structure	Pattern	Structure
(1)	(2)	(3)	(4)	(5)	(6)	(7)	(8)
.774	(.804)	−.100	(.026)	−.089	(−.255)	−.094	(−.223)
.870	(.921)	.189	(.315)	−.100	(−.371)	−.061	(−.309)
.840	(.908)	.103	(.256)	−.231	(−.463)	−.030	(−.267)
.703	(−.775)	−.387	(−.527)	−.077	(.262)	.300	(.551)
.874	(−.810)	.311	(.290)	−.111	(−.015)	−.061	(−.023)
.285	(−.426)	.166	(−.137)	.039	(.201)	.779	(.783)
.278	(.060)	.053	(−.312)	.147	(.256)	1.002	(.959)
.038	(−.140)	−.106	(−.411)	−.018	(.180)	.917	(.943)
.220	(−.360)	−.233	(−.485)	−.140	(.135)	.806	(.901)
.458	(.553)	.229	(.360)	−.394	(−.554)	.085	(−.154)
.124	(.327)	−.127	(.162)	−.976	(−.954)	.061	(−.103)
.105	(.121)	.117	(.409)	−.810	(−.850)	−.151	(−.325)
.129	(.179)	.628	(.634)	.009	(−.212)	.007	(−.230)
.439	(.529)	.738	(.814)	−.080	(−.417)	−.041	(−.392)
.138	(.010)	.841	(.949)	−.152	(−.419)	−.212	(−.503)
.337	(−.261)	.746	(.734)	−.035	(−.190)	−.018	(−.216)

U.S. Bureau of the Census 1971–73, 1973*b*.

Oblique rotations; iterations = 6; delta = 0. Figures in parentheses represent the factor structure coefficients.

Appendix C

Descriptive Statistics
of All Major Variables

Table 20

Variables, 1960 and 1970

Stratification variables, 1960
% families poor
% broken families
Male underemployment rate
Female underemployment rate
% females not working
Nonworker-worker ratio

Stratification variables, 1970
% families poor
% families very poor
% broken families
Male underemployment rate
Female underemployment rate
% females not working
Nonworker-worker ratio

Mass society variables, 1960
% voter participation
Median level of education
% high-school or more education
% upper white-collar employment
Per capita revenue
Per capita taxes
Urbanization index
Industrial index, males
Industrial index, females
% employed nonfarm

Mass society variables, 1970
% voter participation
Median level of education
% high-school or more education
% upper white-collar employment
Per capita revenue
Per capita taxes
Urbanization index
Industrial index, males
Industrial index, females
% employed nonfarm

Descriptive Statistics of All Major Variables, 1960 and 1970

Mean (1)	Standard Error (2)	Standard Deviation (3)	Variance (4)	Kurtosis (5)	Skewness (6)	Minimum (7)	Maximum (8)	Coefficient of Variability V (9)
20.5	1.38	9.6	93.0	.054	.974	8.0	47.9	.471
11.6	.29	2.0	4.2	−.954	.107	7.8	15.7	.176
50.8	.71	5.0	24.6	−.613	.437	42.5	61.5	.098
85.0	.34	2.4	5.8	−.248	−.408	78.5	89.7	.028
67.9	.44	3.1	9.5	.688	.333	61.7	77.1	.045
1.6	.03	.2	.0	.698	.683	1.2	2.2	.111
11.7	.75	5.3	27.6	.941	1.229	5.3	28.9	.450
7.6	.54	3.8	14.6	1.585	1.413	3.6	21.0	.501
13.2	.30	2.1	4.3	−.828	.142	9.7	17.3	.157
43.6	.56	3.9	15.4	−.099	.483	35.0	51.9	.090
78.4	.36	2.5	6.4	1.584	−.635	69.7	84.4	.032
61.1	.49	3.5	12.0	.975	.444	53.2	72.2	.057
1.5	.02	.2	.0	.905	.969	1.2	2.0	.109
64.7	2.21	15.4	235.4	−.124	−1.154	25.7	80.6	.238
10.6	.16	1.1	1.2	−.998	−.369	8.7	12.2	.104
41.5	1.02	7.2	51.3	−.705	−.195	27.6	55.8	.174
19.5	.35	2.4	5.9	−.770	−.031	14.4	24.6	.125
69.7	6.49	45.4	2069.4	1.355	1.234	98.0	314.8	.268
109.2	4.01	28.1	778.3	2.315	1.323	63.6	208.9	.257
37.3	11.81	82.7	6835.2	−.953	.092	97.5	411.0	.348
91.7	2.22	15.5	240.5	−.795	−.302	59.3	116.9	.169
93.6	2.02	15.4	237.5	−.720	.267	62.8	124.6	.165
91.1	1.00	7.0	48.7	2.210	−1.456	67.7	99.3	.077
44.9	1.70	11.9	141.1	−.160	−.755	14.7	63.9	.264
11.8	.10	.7	.5	.375	−1.337	9.9	12.5	.057
52.8	1.13	7.9	62.7	−.798	−.357	37.8	67.3	.150
23.1	.38	2.7	7.1	−1.007	.072	18.5	28.7	.115
46.0	14.44	101.1	10217.9	1.472	1.167	316.5	791.1	.227
32.5	8.05	56.4	3176.8	2.566	1.276	128.8	442.4	.243
245.9	11.27	78.9	6227.1	−.718	−.015	84.7	406.4	.321
93.4	1.78	12.5	156.0	−.840	−.065	67.2	114.2	.134
93.8	1.79	12.5	157.5	−.426	.468	71.2	122.1	.134
95.1	.66	4.6	21.3	4.395	−2.070	78.5	99.6	.049

(continued)

Table 20 (continued)

Variables, 1960 and 1970

Threat variables, 1960
% black
% nonwhite
% native population born in South
% population increase, 1950–60
% total in-migration
% total net migration
% nonwhite in-migration
% nonwhite net migration

Threat variables, 1970
% black
% nonwhite
% native population born in South
% population increase, 1960–70
% total in-migration
% total net migration
% nonwhite in-migration
% nonwhite net migration

Dependent variables
AFDC rolls, 1960
TES, 1960
AFDC, rolls, 1970
TES, 1970

Mean	Standard Error	Standard Deviation	Variance	Kurtosis	Skewness	Minimum	Maximum	Coefficient of Variability V
(1)	(2)	(3)	(4)	(5)	(6)	(7)	(8)	(9)
8.9	1.50	10.5	110.6	1.289	1.458	.1	42.0	1.175
11.3	1.86	13.0	169.8	6.009	2.247	.2	68.0	1.157
9.1	.87	6.1	37.2	−.018	.690	1.2	25.8	.673
19.1	2.68	18.8	352.5	3.247	1.765	−7.2	78.7	—[a]
1.1	.88	6.1	37.6	2.682	1.713	4.0	31.9	.544
−.3	.69	4.8	23.4	4.158	1.797	−8.3	18.0	—[a]
11.3	1.24	8.7	75.4	3.322	1.702	1.9	42.8	.766
1.4	.85	6.0	35.7	1.628	.749	−10.8	22.2	—[a]
8.9	1.33	9.3	86.6	.753	1.228	.2	36.8	1.046
1.5	1.62	11.4	129.4	5.986	2.146	.4	61.2	.993
8.9	.77	5.4	29.2	−.504	.482	1.6	22.8	.607
13.3	1.79	12.5	156.6	7.768	2.179	−6.2	71.3	—[a]
1.7	.69	4.9	23.6	1.468	1.192	4.2	28.1	.419
−.3	.53	3.7	13.7	.542	.101	−9.2	9.6	—[a]
7.4	.63	4.4	19.7	3.096	1.500	1.0	23.8	.595
−.2	.57	4.0	16.1	−.323	−.442	−9.8	6.4	—[a]
1.7	.12	.8	.7	1.573	1.322	.7	4.4	.473
21.8	.59	4.1	17.2	−.382	.487	14.0	31.0	.188
2.9	.16	1.1	1.2	.152	.747	1.1	5.7	.380
13.5	.50	3.5	12.5	−.190	.013	6.0	22.0	.259

U.S. Bureau of the Census 1961–63, 1963, 1971–73, 1973b,c; Book of the States 1962–63; Social Security Bulletin 1960, 1961, 1970, 1971; U.S. Social Security Administration 1960, 1962; U.S. Social and Rehabilitation Service 1971d,f; SPCU Reports.

[a]Coefficients of variability are not appropriate when some of the observations are negative.

Appendix D

Zero-Order Correlations
among Independent
Variables

Table 21

	X_1	X_2	X_3	X_4	X_5	X_6	X_7	X_8	X_9	X_{10}	X_{11}	X_{12}
X_1	1.00	.75[a]	.71[a]	.41[b]	.36[b]	.16	.01	.44[a]	.00	−.23	−.70[a]	−.62[a]
X_2	.57[a]	1.00	.92[a]	.70[a]	.39[b]	.27[c]	.37[b]	.64[a]	.24[c]	−.06	−.81[a]	−.62[a]
X_3	.58[a]	.98[a]	1.00	.71[a]	.51[a]	.32[c]	.33[c]	.59[a]	.19	−.07	−.74[a]	−.68[a]
X_4	.33[c]	.76[a]	.77[a]	1.00	.55[a]	.42[a]	.34[b]	.51[a]	.32[c]	.13	−.47[a]	−.25[c]
X_5	.14	.41[b]	.48[a]	.54[a]	1.00	.79[a]	.10	.35[c]	.26[c]	.06	−.26[c]	−.14
X_6	.04	.36[b]	.37[b]	.50[a]	.78[a]	1.00	.26[c]	.47[a]	.54[a]	.27[c]	−.30[c]	−.12
X_7	.13	.33[c]	.28[c]	.40[b]	−.12	.19	1.00	.56[a]	.62[a]	.39[b]	−.35[b]	.06
X_8	.60[a]	.71[a]	.68[a]	.66[a]	.19	.35[b]	.64[a]	1.00	.78[a]	.46[a]	−.83[a]	−.16
X_9	.36[b]	.46[a]	.41[b]	.47[a]	.01	.35[b]	.77[a]	.86[a]	1.00	.70[a]	−.51[a]	.35[t]
X_{10}	.03	.18	.09	.27[c]	−.12	.25[c]	.61[a]	.56[a]	.71[a]	1.00	−.18	.54[a]
X_{11}	−.75[a]	−.80[a]	−.77[a]	−.59[a]	−.18	−.26[c]	−.54[a]	−.90[a]	−.76[a]	−.42[a]	1.00	.47[a]
X_{12}	−.61[a]	−.69[a]	−.73[a]	−.47[a]	−.33[c]	−.03	.11	−.37[b]	.02	.34[b]	.47[a]	1.00
X_{13}	−.64[a]	−.57[a]	−.59[a]	−.34[b]	−.06	.05	−.31[c]	−.55[a]	−.39[b]	.01	.74[a]	.47[a]
X_{14}	.01	−.18	−.14	−.09	.04	−.25[c]	−.53[a]	−.38[b]	−.66[a]	−.56[a]	.45[a]	−.39[b]
X_{15}	−.02	−.31[c]	−.30[c]	−.09	−.03	−.20	−.37[b]	−.31[c]	−.51[a]	−.36[b]	.46[a]	−.19
X_{16}	−.32[c]	−.53[a]	−.49[a]	−.26[c]	−.02	−.18	−.50[a]	−.56[a]	−.67[a]	−.34[b]	.72[a]	.08
X_{17}	−.87[a]	−.69[a]	−.70[a]	−.48[a]	−.27[c]	−.15	−.19	−.55[a]	−.34[b]	.01	.74[a]	.69[a]
X_{18}	−.73[a]	−.45[a]	−.45[a]	−.28[c]	.13	.30[c]	−.02	−.40[b]	−.13	.02	.52[a]	.61[a]
X_{19}	−.51[a]	−.12	−.14	.25[c]	.04	.20	.11	−.01	.07	.28[c]	.26[c]	.18
X_{20}	−.07	.45[a]	.46[a]	.59[a]	.29[c]	.47[a]	.40[b]	.46[a]	.44[a]	.38[b]	−.34[b]	−.14
X_{21}	−.07	.48[a]	.50[a]	.62[a]	.53[a]	.49[a]	.08	.25[c]	.16	.13	−.20	−.29[c]
X_{22}	−.15	.38[b]	.37[b]	.54[a]	.20	.40[b]	.39[b]	.37[b]	.39[b]	.44[a]	−.27[c]	−.03
X_{23}	.54[a]	.54[a]	.54[a]	.25[c]	.14	−.01	−.07	.27[c]	.15	.09	−.50[a]	−.40[b]
X_{24}	.48[a]	.51[a]	.48[a]	.29[c]	−.12	.01	.42[a]	.54[a]	.55[a]	.34[b]	−.66[a]	−.23

Sources U.S. Bureau of the Census 1961–63,
1963, 1971–73, 1973; *Book of the
States* 1962–63.

Notes   The coefficients below the diagonal
refer to the zero-order correlations
between the independent variables
for 1960. The boldface coefficients
above the diagonal refer to the
zero-order correlations between the
independent variables for 1970.

X_{13}	X_{14}	X_{15}	X_{16}	X_{17}	X_{18}	X_{19}	X_{20}	X_{21}	X_{22}	X_{23}	X_{24}
−.42[b]	.00	−.18	−.33[c]	−.76[a]	−.59[a]	−.54[a]	−.10	.02	−.29[c]	.42[a]	.39[b]
−.47[a]	−.11	−.28[c]	−.46[a]	−.68[a]	−.43[a]	−.20	.30[c]	.35[b]	.12	.43[a]	.57[a]
−.41[b]	−.10	−.26[c]	−.42[a]	−.73[a]	−.42[a]	−.27[c]	.36[b]	.47[a]	.15	.45[a]	.50[a]
−.28[c]	−.08	−.16	−.22	−.41[b]	−.20	.09	.40[b]	.50[a]	.21	.24[c]	.43[a]
−.16	−.14	−.08	−.08	−.38[b]	.11	−.16	.21	.40[b]	−.06	−.02	.04
−.25[c]	−.38[b]	−.33[c]	−.26[c]	−.13	.32[c]	.00	.34[b]	.27[c]	.17	−.12	.26[c]
−.13	−.20	−.27[c]	−.36[b]	−.09	.12	.28[c]	.48[a]	.15	.32[c]	−.05	.57[a]
−.37[b]	−.25[c]	−.38[b]	−.55[a]	−.37[b]	−.19	−.07	.44[a]	.10	.30[c]	.26[c]	.72[a]
−.27[c]	−.52[a]	−.53[a]	−.57[a]	.05	.25[c]	.24[c]	.55[a]	.12	.46[a]	.05	.49[a]
.07	−.28[c]	−.32[c]	−.26[c]	.26[c]	.21	.36	.43	.05	.57[a]	.12	.18
.58[a]	.32[c]	−.52[a]	.72[a]	.65[a]	.45[a]	.32[c]	−.33[b]	−.16	−.24[c]	−.58[a]	−.68[a]
.25[c]	−.24[c]	−.09	.11	.77[a]	.61[a]	.40[b]	.04	−.25[c]	.14	−.37[b]	−.27[c]
1.00	.74[a]	.68[a]	.70[a]	.25[c]	−.02	.16	−.17	−.16	.04	−.31[c]	−.38[b]
.40[b]	1.00	.91[a]	.78[a]	−.13	−.44[a]	−.05	−.36[b]	−.20	−.27[c]	−.14	−.21
.44[a]	.89[a]	1.00	.90[a]	.01	−.21	.05	−.45[a]	−.22	−.39[b]	−.30[c]	−.44[a]
.63[a]	.80[a]	.87[a]	1.00	.21	.02	.09	−.45[a]	−.24[c]	−.40[b]	−.36[b]	−.56[a]
.55[a]	−.04	.01	.33[b]	1.00	.67[a]	.54[a]	.00	−.23	.14	−.48[a]	−.29[c]
.47[a]	−.28[c]	−.15	.13	.69[a]	1.00	.42[a]	.09	.05	.09	−.58[a]	−.22
.43[a]	.04	.10	.17	.44[a]	.33[c]	1.00	.41[b]	.35[b]	.42[a]	−.37[b]	.01
−.02	−.24[c]	−.34[b]	−.32[c]	−.06	.04	.55[a]	1.00	.71[a]	.78[a]	.16	.38[b]
.09	−.05	−.20	−.19	−.18	.03	.51[a]	.82[a]	1.00	.51[c]	.15	.05
.07	−.26[c]	−.35[b]	−.28[c]	.00	.09	.58[a]	.94[a]	.79[a]	1.00	.22	.31[c]
−.43[a]	−.16	−.32[c]	−.38[b]	−.58[a]	−.57[a]	−.40[b]	.11	.24[c]	.13	1.00	.19
−.54[a]	−.46[a]	−.53[a]	−.63[a]	−.46[a]	−.45[a]	−.19	.37[b]	.18	.39[b]	.71[a]	1.00

X_1 = % voter participation
X_2 = median level of education
X_3 = % high-school or more education
X_4 = % upper white-collar employment
X_5 = Per capita revenue
X_6 = Per capita taxes
X_7 = Urbanization index
X_8 = Industrial index, males
X_9 = Industrial index, females
X_{10} = % employed nonfarm
X_{11} = % families poor
X_{12} = % broken families
X_{13} = Male underemployment rate

X_{14} = Female underemployment rate
X_{15} = % females not working
X_{16} = Nonworker-worker ratio
X_{17} = % black
X_{18} = % nonwhite
X_{19} = % native population born in South
X_{20} = % population increase
X_{21} = % total in-migration
X_{22} = % total net migration
X_{23} = % nonwhite in-migration
X_{24} = % nonwhite net migration

[a] $p < .001$.　　[b] $p < .01$.　　[c] $p < .05$.

Table 22

Zero-Order Correlations between 1960 and 1970 Independent Variables

	Z_1	Z_2	Z_3	Z_4	Z_5	Z_6	Z_7	Z_8	Z_9	Z_{10}	Z_{11}	Z_{12}
Y_1	**.82**[a]	.64[a]	.63[a]	.31[c]	.24[c]	.10	.01	.51[a]	.04	−.17	−.72[a]	−.64[a]
Y_2	.66[a]	**.90**[a]	.97[a]	.70[a]	.45[a]	.29[c]	.34[b]	.59[a]	.22	.01	−.72[a]	−.62[a]
Y_3	.68[a]	.90[a]	**.98**[a]	.72[a]	.47[a]	.28[c]	.32[c]	.55[a]	.16	−.08	−.70[a]	−.67[a]
Y_4	.38[b]	.71[a]	.75[a]	**.93**[a]	.53[a]	.37[b]	.44[a]	.53[a]	.30[c]	.11	−.44[a]	−.34[b]
Y_5	.24[c]	.34[b]	.47[a]	.50[a]	**.84**[a]	.55[a]	−.00	.10	−.05	−.19	−.08	−.28[c]
Y_6	.07	.27[c]	.39[b]	.46[a]	.80[a]	**.84**[a]	.27[c]	.36[b]	.40[b]	.21	−.19	.03
Y_7	.11	.38[b]	.30[c]	.36[b]	.10	.28[c]	**.91**[a]	.69[a]	.71[a]	.52[a]	−.48[a]	.16
Y_8	.55[a]	.73[a]	.70[a]	.60[a]	.39[b]	.40[b]	.54[a]	**.94**[a]	.65[a]	.39[b]	−.80[a]	−.27[c]
Y_9	.31[c]	.49[a]	.44[a]	.46[a]	.32[c]	.48[a]	.64[a]	.92[a]	**.92**[a]	.60[a]	−.71[a]	.08
Y_{10}	−.06	.13	.10	.26[c]	.12	.28[c]	.45[a]	.61[a]	.74[a]	**.96**[a]	−.37[b]	.39
Y_{11}	−.73[a]	−.85[a]	−.80[a]	−.58[a]	−.36[b]	−.34[b]	−.41[b]	−.87[a]	−.51[a]	−.21	**.97**[a]	.46[a]
Y_{12}	−.60[a]	−.65[a]	−.71[a]	−.34[b]	−.17	.09	−.02	−.21	.30[c]	.50[a]	.43[a]	**.95**[a]
Y_{13}	−.68[a]	−.70[a]	−.61[a]	−.43[a]	−.12	−.14	−.18	−.55[a]	−.17	.18	.74[a]	.47[b]
Y_{14}	−.08	−.23	−.18	−.25[c]	−.16	−.42[a]	−.37[b]	−.54[a]	−.75[a]	−.53[a]	.50[a]	−.35[b]
Y_{15}	−.20	−.34[b]	−.30[c]	−.24[c]	−.14	−.32[c]	−.27[c]	−.43[a]	−.56[a]	−.34[b]	.53[a]	−.17
Y_{16}	−.42[a]	−.58[a]	−.51[a]	−.33[b]	−.17	−.31[c]	−.39[b]	−.64[a]	−.62[a]	−.23	.78[a]	.10
Y_{17}	−.78[a]	−.71[a]	−.74[a]	−.43[a]	−.38[b]	−.16	−.15	−.46[a]	−.04	.21	.71[a]	.74[a]
Y_{18}	−.61[a]	−.46[a]	−.44[a]	−.23	.10	.28[c]	.05	−.26[c]	.18	.18	.49[a]	.59[a]
Y_{19}	−.50[a]	−.14	−.21	.14	−.13	.01	.31[c]	−.05	.21	.34[b]	.30[c]	.33[b]
Y_{20}	−.02	.40[b]	.41[b]	.50[a]	.23	.33[c]	.53[a]	.42[a]	.44[a]	.32[c]	−.29[c]	−.01
Y_{21}	.02	.38[b]	.46[a]	.53[a]	.38[b]	.26[c]	.27[c]	.14	.14	.08	−.13	−.20
Y_{22}	−.12	.34[b]	.34[b]	.49[a]	.18	.29[c]	.49[a]	.35[b]	.42[a]	.41[b]	−.23	.07
Y_{23}	.51[a]	.52[a]	.58[a]	.33[c]	.19	−.02	−.11	.20	−.03	−.01	−.49[a]	−.44[a]
Y_{24}	.39[b]	.57[a]	.52[a]	.34[b]	−.01	.03	.34[b]	.55[a]	.38[b]	.22	−.65[a]	−.21

Sources U.S. Bureau of the Census 1961–63, 1963, 1971–73, 1973; *Book of the States* 1962–63.

Z_{13}	Z_{14}	Z_{15}	Z_{16}	Z_{17}	Z_{18}	Z_{19}	Z_{20}	Z_{21}	Z_{22}	Z_{23}	Z_{24}
−.26[c]	.15	−.03	−.23	−.84[a]	−.71[a]	−.58[a]	−.12	−.06	−.21	.52[a]	.40[b]
−.37[b]	−.08	−.26[c]	−.45[a]	−.68[a]	−.43[a]	−.18	.37[b]	.46[a]	.20	.43[a]	.52[a]
−.40[b]	−.07	−.25[c]	−.42[a]	−.69[a]	−.43[a]	−.20	.38[b]	.48[a]	.15	.41[b]	.51[a]
−.14	.09	.00	−.15	−.46[a]	−.24[c]	.18	.44[a]	.54[a]	.21	.14	.44[a]
−.13	−.02	.05	.05	−.30[c]	.12	.00	.21	.56[a]	−.09	−.07	−.03
−.13	−.23	−.16	−.17	−.14	.32[c]	.18	.47[a]	.51[a]	.28[c]	−.12	.22
−.17	−.25[c]	−.37[b]	−.44[a]	−.12	.06	.09	.37[b]	−.02	.29[c]	.02	.62[a]
−.29[c]	−.07	−.23	−.43[a]	−.47[a]	−.33[b]	−.06	.40[b]	.17	.20	.28[c]	.68[a]
−.33[c]	−.38[b]	−.47[a]	−.60[a]	−.25[c]	−.06	.06	.49[a]	.11	.34[b]	.20	.63[a]
−.02	−.25[c]	.32[c]	−.33[b]	.07	.06	.28[c]	.45[a]	.09	.52[a]	.20	.29[c]
.49[a]	.21	.41[b]	.62[a]	.67[a]	−.47[a]	.30[c]	−.33[b]	−.19	−.18	−.50[a]	−.69[a]
.20	−.31[c]	−.16	.05	.70[a]	.61[a]	.26[c]	−.03	−.28[c]	.13	−.30[c]	−.33[b]
.71[a]	.31[c]	.43[a]	.54[a]	.49[a]	.42[a]	−.01	.08	.15		−.44[a]	−.56[a]
.60[a]	.87[a]	.86[a]	.79[a]	−.10	−.33[c]	−.02	−.44[a]	−.12	−.36[b]	−.23	−.37[b]
.60[a]	.84[a]	.93[a]	.86[a]	−.03	−.18	.03	−.52[a]	−.27[c]	−.42[a]	−.32[c]	−.38[b]
.65[a]	.69[a]	.83[a]	.95[a]	.27[c]	.09	.14	−.47[a]	−.24[c]	−.34[b]	−.38[b]	−.54[a]
.29[c]	−.10	.04	.26[c]	.99[a]	68[a]	.53[a]	−.02	−.19	.13	−.48[a]	−.36[b]
.01	−.42[a]	−.18	.06	.67[a]	.99[a]	.41[b]	.08	.08	.09	−.56[a]	−.28[c]
.20	.03	.12	.14	.44[a]	.35[b]	.99[a]	.40[b]	.37[b]	.40[b]	−.36[b]	.01
−.08	−.13	−.24[c]	−.25[c]	−.04	.06	.52[a]	.85[a]	.68[a]	.62[a]	.01	.39[b]
−.06	−.08	−.11	−.13	−.20	.02	.46[a]	.72[a]	.94[a]	.45[a]	.05	.08
.02	−.13	−.25[c]	−.22	.01	.10	.54[a]	.80[a]	.66[a]	.72[a]	.04	.32[c]
−.27[c]	−.11	−.24[c]	−.30[c]	−.60[a]	−.59[a]	−.44[a]	.23	.32[c]	.18	.88[a]	.02
−.33[c]	−.27[c]	−.43[a]	−.52[a]	−.42[a]	−.42[a]	−.22	.43[a]	.15	.36[b]	.71[a]	.47[a]

Notes   The boldface coefficients along the diagonal refer to the zero-order correlations between a given independent variable in 1960 and that same independent variable in 1970. The subscripts for the **Y** and **Z** variables are identical to the subscripts for the **X** variables in table 21 and refer to the same variables (see notes to table 21). The **Y** variables stand for 1960 variables, the **Z** variables for 1970 variables.

[a]**p**<.001.   [b]**p**<.01.   [c]**p**<.05.

Appendix E

Zero-Order Correlations
between Dependent and
Independent Variables,
1960 and 1970

Table 23

Independent Variables
1960 and 1970

% families poor
% broken families
Male underemployment rate
Female underemployment rate
% females not working
Nonworker-worker ratio

% voter participation
Median level of education
% high-school or more education
% upper white-collar employment
Per capita revenue
Per capita taxes
Urbanization index
Industrial index, males
Industrial index, females
% employed nonfarm

% black
% nonwhite
% native population born in South
% population increase
% total in-migration
% total net migration
% nonwhite in-migration
% nonwhite net migration

Zero-Order Correlations between AFDC Rolls and Policies and All Independent Variables, 1960 and 1970

1960 Correlations				1970 Correlations			
AFDC Rolls	TES	Cost Standard	Maximum Paid	AFDC Rolls	TES	Cost Standard	Maximum Paid
(1)	(2)	(3)	(4)	(5)	(6)	(7)	(8)
.61[a]	.47[a]	−.62[a]	−.73[a]	.28[c]	.42[a]	−.62[a]	−.72[a]
.43[a]	.34[b]	−.50[a]	−.44[a]	.58[a]	.29[c]	−.25[c]	−.33[b]
.70[a]	.35[b]	−.49[a]	−.65[a]	.39[b]	.33[b]	−.26[c]	−.41[a]
.37[b]	.03	−.10	−.19	.15	.13	−.11	−.15
.50[a]	.07	−.25[c]	−.21	.23	.12	−.19	−.30[c]
.67[a]	.24[c]	−.44[a]	−.45[a]	.31[c]	.27[c]	−.38[b]	−.47[a]
−.32[c]	−.48[a]	.47[a]	.67[a]	−.16	−.39[b]	.51[a]	.63[a]
−.48[a]	−.40[b]	.64[a]	.57[a]	−.20	−.41[a]	.53[a]	.60[a]
−.47[a]	−.45[a]	.65[a]	.59[a]	−.16	−.49[a]	.51[a]	.52[a]
−.18	−.33[b]	.42[a]	.48[a]	.17	−.35[b]	.32[c]	.44[a]
.07	−.40[b]	.19	.22	.30[c]	−.42[a]	.18	.27[c]
.13	−.36[b]	.16	.17	.35[b]	−.34[b]	.18	.24[c]
−.21	−.14	.30[c]	.37[b]	.17	.07	.17	.15
−.37[b]	−.36[b]	.55[a]	.63[b]	.05	−.30[c]	.58[a]	.58[a]
−.30[c]	−.22	.40[b]	.50[a]	.28[c]	−.15	.40[b]	.32[c]
−.01	.07	.01	.05	.33[b]	.14	.03	−.05
.36[b]	.51[a]	−.54[a]	−.68[a]	.23	.49[a]	−.48[a]	−.59[a]
.33[b]	.25[c]	−.38[b]	−.43[a]	.25[c]	.15	−.40[b]	−.40[b]
.28[c]	.35[b]	−.27[c]	−.43[a]	.14	.38[b]	−.40[b]	−.55[a]
−.09	−.09	.40[b]	−.01	−.05	−.01	.13	−.05
.01	−.14	.29[c]	−.03	−.20	−.13	−.09	−.09
−.05	.03	.32[c]	−.03	−.08	.14	.01	−.08
−.32[c]	−.23	.41[a]	.30[c]	−.24	−.25[c]	.40[b]	.34[b]
−.44[a]	−.25[c]	.49[a]	.43[a]	−.07	−.22	.29[c]	.48[a]

U.S. Bureau of the Census 1961–63, 1963, 1971–73, 1973b,c; Book of the States 1962–63; Social Security Bulletin 1960, 1961, 1970, 1971; Social Security Administration 1960, 1962; Social and Rehabilitation Service 1971d, f; SPCU Reports.

[a] $p < .001$. [b] $p < .01$. [c] $p < .05$.

Notes

Chapter 1

1. It is even possible that the "crisis" may be a function of how statistical data have been analyzed. Thus Rein and Heclo (1973) indicate that public assistance payments have decreased relative to income-security program payments. They argue that the "crisis" reflects the inappropriate tendency to blame nonwhites and single parents for the growth in welfare which should be blamed on the expansion in Medicare and Medicaid, as well as on the growth in social-service expenses (see also Derthick 1975).

2. See for example Banfield (1969), Rein and Heclo (1973), Durbin (1973), Honig (1973, 1974), Piven and Cloward (1971), Kasper (1968), and Winegarden (1973).

3. I am deliberately limiting the discussion to causes associated with poverty in industrial societies, since poverty in the agrarian or feudal society often was attributed to nature, fate, or acts of God with no necessary intervention by man.

4. The explanation is recent primarily in terms of its widespread acceptance. As early as the beginning of the nineteenth century Paine (1792, new edition 1894), Owen (1817), and Godwin (1820) advanced essentially the same argument about why poverty existed and how government should respond to it.

5. Mohl (1972), however, found evidence of a culture of poverty perspective in American cities in 1780–1840.

6. See Jensen (1967, 1969, 1970) and Herrnstein (1971).

7. This notion is related to Rainwater's (1970*b*, pp. 21–22) apothesizing perspective—a view of the poor as the natural or heroic man.

8. See Herzog (1963), Rainwater (1967, 1970*a*), Liebow (1967), Goodwin (1972), Rodman (1971), Hylan Lewis (1967), Kriesberg (1970), Hannerz (1969), as well as Billings (1974), Coward, Feagin, and Williams (1974), Davidson and Gaitz (1974), Elesh (1973), Goering and Coe (1971), Gruber (1972), Irelan, Moles, and O'Shea (1969), Kaplan and Tausky (1972), Rodman, Voydanoff, and Lovejoy (1974), and Stewart, Lauderdale, and Shuttlesworth (1972).

9. See Alger et al. (1906-7), Addams (1903), United States Bureau of Labor (1910-13), Seager (1921), Downey (1924), Weiss (1918-35), Hurry (1917), and Robinow (1913).

10. This remains true although both the USSR and Communist China maintain subsistence economies to fall back on.

11. Durkheim (1964), for example, was one of the first sociologists to point to the changing forms of solidarity in societies experiencing increasing division of labor—e.g., industrialization.

12. See Almond and Verba (1965), Benjamin, Blue, and Coleman (1971), Inkeles (1969), Nie, Powell, and Prewitt (1969), Olsen (1968), and

Verba and Nie (1972) for such analyses of political participation in relation to economic structure and socioeconomic status.

13. Thus in 1860 only about 17 percent of the total population of the United States was eligible to vote (Gendell and Zetterberg 1964, p.5; also reported in Bendix 1968, p. 75).

14. This use of the term "mass society" is quite different from that of William Kornhauser (1959), which emphasizes negative and anti-democratic tendencies in modern societies. I believe that Shils is correct in criticizing Kornhauser and his followers for an overly simple interpretation of modern processes, which fails to distinguish between democratic and totalitarian societies. The former type of society is characterized by short distance between the center and periphery, while the latter tend to have restricted centers far removed from the periphery (Shils 1975, pp. 34–47).

15. See Janowitz (1961), Brazer (1958), and Hawley and Zimmer (1961). Stephens (1974) presents data indicating the increasingly prominent role of state governments and state centralization at the expense of local autonomy.

16. For discussions of the importance of such federal grants-in-aid for the viability of state governments and the type and extent of their activities, see Bahl and Saunders (1965), Break (1967), Clement (1962), Crittenden (1967), Derthick (1970, 1975), Gayer (1972), Gramlich (1968), Osman (1966), Pogue and Sgontz (1968), Smith (1968), Steiner (1966), and Strouse and Jones (1974).

17. State socioeconomic development is almost always included by political scientists and economists alike in explaining state expenditures and other policy outcomes. See for example Cnudde and McCrone (1969), Dawson and Gray (1971), Dawson and Robinson (1963), Dye (1966, 1969a), Hofferbert (1966a, 1968), Sharkansky and Hofferbert (1969), Sharkansky (1967a,b, 1968a,b, 1971a,b), Crittenden (1967), Luttbeg (1971), Morgan and Lyons (1975), Cowart (1969), Jones (1974), Morss, Fredland, and Hymans (1967), Cowart and Jones (1974), Baer and Jaros (1974), Gary (1973), Grumm (1971), Fabricant (1952), and Fisher (1964) to mention only some such studies.

18. Bell illustrates this point in her study of the "suitable home" clause in the ADC program. She especially emphasized how the states originally used the clause to limit ADC to the respectable poor: white, middle-class widows, especially war widows, with small children. Piven and Cloward (1971) also document restrictive eligibility requirements which, as they argue, operate to exclude blacks from public assistance, especially in southern agricultural states.

19. For a study which is a direct attempt to deal with this issue, see Tropman (1974). See also Tropman (1973).

20. See discussion in chapter 6.

Chapter 2

1. This point was made very early by Fabricant (1952) and Key (1949, 1956). Both these writers were in some ways pioneers in the study of state politics and can take much of the credit for subsequent interest in the study of state economies (Fabricant) and politics (Key).

2. Most social scientists who have engaged in cross-national studies have been acutely aware of some of these problems; see for example Rokkan (1968).

3. Much of the political science literature on state politics has addressed the issue of regionalism. Some writers have concluded that regional characteristics are important determinants of state politics (Sharkansky 1967*b*, 1968*a,b*, 1970*a,b*; Luttbeg 1971; and Bahl and Saunders 1965). Other writers have questioned the usefulness of region as an explanatory factor (Coulter 1970) or have found little support for region as a separate factor (Clynch 1972). A number of political scientists have also argued that over time the states have become more similar in their policies because of increased interaction between state politicians and administrators, which may act as an incentive for the most backward states and as a brake for the most progressive ones.

4. Bahl and Saunders 1965; Crittenden 1967; Derthick 1970; Hofferbert 1966*a*; Jones 1974; and especially Strouse and Jones 1974.

5. International Labor Organization 1958, 1961; Gordon 1963; Aaron 1967; Tanzi 1968.

6. Discussion of the literature on the relationship between work and welfare will be reserved for chapters 6 and 7.

7. Fabricant 1952; Merriam 1957; Fisher 1964; Collins 1967; Sacks and Harris 1964.

8. Bahl and Saunders 1965; Clement 1962; Gayer 1972; Osman 1966; Pogue and Sgontz 1968. Among the political scientists Crittenden (1967), Hofferbert (1966*a*), and Strouse and Jones (1974) have examined the impact of federal aid.

9. This last finding may perhaps be seen as confirming Michel's iron law of oligarchy, but more simply it illustrates the reality of budget-making processes, where previous levels of expenditures are seen both as political commitments to be upheld and as the safest guidelines for planning (See Sharkansky 1967*a,c*). However, this may well be a trivial finding if the primary concern is to explain why some states spend more than others (Harlow 1968).

10. See Gold 1969; Collins 1967; Paulson, Butler, and Pope 1969; Pogue and Sgontz 1968.

11. In contrast to the economists, political scientists do not usually include population density as a measure of economic development, but instead use median level of education. Both groups include per capita income, urbanization, and percentage employed in nonfarm industries as economic development variables.

12. Thus Dawson and Robinson (1963), Dye (1965, 1966, 1969b), Hofferbert (1966b), Grumm (1971), Dawson and Gray (1971), Prothro (1972), and Baer and Jaros (1974) all concluded that socio-economic development was the primary determinant of state welfare expenditures or payments or both. Jones (1974) arrived at a similar conclusion in his study of changes in the level of expenditures and in the distribution of expenditures for various purposes.

13. Some studies have found limited support for some influence of political variables. See, for example, Pulsipher and Weatherby (1968). However, in this case the conclusion was obtained at the cost of using a somewhat questionable level of significance (.10 and .20). Using path analysis, Tompkins (1975) found that only interparty competition had a direct impact on welfare payments.

14. For a typical statement see the opening paragraphs of Cnudde and McCrone (1969).

15. Some of these attempts have included the use of federal grants-in-aid as an increasingly important *political* variable (Strouse and Jones 1974). Coulter and Gordon (1968) established a new dimension of political structure, ranging from states controlled by the Democratic party, to states with a competitive party structure, to states controlled by the Republican party. The strength of interest groups and the degree of popular participation in various organizations have been suggested as more appropriate than voter participation for measuring the pressure on state politicians to produce a given policy (Baer and Jaros 1974).

16. Measures of state public assistance expenditures or average benefits levels or both have been included as measures of policy outputs by at least the following twenty-eight political science studies: Crew 1969; Dawson and Robinson 1963; Dye 1965, 1966, 1969a; Jones 1974; Carmines 1974; Sharkansky 1967a,b,c, 1968b, 1970a,b, 1971a,b; Sullivan 1973; Cowart 1969; Paulson, Butler, and Pope 1969; Pulsipher and Weatherby 1968; Baer and Jaros 1974; Dawson and Gray 1971; Gary 1973; Grumm 1971; Broach 1973; Cnudde and McCrone 1969; Sharkansky and Hofferbert 1969; Hofferbert 1966a.

17. I find particularly troublesome the assumption that state income taxes are graduated at the same rate as the federal income tax.

18. By examining the net benefits to the lowest 60 percent of the population, both studies fail to distinguish between at least three hypothetical cases: (1) where the lowest and highest income groups both

subsidize the middle, (2) where the high income groups subsidize both the low- and middle-income groups, and (3) where the major redistribution is within the lowest 60 percent.

19. The President's Commission on Income Maintenance (1970) found that public assistance is the program most likely to benefit primarily the poor.

20. The failure of some writers (especially Dye 1965, 1966, 1969c) to consider the extent of need for welfare in studies of state welfare rolls is surprising. But the problem is by no means limited to the study of welfare policy, and several writers have been concerned about the failure to consider the need for a given policy. Thus Riley (1971) and Albin and Stein (1968) indicated the necessity of looking at the demand for each specific type of policy outcome, while Hofferbert (1966b) expressed a similar concern when he emphasized the need to examine the relationship between the "environment" and policy.

21. Welfare effort may refer both to welfare rolls and to welfare payments and expenditures. Only a few writers have included need in studies of welfare benefits (Baer and Jaros 1974; Dawson and Gray 1971) or welfare expenditures (Pogue and Sgontz 1968).

22. There exist only national surveys and isolated state surveys. The latter usually cannot be compared among the states, because of differences in methodology, timing, and wording of questions. A number of political scientists have attempted to use national survey responses to obtain simulated state public opinion data. This involves a rather complicated procedure of decomposing survey responses by demographic characteristics of the respondents and reassembling them again to conform to a given state's demographic characteristics (Weber and Schaffer 1972; Sutton 1973; Hopkins 1974).

23. Elazar (1972) attempted to categorize the states along these lines; however, his procedure is admittedly quite impressionistic. Although his dimension of state culture has been quite widely used (see for example Sharkansky 1970b, Luttbeg 1971), certain aspects of it have not been supported by further data analysis (Stephens 1974).

24. I will discuss each of these different explanations, along with the appropriate literature, in detail in chapters 6, 7, and 8.

25. Multiple regression analysis, of which partial and stepwise regression analysis are special cases, is a general statistical technique through which the relationship between a dependent or criteria variable (policy output) and a set of independent or predictor variables (economic development and political structure variables) can be analyzed. Multiple regression may be seen as a descriptive tool by which the linear dependence of one variable on all others included in the analysis is summarized and decomposed (Nie, et al. 1975, p. 321). Partial regression analysis allows the researcher to evaluate the

contribution of a particular independent variable (for example, median income) to explaining the dependent variable (the policy variable) with the influence of all other independent variables (i.e., other economic development variables and political structure variables) controlled (see Nie, et al. 1975, p. 332). Stepwise regression analysis will be discussed in greater detail below.

26. The attempts to group variables through factor analysis to produce dimensions of policy outcomes, political conditions, and socio-economic conditions (Crew 1969; Sharkansky and Hofferbert 1969; Grumm 1971) are particularly questionable. The results of these procedures generally have been unsatisfactory, especially because very different policies often are grouped together. Thus Sharkansky and Hofferbert (1969) and their followers grouped among other variables the number of high-school graduates with average old-age assistance payments, but excluded the size of welfare rolls. It has therefore been rather difficult to interpret these findings, even when they do suggest that elements of the political structure may be important in shaping some policy outputs.

27. Some writers have suggested using more sophisticated statistical procedures when trying to determine how strongly policies are related to standard measures of economic development and political structure. Kurnow (1964) and Broach (1973), for example, suggested that an interactive rather than a linear regression model might be more appropriate for predicting policy outcomes. However, the improvements in prediction when using such revised models generally have been found to be quite small or negligible. Tompkins (1975) used path analysis, which is a more sophisticated version of partial regression analysis, in his study of average AFDC benefits. Tompkins's procedure deliberately assumes that a given economic development variable is important only because it causes a given political structure and population heterogeneity. I am not convinced that such assumptions of causality are warranted in the analysis of state politics.

28. Stepwise regression analysis is a powerful variant of multiple regression analysis where only those independent variables which are important in determining the dependent variable (i.e., the policy output) are included in the analysis, in the order of their importance. The decision to include a given variable depends on how much that variable can contribute independently of all other variables already included. See also chapter 5 for a more complete discussion of this procedure.

29. AFDC stands for Aid to Families with Dependent Children. However, before 1961 the same program was known as ADC, Aid to Dependent Children. The abbreviation AFDC will be used throughout.

30. This interpretation is commonly accepted in the literature (Steiner

1966) and is also supported by a recent study (Williamson 1974*b*) which found the AFDC program to be the most stigmatized.

31. Back in the early 1950s, however, Ohio discovered that a number of corpses were collecting Old Age Assistance (OAA). This created quite an uproar at the time and precipitated several legislative changes, especially the passing of the Jenner Amendment to the Social Security Act, which required that public assistance rolls be open to public inspection to deter fraud (Steiner 1966).

32. The number of AFDC recipients increased by 214 percent between 1960 and 1970, compared with 38 percent between 1950 and 1960. For both periods, AFDC rolls increased at more than twice the rate of all public assistance programs combined. In 1950 there were a total of 6.1 million public assistance recipients. This increased to 7.1 million in 1969 and 13.8 million in 1970, an increase of 17 percent between 1950 and 1960 and 95 percent between 1960 and 1970. Aid to the Blind (AB) increased only minimally between 1950 and 1960 (10 percent) and decreased by 24 percent between 1960 and 1970. OAA decreased in both periods: a 17-percent decrease between 1950 and 1960, and a 10-percent decrease for 1960–70. Both of these programs lost recipients because of the increased coverage and benefit levels in Social Security (OASDHI). General Assistance (GA) increased more than AFDC in the 1950s (44 percent) but declined in the 1960s (15 percent). The only program other than AFDC which increased between 1960 and 1970 is Aid to the Permanently and Totally Disabled (APTD), which grew by 153 percent. However, this program is likely to experience the fate of OAA and AB as Social Security expands further (*Social Security Bulletin* Sept. 1973, p. 54).

33. These records are maintained by the State Program Characteristics Unit of the Assistance Payments Administration and will hereafter be referred to as SPCU Reports.

34. The number of AFDC families was collected from various issues of the *Social Security Bulletin*, which carries monthly statistics on Social Security and public assistance programs.

35. The importance of level of unemployment for size of AFDC rolls has been clearly established by Collins (1967) and others.

Chapter 3

1. Students of organizations will be quick to point out that formal policies may be subverted or sidetracked in many ways by bureaucratic and organizational factors. Thus they might argue that similar formal policies may be implemented differently in different agencies or organizations. However, this argument leaves two important questions unresolved: (1) If formal eligibility requirements do not determine the relative size of welfare rolls, what factors do? (2) What

is the significance of formal eligibility requirements if they have no practical effects on which and how many people receive state support? Both these questions will be explored in the following chapters.

2. Other requirements also mandate administrative components of state public assistance plans: (1) state financial participation, (2) opportunity for fair hearing, (3) administration to insure proper and efficient operation of the plan, including a merit system for personnel administration and quality control of case action, (4) required reports, (5) confidentiality of information, and (6) opportunity for application, including a time limit for processing applications (see Advisory Commission on Intergovernmental Relations 1964).

3. Handler and Hollingsworth (1971, p. 11) report that a similar study by Lawrence Podell of AFDC agencies in New York has arrived at the same conclusion.

4. In the thirty states which had some form of old-age assistance before 1935, one-third of the counties had no such provisions. In the forty-five states with children's aid or mothers' pension programs, less than one-half the counties provided this aid, and in the twenty-four states with public pensions for the blind, only two-thirds of the counties participated (see Advisory Commission on Intergovernmental Relations 1964).

5. The Social Security Amendment of 1972 (PL 92-603), effective January 1974, replaced the state programs of ABD or OAA, AB and APTD with a wholly federal program, Supplemental Security Income (SSI), with federal standards of eligibility (lower than most earlier state standards). However, the law gives state and local political jurisdictions the possibility of supplementing federal grants. States or local political jurisdictions may also require a period of residence in the state or locality as a condition of eligibility for such supplemental aid. In other words, it is now again possible to have local variation within the state, although Bell (1965, p. 202, n.3) points out that some states, in spite of federal requirements of "equitable treatment," discriminated between localities in terms of size of benefits). However, the states must supplement the SSI payments if they want any federal matching funds for their Medicaid programs. Furthermore, the state SSI supplements must be so high that recipients receive benefits at least as high as they did in December 1973 as recipients of any of the adult assistance programs.

6. Under this method, the federal government pays (1) five-sixths of the first $18 of the AFDC grant per recipient, plus (2) 50 to 60 percent (depending on the state's per capita income; the poorer the state the higher the percentage) of the next $14 of a maximum average monthly payment of $32 per recipient. The aggregate of payments in

excess of an average payment of $32 must be financed entirely from state and local funds. Using this formula, the federal government in 1971 would pay 83 percent of Mississippi's average grant of $13.75; 75 percent of West Virginia's average grant of $27.98; and 29 percent of New York's average grant of $75.83. Thus the lower the level of payments and the poorer the state, the higher is the federal financial participation (FFP).

7. Under this method, the federal share is computed by applying the "federal medical assistance percentage" to the aggregate amount spent for money payments for all federally supported public assistance programs combined. The "federal medical assistance percentage" varies among the states from 50 to 83 percent, depending upon each state's per capita personal income. Again, the poorer the state, the higher is the FFP (U.S. Social and Rehabilitation Service 1972, pp. 3–4).

8. This early rush may also be at least partly explained by the termination of the Work Projects Administration (WPA) in 1935. As a result, many states found themselves with a large number of families on their caseloads whose members previously had been employed by WPA.

9. At least seven of the remaining eleven states followed suit by 1941 (Connecticut, Florida, Illinois, Mississippi, South Dakota, Texas, and Virginia). Kentucky joined in 1942, Iowa in 1943, and Alaska in 1945. Nevada was the last state in the union to join the program, entering in 1955, twenty years after the program was initiated by the federal government (U.S. Social and Rehabilitation Service 1971e).

10. Calculated from U.S. Bureau of the Census 1973b, p. 278, table 451, "Social Welfare Expenditures under Public Programs: 1935 to 1971."

11. Calculated from U.S. Bureau of the Census 1973b, p. 299, table 486, "Public Assistance—Payments and Recipients: 1950–1971."

12. No local funds were used in ten states for General Assistance (GA), in twenty-five states for AFDC, in twenty-seven states for APTD, in thirty-one states for AB, and in thirty states for OAA programs in 1967 (U.S. Social and Rehabilitation Service 1968).

13. The inclusion of unemployed parents in the AFDC program clearly showed the extent to which states may be anxious to share their financial burdens with the federal government. Thus West Virginia, in the middle of an extensive coal miners strike and with large pockets of industrial unemployment, called a special legislative session during the summer of 1961 to adopt the plan as soon as federal financial participation became available. Subsequently 18,000 families became immediately eligible for AFDC-U, and there was a corresponding reduction in the state-funded General Assistance program (GA).

14. In 1971 the Supreme Court ruled in *Townsend* v. *Swank* that any person under eighteen was a "child." Consequently, AFDC must be available to an otherwise eligible child until his eighteenth birthday. Before 1971, there had been no such definition of "child," although there seems to have been a general acknowledgment that anyone under fourteen was a child, especially since child labor laws prohibited children below that age from working in most jobs.

15. The recent Supreme Court ruling liberalizing abortion laws in the United States has been problematic for those states which provide aid to a mother on behalf of her unborn child. As a recipient of such assistance an expectant mother would be eligible for medical assistance in most states, possibly including abortion. It is difficult to argue that aborting a fetus should be considered an aid to that dependent, but still unborn, child.

16. In what are called the adult programs, OAA, AB, APTD, or ABD, the states were allowed to use a maximum residency requirement of five out of the preceding nine years, including one year immediately before application.

17. Several states, notably New York, have attempted to get around this ruling by making persons who enter the state for the purpose of obtaining public assistance ineligible for such aid. This is a considerably less straightforward requirement than the durational residency requirement, since it is difficult to get an objective determination of "purpose."

18. Arizona adopted the most restrictive definition of unemployment; a person was considered unemployed for AFDC purposes only if he (1) had been employed for at least one month prior to ninety days before applying for AFDC-U; (2) was not eligible for unemployment compensation; (3) while employed had worked at least twenty hours a week or had an income which brought the family above eligibility standards; (4) had exhausted unemployment compensation sixty days before application; *and* (5) had not been employed since. These requirements effectively excluded most Indians and other long-term poor families, and by May 1963, almost one year after the plan went into effect, only two families had become eligible for AFDC-U. In June of the same year the plan was further restricted by limiting the length of time that AFDC-U payments could be granted to two months, since it was explicitly assumed than no person seeking employment for two months would be unable to find work. This was, however, too restrictive for the federal agency, and the plan was not approved in July 1963; but Arizona did not withdraw the plan until January 1964. In January 1966 Arizona made another try. The new plan defined as unemployed anyone who (1) had been employed full-time (twenty hours a week or more) for five of the last seven years before

application; (2) was not eligible for unemployment compensation; (3) had some vocational training; (4) had been registered with an employment agency for a minimum of thirty days before application; *and* (5) had not been dismissed for cause less than one year before application. By May one family had become eligible. In June the requirement of full-time work under point (1) was limited to two out of the last three years. By September 1967 fifteen families were eligible for AFDC-U. At this point Arizona discontinued payments to AFDC-U parents. In comparison, the West Virginia plan was quite liberal: a person was considered unemployed if he or she (1) had not been employed full time (160 hours a month) for three months before application; (2) was not eligible for unemployment compensation or had exhausted such benefits; and (3) was seeking work. In the first month the program was in operation, 18,000 families became eligible for AFDC-U payments (SPCU Reports).

19. Thus Georgia had a ruling considering paramours substitute fathers. If a child receiving AFDC was found to be illegitimate, this was considered evidence of a substitute father and the case would be closed. If the mother reapplied, she had to prove that her pattern of living had changed and that there was no substitute father (SPCU Reports).

20. This was the case in Missouri, 1963 (SPCU Reports).

21. Thus in 1963 Illinois instituted a ruling that the birth of a second illegitimate child to any woman living in the same house as a child receiving AFDC was prima facie evidence that the home was not suitable (SPCU Reports). See also Bell (1965) for a particularly good analysis and evaluation of the suitable home clause and its use in various states.

22. Personal communication, Catherine M. Miller, head of State Program Characteristics Unit of HEW.

23. For statistical purposes, the cost standard is reported for a standard AFDC family which consists of a mother aged thirty-five, a boy aged fourteen, a girl aged nine, and a girl aged four, living in rented quarters. This cost standard is the sum of what the state considers the minimum amount of money such a family would need in each of the following categories: rent, food, clothing, personal incidentals and medicine, utilities, and other, usually unspecified, items.

24. For a description of the monthly cost standard, see, for example, U.S. Social Security Administration (1962).

25. The variation in increased cost standards does not reflect variations in increased per capita incomes in the states. The per capita income in the state with the lowest increase in cost standard—Florida—increased more between 1960 and 1970 (from $1,988 to $3,642, or by 83.1 percent) than did the per capita income in the state with the

highest increase in cost standard—Pennsylvania—where the per capita income increased by 64 percent, from $2,259 to $3,705.

26. See monthly issues of the *Social Security Bulletin* and *Welfare in Review*. The latter journal was terminated in 1972.

27. The combined effect of how, when, and to what extent a state allows income and earnings "disregards" and how it limits payments to welfare recipients is crucial, because these interactions result in considerable variation in how a recipient's nonwelfare income is "taxed" by a corresponding reduction in welfare payments (Lurie 1974; Heffernan 1973). Most studies that have included welfare "tax rates" have been done by economists who have been interested primarily in how these rates affect work incentives among welfare recipients (Hausman 1970; Garfinkel and Orr 1974) rather than in considering the rates themselves as a policy output to be explained. On the other hand, the existence of differential tax rates for nonwelfare income makes political scientists' use of average payments as an index of welfare policy particularly questionable.

28. For example, it is reported that California had an eleven-page set of instructions just for evaluating a kitchen stove (personal communication, Catherine M. Miller).

29. The federal government has placed an upper limit on property reserves (other than home, household and personal effects, and a car needed for transportation) which at the end of 1973 stood at $2,000 per recipient, including the cash value of life insurance. Most states are considerably less liberal than these federal requirements permit.

30. Comparisons among the states are therefore next to impossible. How, for example, is a limitation of $2,500 equity on home ownership in Mississippi comparable to a $25,000 market value limitation in Hawaii and to a $3,000 limitation on assessed value in Wyoming? (U.S. Social and Rehabilitation Service 1971*e*).

31. Both provisions against transferring property in order to obtain assistance and the use of liens, recoveries, or assignments on property are found mainly in the "adult categories" of public assistance (OAA, AB, and APTD). In these programs recipients tend to be old, have high mortality rates, and generally receive aid for long periods of time. Nevertheless, each of these types of provisions is currently used by about 20 percent of the states in the AFDC program.

32. See Appendix A for greater detail.

33. One might argue that a single index of eligibility restrictiveness is too gross a measure and that, instead, several indexes should be used to reflect the different political concerns which may be reflected in the eligibility requirements. Thus Gary (1973) developed six different measures of welfare policies: a "direct" measure (money payments

and percentage of need met) and five "indirect" measures (residency requirements, property rules, maximum earnings allowed, maximum grant, and "sociomoral" constraints). I also experimented with developing several dimensions of eligibility requirements by using various forms of clustering techniques but found the resultant dimensions less usefull than a single summary index. Specifically, I found that a large number of clusters were implicit in the data, but that most of these were closely interrelated and difficult to interpret. More important, the indexes produced in this way were either highly skewed or had uncomfortably low indexes of variability. Furthermore, when included in the various analyses, most of these dimensions behaved much like the single summary index, TES.

34. This pattern of change in the TES between 1950 and 1970 supports to some extent the view that the 1960s was an unusual period in the recent history of public assistance in the United States.

35. The Department of Health, Education, and Welfare has undertaken several studies of recipients of the various federally supported public assistance programs, including studies of the AFDC program in 1961, 1967, 1969, and 1973. However, information on even limited demographic and economic characteristics of recipients by state is available for no more than twenty states. Furthermore, there is no similar information on nonrecipient poor people in each state. The relationship between eligibility requirements and the composition of AFDC rolls therefore cannot be adequately examined by using these data sources.

36. The TES ranged between 64 percent and 141 percent of the mean in 1960. The range for AFDC rolls in 1960 was between 41 percent and 259 percent of the mean. The situation in 1970 was very similar: the TES ranged between 46 percent and 162 percent of the mean, while AFDC rolls ranged between 38 percent and 197 percent of the mean.

37. Alaska was eliminated from this study because it persistently had extreme measures on many of the variables being considered. This was particularly true for all the variables measuring economic conditions: income, revenue, cost standards, and payment standards. Washington, D.C., was excluded for similar reasons, although the extreme measures occurred on different variables: percentage of broken families, percentage black, urbanization index, female underemployment, and male underemployment.

38. Pearson's product-moment (correlation) coefficient is used throughout this study. A correlation coefficient which approaches ± 1 indicates a perfect relationship between two variables; that is, one variable can be used to give an almost perfect prediction of the other variable. When the correlation coefficient approaches zero, there is no determinate relationship between the two variables.

39. The maximum level of benefit is very closely related to the variable used by most political scientists to measure public assistance policy outcomes: the size of the state's average grant to various recipient groups.

40. The 1960 correlation coefficient between AFDC rolls and the cost standard is $r = -.38$, and that between AFDC rolls and maximum payment is $r = -.44$; both coefficients indicate a substantial relationship.

Chapter 4

1. This poverty level is calculated on the basis of the cost of food for a temporary, emergency diet (the "economy plan") as estimated by the Department of Agriculture. The level is adjusted for farm-nonfarm residence, family size, sex of family head, and number of children under eighteen years of age. The cost of feeding a family with any given composition of characteristics is then multiplied by three to obtain the Social Security Administration's (SSA) low-income level. The original poverty levels were calculated for 1963 and have been adjusted for changes in the Consumer Price Index (CPI) for use in other years (see U.S. Bureau of the Census 1972a, pp. 16–19).

2. The percentage of families poor in 1970 was calculated for each state in the 1970 census of population (U.S. Bureau of the Census 1971–73). The 1960 census has been reanalyzed to calculate the percentage of families which at that time would have been defined as poor (U.S. Bureau of the Census 1973b, p. 331).

3. This measure is the proportion of families in the state which had incomes less than 75 percent of the SSA poverty level.

4. Over the age of fourteen in 1960, over the age of sixteen in 1970. These are the cutoff points used by the Census Bureau for these two years. The number of employed people between the ages of fourteen and sixteen is very small relative to the total number employed at all ages.

5. Underemployed in this sense should not be confused with other, more standard definitions of underemployment, which include not only those working less than full time but also those working in jobs for which they are overqualified. I have no way of obtaining this last piece of information for the states.

6. A number of people would of course argue that it is the availability of welfare which encourages women to stay out of the labor force. There are several reasons for thinking that this is a questionable assumption, and I will discuss these issues in greater detail in chapter 6 (see also Rein and Wishnov 1971).

7. It is to a large extent because of this argument, as well as the fact that most eligibility requirements concern either the family as a unit

(cost standards, property limitations) or the characteristics of the adult members of the family (man-in-the-house rules, employment requirements) that welfare rolls have been measured in terms of the proportion of *families*, rather than the proportion of *children* or total population, in the state that receives AFDC (see also chapter 3).

8. In 1969, 5.5 percent of all of AFDC fathers were dead, 75.4 percent were absent for other reasons, 11.5 percent were incapacitated, and 4.8 percent were unemployed. In 1961, 7.7 percent of all AFDC fathers were dead, 66.7 percent were absent for other reasons, 18.1 percent were incapacitated, and 5.2 percent were unemployed (Eppley 1970).

9. However, equally important in the relationship between family status and economic conditions may be the fact that families headed by females tend to have lower incomes simply because females generally earn less than males and thus these families are more likely to need some form of economic assistance.

10. Thus no adequate voter registration data were available for seventeen states in 1960 (*Book of the States* 1962–63 p. 30) and for seven states in 1970 (*Book of the States* 1972–73, p. 44).

11. Resident population aged twenty-one and over, except for four states: Alaska, aged nineteen and over; Georgia and Kentucky, aged eighteen and over; Hawaii, aged twenty and over (Bureau of the Census 1973*b*, p. 375).

12. The correlation between participation in the presidential election and the congressional election in 1960 is $r = .98$, and the correlation between participation in the presidential election in 1968 and the congressional election in 1970 is $r = .82$. Thus either measure of voter participation may be assumed to be useful for our purposes.

13. Age twenty-five is used as a cutoff point in order to find the educational level of the population which is likely to have completed its schooling. There are, of course, a number of individuals over twenty-five who are still attending school: In October 1971, 8 percent of those aged twenty-five to twenty-nine and 4.9 percent of those aged thirty to thirty-four were attending school (U.S. Bureau of the Census 1972*b*, p. 15). Consequently, using the population aged twenty-five and over as the base population may underestimate the level of education in a state. However, the error is likely to be relatively small.

14. This particular variable is less likely to underestimate the level of education in the state than is the median level of education: Only 1.1 percent of the population aged twenty to twenty-one were attending school below the college level, and the corresponding percentages for older population cohorts are even smaller: 0.5 percent of the population aged twenty-two to twenty-four, 0.4

percent of the population aged twenty-five to twenty-nine, and 0.3 percent of the population aged thirty to thirty-four (U.S Bureau of the Census 1972*b*). Consequently, the population aged twenty-five and older has almost completely finished its high-school education, although a large number of people in this age group have not finished their college education.

15. $r = .98$ in 1960, $r = .92$ in 1970.

16. Urbanization Index = 6x(percentage of population living in places 100,000 or more inhabitants)+5x(percentage of population living in places with 50,000 to 100,000 inhabitants)+4x(percentage of population living in places with 25,000 to 50,000 inhabitants)+3x (percentage of population living in places with 10,000 to 25,000 inhabitants)+2x(percentage of population living in places with 5,000 to 10,000 inhabitants)+1x(percentage of population living in places with 2,500 to 5,000 inhabitants).

17. $r = .86$ in 1960 and $r = .78$ in 1970. The changes in the relationship between 1960 and 1970 is probably due to the increasing suburbanization during that decade, particularly around large metropolitan areas, or SMSAs. A SMSA is defined as a large city, or twin cities, with at least 50,000 inhabitants plus the surrounding counties which are economically integrated with the central city or cities. The suburban population is usually defined as the population residing in those surrounding counties of the SMSA.

18. $r = .93$ in 1960 and $r = .85$ in 1970.

19. I.e., the percentage of all employed who worked as professionals or as managers, officials, and proprietors, except farm.

20. Developed by Lester Thurow of the Committee of Economic Advisors (reported by Eckstein 1966, p. 206). Industrial Index = $\Sigma_{i=1}^{n} X_i W_i$, where X_i is the percentage of all males (or females) with earnings who worked in industry i, and W_i is the ratio of the median income of males (or females) with earnings in industry i, divided by the overall median income for males (or females) in the United States. The base population is thus all males (or females) with earnings in 1959 and 1969. The index is calculated separately for each state.

21. The specific formula is as follows: 100 minus the percentage employed as farmers, farm managers, or farm laborers.

22. The forty-nine states do not constitute a random sample but make up almost the entire universe of American states. Under these circumstances it is inappropriate to use significance levels as such, which are designed to test whether an observed relationship for the sample is likely to hold in the larger universe. I am using significance levels here primarily as a shorthand way of indicating the strength of a relationship; that is, the smaller p is (or the greater

the level of significance), the more substantial is the relationship.

23. The correlation between female underemployment rate and percentage of broken families is negative ($r = -.39$, $p < .01$ in 1960; $r = -.24$ in 1970), as are the correlations between percentage of females not working and percentage of broken families ($r = -.19$ in 1960; $r = -.09$ in 1970).

24. Factor analysis is a statistical procedure used to determine whether there are underlying dimensions among a number of different variables. It essentially creates a new and smaller set of variables on the basis of the intercorrelations among the original variables. It is assumed that these original correlations are the result of underlying regularity in the data. Thus the observed variable is assumed to be influenced both by common determinants of all the variables included in the analysis and by determinants unique to the particular variable. The purpose of factor analysis is to separate out the common determinants.

25. A brief description of the type of factor analysis used in this study is presented in Appendix B, along with the results of the analyses for 1960 and 1970 (tables 18 and 19).

26. Bonjean, Browning, and Carter (1969) arrived at a similar conclusion in their study of counties in the United States, and Benjamin, Blue, and Coleman (1971) made the argument for India.

27. There were three major differences between the clustering patterns for 1960 and those for 1970: (1) the order of the factors was changed somewhat; (2) the composite factor became even more of a composite factor in 1970 than it was in 1960, contributing to one additional mass society variable; and (3) the male underemployment rate in 1970 no longer received its largest direct contribution from the composite factor, as it did in 1960, but instead joined the female underemployment factor.

28. Both the culture of poverty theory and the regulation-of-the-poor argument (Piven and Cloward 1971) must be evaluated in this context.

29. This was one of the major elements in the Newburgh crisis in 1961 and was the explicit reason for the New York ruling that no person who enters the state for the purpose of obtaining public assistance is eligible for such aid.

30. This is also reflected in several public opinion polls and special studies (Schiltz 1970, pp. 151–76; Alston and Dean 1972; Feagin 1972; Kallen and Miller 1971; Meyers and McIntyre 1969; Goodwin 1972; Williamson 1973, 1974*a*).

31. Some of these "threat variables" are highly skewed and must be interpreted with caution.

Chapter 5

1. The relationship between the dependent variable and a series of independent variables in this study is highly complex, because the independent variables themselves are quite highly intercorrelated at times. In order to isolate specifically which factors determine welfare rolls or policies it is necessary to establish which combination of independent variables best explains the variation in the dependent variable. The purpose, then, is to arrive at a subset of independent or predictor variables (percentage poor, nonworker-worker ratio, etc.) which can explain a maximum amount of variation in the dependent variable (AFDC rolls). A number of preconditions are important: (1) only those variables which contribute significantly to the explanation of variation in the dependent variable should be included in the analysis; (2) the independent contribution of each variable should be assessed and maximized as far as possible. The statistical technique which best fulfills each of these conditions is the stepwise regression model. Stepwise regression analysis is a powerful variation of multiple regression. It is a means of choosing independent variables that will provide the best possible prediction of the dependent variable with the fewest independent variables. The stepwise regression equation is the one which provides the best prediction in conjunction with the first variable selected. The analysis proceeds in this fashion until no other variable will make a significant contribution to the prediction equation. This process does not always yield the optimum solution, but it usually does fairly well. The analysis carried out in this study was done using the SPSS (Statistical Package for the Social Sciences) computer program (see Nie et al. 1975, pp. 320–48). For a more complete statistical discussion of multiple and stepwise regression analyses, see Johnston (1963).

2. These coefficients are listed in the top section of table 5. Most of the analysis for this preliminary model will be based on the data reported in the first four columns of that table.

3. The zero-order correlation coefficient is identical to the correlation coefficients examined so far in chapters 3 and 4. The name indicates that it is the lowest order of coefficient with only one independent variable (percentage poor, for example) included in the computation of the coefficient with the dependent variable (AFDC rolls).

4. The top part of column 2 in table 5 shows the partial correlation coefficients between the independent stratification variables and the dependent variable, AFDC rolls, controlling for the underemployment rate for males.

5. The significance of the partial correlation coefficient, controlling for

independent variables already selected into the prediction equation, is measured by the F-statistic, which indicates whether adding this particular variable will contribute significantly to explaining the variation in the dependent variable. In general, if the F-statistic is very small there is little reason to add that particular variable to the prediction equation. However, it should be kept in mind that in this study I am using significance levels not to test hypotheses, but as one way to indicate the strength of various relationships. Specifically, significance levels are used in the stepwise regression analysis mainly as benchmarks for determining whether a particular independent variable should be included in the prediction equation. The specific limitations on stepwise regression analysis used in this study are: (1) no variable is added to the equation if the significance of the particular correlation is less than .05 (using a two-tailed test); and (2) no variable is allowed to enter the prediction equation if its tolerance is below .15. Generally, the combined effect of these requirements is that no variable has been selected unless it can increase the total amount of explained variation at least three percentage points. Usually five percentage points are added.

6. The unstandardized regression coefficient, b in this case, measures the expected change in AFDC rolls if the nonworker-worker ratio is increased one unit while male underemployment is controlled or held constant. The standardized regression coefficient β indicates the corresponding changes if all variables were standardized to have a mean of zero and a standard deviation of one. Thus the size of the standardized regression coefficient does not depend on the type of units used in the analysis and will allow us to compare directly the effects of changing variables which are measured in different units; for example, education in number of years, families in percentages, and per capita taxes in dollars.

7. The tolerance is the pivotal element involved in bringing this particular variable into the equation: the smaller the tolerance, the closer is the variable to a linear combination of variables already entered in the equation—in this case, the full-year employment rate for males. The statistical technique of stepwise regression makes possible the selection of a variable which will reduce the amount of unexplained variation the most without entering a variable which is highly correlated with variables already selected into the equation. Only variables which will contribute significantly to the prediction of the dependent variable are entered.

8. The amount of additional variation explained by any given variable, if that variable was included in the regression equation, equals the product of the squared standardized regression coefficient β and the tolerance; i.e., $\beta_{\mathrm{f}}^2 \times$ tolerance.

9. See top section of column 3 table 5 for these partial correlation coefficients.

10. This correlation mainly reflects the fact that southern states have high welfare rolls, high poverty rates, and large black populations. The zero-order correlation between the percentage black and AFDC rolls is $r = .05$ in the southern states and $r = .00$ in the non-southern states in 1960.

11. This is the major reason why the tolerance of the variable percentage black (given the presence of the three independent stratification variables already entered into the regression equation) is relatively low (tolerance = .44).

12. The examination of this model, which includes both stratification and mass society variables, is based essentially on the data reported in the top two sections of table 5. See the first five columns of this table for the specific coefficients.

13. The material presented in chapter 7 indicates that the presence of such "threatening" groups clearly is related to welfare policies.

14. This argument has been made particularly explicit in New York State, where a person is ineligible for public assistance if he or she entered the state for the *purpose* of obtaining aid. Various public opinion polls have also documented the widespread endorsement of that argument (Feagin 1972; Williamson 1973).

15. The importance of economic opportunity in determining migration patterns is one of the major conclusions of the literature on migration. See Beshers 1965, chap. 5; Lee 1966; Goodrich et al. 1936; Bogue, Shryock, and Hoermann 1957, vol. 1; Bogue 1957, pp. 24–29, 1959, pp. 375–418; Lee et al. 1957, vol. 1; George 1961; Schultz 1960; Barth 1970; Lurie 1968; Gallaway, Gilbert, and Smith 1967; Lansing, Morgan, and Mueller 1967; Lansing and Morgan 1967; Bramhall and Bryce 1969; Raymond 1972; Rutman 1970; Startup 1971. However, at least one author (Uhlenberg 1973) has warned against overemphasizing the role of economic incentives for migration.

16. In some studies, findings have been reported in terms of partial correlation coefficients instead of standardized regression coefficients. I am therefore listing the fourth-order partial correlation coefficients between AFDC rolls and each of the five variables included in the regression equation, in each case controlling for the other four variables: underemployment rate for males, partial $r = .25$ ($p < .05$); nonworker-worker ratio, partial $r = .63$ ($p < .001$); percentage of broken families, partial $r = .59$ ($p < .001$); percentage of voter participation, partial $r = .49$ ($p < .001$); and percentage total in-migration, partial $r = .43$ ($p < .002$). All of these fourth-order partial correlation coefficients have 43 degrees of freedom.

17. We arrive at similar conclusions when we look separately at the determinants of AFDC rolls in the southern and non-southern states. In the southern states the nonworker-worker ratio is the only variable that enters the regression equation ($r = .78$, $p < .001$). However, only

sixteen states are included in this regression analysis, and the conclusions we can draw from such a small sample are quite tentative. It is obvious, however, that objective economic dependency clearly is the most important determinant of AFDC rolls in the southern states in 1960. In the non-southern states we find that, controlling for all other variables in the equation, the higher the underemployment rate for males ($\beta = .18$, $p < .05$); the greater the proportion of poor families ($\beta = 1.00$, $p < .001$); the greater the proportion of all workers employed in nonfarm occupations ($\beta = .63$, $p < .001$); the greater the percentage employed in upper white-collar occupations ($\beta = .28$, $p < .001$); and the greater the urbanization index ($\beta = .25$, $p < .05$), the higher are AFDC rolls. In the non-southern states, then, the two models seem to operate in about the same way as in the total United States, but the mass society model is more prominent, as we should expect in these states where economic dependency is less prevalent: stratification variables are still the most important determinants of AFDC rolls, but three mass society variables enter into the regression equation, instead of just two for the total United States. However, there is an important difference: two of the mass society variables selected into the equation for the non-southern states are from the urbanization-industrialization factor (percentage employed nonfarm and urbanization index). This is the only place in this study where that particular factor has any explanatory power. The reasons for this are not entirely clear. It is possible that the pattern is one involving changes over time: urbanization and industrialization may be necessary preconditions for other aspects of mass society to develop fully. Thus the pattern which is evident in the non-southern states in 1960 may reflect less "mature" mass society conditions in these states than had been achieved nationally by 1970 (see chapter 6).

Chapter 6

1. This was done by using the z transformation for each correlation coefficient and the formula:

$$z = \frac{z_1 - z_2}{\sqrt{\dfrac{1}{N_1 + 3} + \dfrac{1}{N_2 + 3}}}$$

Where z_1 is the z transformation of the zero-order correlation between AFDC rolls and an independent variable in 1960 and z_2 is the z transformation of the zero-order correlation between AFDC rolls and the corresponding independent variable in 1970 (Walker and Lev 1953, pp. 255–56).

2. This was particularly the case with female underemployment rate (correlation with urbanization from $r = -.53$ in 1960 to $r = -.20$ in 1970, $p \leqslant .031$), and two sets of correlations involving the industrial index for females also changed significantly between 1960 and 1970 (correlation with percentage of families which are poor from $r = -.76$ in 1960 to $r = -.51$ in 1970, $p \leqslant .019$; and correlation with percentage of broken families from $r = .02$ in 1960 to $r = .35$ in 1970, $p \leqslant .049$). See table 21 in Appendix D for the remaining correlation coefficients.

3. The other variables are the per capita revenue, which increased from $r = .07$ in 1960 to $r = .30$ in 1970, and per capita taxes, which increased from $r = .13$ in 1960 to $r = .35$ in 1970. One possible reason for the increased significance of the percentage of broken families in determining AFDC rolls in 1970 relative to 1960 may be a corresponding increase in the proportion of AFDC fathers who were absent from the home: 80.9 percent in 1969, an increase of 6.5 percentage points from 1961 (74.4 percent). See Eppley (1970). The changing role of women in the economic area may be a more basic factor. This problem will be dealt with later in this chapter.

4. Partial $r = .39$ for percentage with at least a high-school education ($p \leqslant .01$); partial $r = .40$ for percentage employed in upper white-collar occupations ($p \leqslant .01$); partial $r = .31$ for percentage voter participation ($p \leqslant .05$); see column 2 of table 8.

5. Male underemployment rate (partial $r = .31$, $p < .05$); female underemployment rate (partial $r = .36$, $p < .05$); percentage of females not working (partial $r = .35$, $p < .05$); and nonworker-worker ratio (partial $r = .30$, $p < .05$).

6. Note that the percentage black also has a partial correlation significantly different from zero (partial $r = -.41$, $p < .01$). Thus the 1960 pattern of the relative size of the black population being inversely related to AFDC rolls is repeated in 1970: $\beta = -.52$, which is higher than any of the other βs, but the tolerance for this variable is relatively low (.42), and the percentage black would contribute less to the reduction of unexplained variation than the per capita revenue. The low tolerance occurs because the percentage black is quite highly correlated with the percentage of broken families ($r = .77$), which entered the regression equation on the first step.

7. For the five variables selected into the regression equation, the fourth-order partial correlations with AFDC rolls—in each case controlling for the remaining four independent variables—are as follows: percentage of broken families (partial $r = .77$, $p \leqslant .001$); per capita revenue (partial $r = .44$, $p \leqslant .001$; female underemployment rate (partial $r = .60$, $p \leqslant .001$); percentage of high-school graduates (partial $r = .47$, $p \leqslant .001$); and percentage total in-migration (partial $r = -.33$, $p \leqslant .013$).

8. A similar shift is evident when the determinants of AFDC rolls are examined separately for southern and non-southern states. In 1960 only the nonworker-worker ratio entered the regression equation for

the southern states ($\beta = .78$), explaining 61 percent of the variation in AFDC rolls in the South. In 1970, however, two variables enter into the regression equation, a stratification variable (nonworker-worker ratio, $\beta = .49$, $p < .001$) and a mass society variable (per capita revenue, $\beta = .47$, $p < .05$), explaining about 61 percent of the variation in AFDC rolls in the South. Thus the South clearly has moved in the direction of mass society status. For non-southern states, however, the situation is somewhat more complex. In 1960 the first two variables to enter the equation were stratification variables (male underemployment rate, $\beta = -.18$, and percentage of families which are poor, $\beta = 1.08$) followed by three mass society variables (percentage employed nonfarm, $\beta = .63$; percentage employed in upper white-collar occupations, $\beta = .28$; and urbanization index, $\beta = .25$). In 1970, five variables also enter the equation, explaining 80 percent of the variation in AFDC rolls (compared with 83 percent in 1960). The first variable to enter in 1970 is the percentage of broken families ($\beta = .58$, $p < .001$), followed by a mass society variable, percentage employed in upper white-collar occupations ($\beta = .30$, $p < .01$); a stratification variable, the percentage of families which are poor ($\beta = .45$, $p < .001$); a "threat" variable, percentage of total out-migration 1965–70 ($\beta = -.47$, $p < .001$); and a second mass society variable, per capita revenue ($\beta = .31$, $p < .01$). Thus the stratification and mass society variables still operate in the same direction in the two regions as they do in the total United States: high mass society and high level of economic need are both associated with high AFDC rolls. However, the shift toward mass society in the non-southern states is less clear than in either the southern states or in the total United States. This perhaps reflects the fact that the non-southern states already had relatively high mass society status in 1960.

9. See table 21 in Appendix D for the specific correlations.

10. Median level of education, percentage of high-school or more education, percentage employed in upper white-collar occupations, per capita taxes, and per capita revenue.

11. Urbanization index, industrial index for males, industrial index for females, and percentage employed nonfarm.

12. Median income in 1970 was $4,962 for female-headed families, but $9,596 for male-headed families; 85.3 percent of male heads of households were working in 1970 compared with 55.7 percent of female heads of households (U.S. Bureau of the Census 1971–73).

13. Percentage of families poor: $r = .47$ in 1970 and 1960; percentage of males employed full year: $r = .47$ in 1960, $r = .25$ in 1970; see table 21 in Appendix D.

14. In no state do females actually earn more overall than males. We are

speaking of the relative size of the distance between male and female levels of earnings.

15. See Appendix C for the specific levels of employment in each year from which these changes were calculated, with appropriate adjustments for changes in age definitions.

16. Female employment and income may be more sensitive measures of economic conditions, since females are less dependent on the labor market and tend to enter employment in large numbers when economic conditions are especially good and withdraw quickly from the labor market when economic opportunities decline (Hauser 1964).

17. While a correlation coefficient of .64 would normally be considered very high, in time series analysis of this type the best single predictor of a variable at one point in time (t) generally is the corresponding variable at time t-1. Often such correlations between two corresponding variables relatively close in time are on the order of .80 to .98. In fact, the correlations between, for example, each of the mass society variables in 1960 and the corresponding variables in 1970 all are of that magnitude (see table 22 in Appendix D).

18. The majority of state revenue is in fact being spent on social welfare programs.

19. One may assume that rates of migration do not change drastically from year to year in the United States. Therefore it is likely that nonwhite net migration rates during the total decade also would be positively related to increases in AFDC rolls during the same period, although presumably less strongly so.

20. In 1970, 50.8 percent of all families receiving some form of public assistance had total incomes above the Social Security Administration's low-income limit and thus would not be classified as poor according to my criteria (U.S. Bureau of the Census 1971, table 1, p. 12). However, the very fact that there is a significant negative correlation between percentage of families in a state which are poor and the percentage of poor families which receive some form of public assistance ($r = -.75$) also indicates that in 1970 the extent of poverty in a state was not a primary factor in determining the size of the public assistance rolls.

Chapter 7

1. However, in 1971 there were still cases reported in the news media of people literally freezing to death rather than applying for public assistance. Most people today seem rather unsympathetic with such heroism. The day of admiration for the starving but proud pauper seems to have gone.

2. As was emphasized in chapter 3, the TES is a composite index of all AFDC eligibility requirements. The higher the TES, the more restrictive is the state. See Appendix A.

3. Some of the variables from the urbanization-industrialization factor are not very highly correlated with TES. This is the case with the index of urbanization, the industrial index for females, and the percentage employed in nonfarm occupations. However, the industrial index for males is significantly related to TES in both years. It is clear that it is not necessarily the large, urban states that are the most lenient in terms of AFDC policies, contrary to what is often stated by sociologists and political scientists alike. I will deal with these differences in findings in greater detail later in this chapter, but for the present it should be emphasized that these contradictions are due mainly to the way welfare policies are operationalized.

4. The relationship between other measures of welfare policies and all the independent variables will be discussed in greater detail later in this chapter.

5. None of the measures of female labor force participation are highly correlated with the TES in either 1960 or 1970, which is to be expected, since the work of females is much less crucial in determining overall rates of economic dependency in these states. Measures of female working activity are, however, fairly highly correlated with economic eligibility requirements.

6. The βs given here are the standardized regression coefficients in the final regression equation.

7. Georg Simmel (1965) considered the necessity of having both rights and duties essential for full citizenship in any society.

8. Durational residency requirements were declared unconstitutional by the Supreme Court ruling in *Shapiro* v. *Thompson*, 1969. Most states now require instead an "intent to remain" before such rights are granted.

9. This suggests that there is probably another important avenue to full status in American society—participating on a voluntary basis in wars, particularly wars fought against the country of one's national origin. Thus the Germans, the Italians, and particularly the Japanese gained considerable acceptance in the United States after World Wars I and II (see Grønbjerg, Street, and Suttles, forthcoming).

10. It should be emphasized, however, that these correlations are of about the same magnitude as the correlations between the TES and mass society and stratification variables.

11. Sharkansky and Hofferbert (1969) and a number of their followers attempt to deal with some of these state characteristics. However, most of these analyses are based on measures of policy outcomes which are of questionable relevance. See also Uslaner and Weber (1975) and Carmines (1974).

12. The correlation coefficients between the TES and Walker's Index of Innovation are small, $r = -.23$ (n.s.) in 1970 and $r = -.27$ ($p < .05$) in 1960, but nevertheless provide a slight indication that innovative states also tend to have lenient welfare policies.

13. This is the case for all the studies included in the following incomplete list: Collins 1967; Cnudde and McCrone 1969; Dawson and Gray 1971; Dawson and Robinson 1963; Dye 1965, 1966; Hofferbert 1966*b*; Sharkansky and Hofferbert 1969; Sharkansky 1967*a*.

14. A composite measure like the TES necessarily has a lower variability than its component parts (cost standards, etc.), unless these subparts are perfectly correlated with one another.

15. In 1959 the United States average for TES was 22. California scored 22 while New York scored 19. In 1970 the average was 13, California 12 and New York 10.

16. In 1959 Illinois had a TES of 27, in 1970, 15.

17. One is almost tempted to conclude that a major reason why average payments have been selected in previous studies as a measure of welfare policies in the states is that this particular item happens to be handily available in *Statistical Abstracts of the United States*. It is surprising how often all the data used in given studies have been limited to what is available in these volumes.

18. In 1970 the zero-order correlation between maximum payments and average payments was $r = .94$.

19. Including party competition, voter participation, democratic party control, and malapportionment. See Dye (1966) for a summary of these findings.

20. This interpretation is even more striking if Wisconsin is exluded from the analysis. In this case the zero-order correlation between the TES in 1960 and the TES in 1970 increased to $r = .76$.

21. However, one study of public assistance in New York City (Gordon 1969) found no evidence of an increase in the rate of participation between 1960 and 1967.

22. Durman (1973, pp. 356–57) estimates that 65 percent of the increase in applications approved in 1964–68 over 1960–63 could be attributed to additional applications, about 26 percent to increased rates of approval, and about 9 percent to increases in both applications and rates of approval.

23. Public welfare workers have considerable discretion in how they conduct the intake procedure and whether they approve applications (Gordon 1972). However, once an application has been approved and the family is receiving aid, the actions of the caseworker have very little effect on the size or costs of the public assistance programs (Kroeger 1971).

24. This is particularly true of the percentage with at least a high-school

education ($r = .26$) and the percent employed in upper white-collar occupations ($r = .37$).

25. During the 1960s a number of social workers became very active in community action programs, community organizations, and other advocacy activities (see Cloward and Piven 1966, 1968). However, it is uncertain how much of this trend also extended to public assistance caseworkers, who tend to have relatively tenuous ·association with professional social work.

26. There is some disagreement among these studies about the rate of participation and changes therein, which may reflect the time or location of the investigation as well as procedures used to determine the pool of eligible persons. See Greenleigh Associates 1965; Cloward and Piven 1966, 1968; Sauber and Rubinstein 1965; Anderson and D'Amico 1969; Boland 1973; Gordon 1969; Moles 1969, 1971; Moles, Hess, and Fascione 1968; Powers and Bultena 1974.

27. A somewhat similar notion lies behind Elman's use of the term "poorhouse state" (Elman 1966).

Chapter 8

1. This is what Nisbet (1974) calls the tradition of citizenship originating in Rousseau and unitary democracy, where a close and direct relationship is established between the state and the individual, with no competing ties. Nisbet generally deplores that form of citizenship and argues that the United States has gone too far in that direction and needs to return to decentralization of government and indirect administration. This is in direct contrast to Palley and Palley (1972), who argue that only a national approach to welfare will be effective in overcoming inequities. Instead, Nisbet favors the tradition he attributes to Burke and social pluralism, in which citizenship is established through other groups and may be used against the political power of the state. The latter tradition is clearly within the laissez-faire ideology.

2. It is illuminating here to contrast the inaugural address of President Kennedy in 1961 with that of President Nixon in 1973. Kennedy emphasized the system of rights and obligations between the individual and the nation: "Ask not what your country can do for you; ask what you can do for your country." Nixon seemed to reject that relationship: "Do not ask what the country can do for you, but what you can do for yourself."

3. For a complete listing of the structural factors discussed by Wilensky, see Wilensky (1975, pp. 50–69).

4. Such national emergencies seem to be the primary conditions under which developments in the welfare system occur in the United States (Grønbjerg, Street, and Suttles, forthcoming).

5. The need for inequality should not necessarily be interpreted to mean that the poor are necessary as pawns in the struggles of other social strata (Halper 1973); it simply indicates that some differentiation is necessary within the social structure. Social differentiation almost always involves inequality in some form as well.

Bibliography

Aaron, Henry. 1967. Social Security: International comparisons. In *Studies in the economics of income maintenance*, ed. Otto Eckstein, pp. 13–48. Washington, D.C.: Brookings Institution.

Addams, Jane. 1903. Child labor and pauperism. *Proceedings of the National Conference of Charities and Correction*, pp. 114–21.

Advisory Commission on Intergovernmental Relations. 1964. *Statutory and administrative controls associated with federal grants for public assistance*. Washington, D.C.: U.S. Government Printing Office.

Albin, Peter S., and Stein, Bruno. 1968. The constrained demand for public assistance. *Journal of Human Resources* 3 (Summer):300–311.

———. 1971. The determinants of relief policy at the sub-federal level. *Southern Economic Journal* 37:445–57.

Alger, George W., et al. 1906–7. Industrial accidents and their social cost. *Charities and the Commons* 27:791–844.

Almond, Gabriel A., and Powell, G. Bingham, Jr. 1966. *Comparative politics: A developmental approach*. Boston: Little, Brown.

Almond, Gabriel A., and Verba, Sidney. 1965. *The civic culture: Political attitudes and democracy in five nations*. Boston: Little, Brown.

Alston, Jon P., and Dean, Imogene. 1972. Socioeconomic factors associated with attitudes toward welfare recipients and the causes of poverty. *Social Science Review* 46 (March):13–23.

Anderson, Jacqueline, and D'Amico, Rocco. 1969. Use of AFDC by eligible families. *Welfare in Review* 7 (November–December):25–26.

Arieli, Yehoshua. 1964. *Individualism and nationalism in American ideology*. Baltimore: Penguin Books.

Bacon, Lloyd. 1971. Poverty among interregional rural-to-urban migrants. *Rural Sociology* 36 (June):125–40.

———. 1973. Migration, poverty, and the rural South. *Social Forces* 51 (March):348–55.

Baer, Michael A., and Jaros, Dean. 1974. Participation as instrument and expression: Some evidence from the states. *American Journal of Political Science* 18:365–83.

Bahl, Roy W., and Saunders, Robert J. 1965. Determinants of changes in state and local government expenditures. *National Tax Journal* 18:50–57.

Bailis, Lawrence N. 1972. Bread and justice: Grass-roots organizing in the welfare rights movement. Ph.D. diss. Department of Sociology, Harvard University.

Banfield, Edward. 1968. *The unheavenly city: The nature and future of our urban crisis*. Boston: Little, Brown.

———. 1969. Welfare: A crisis without "Solutions." *Public Interest* 16 (Summer):89–101.

Barth, Michael C. 1970. Migration and income maintenance. In *The President's Commission on Income Maintenance: Technical Studies*, pp. 187–206. Washington, D.C.: U.S. Government Printing Office.

Beale, Calvin L. 1971. Rural-urban migration of blacks: Past and future. *American Journal of Agricultural Economics* 53:302–7.

Bell, Winifred. 1965. *Aid to Dependent Children*. New York: Columbia University Press.

Bendix, Reinhard. 1968. Concepts in comparative historical analysis. In *Comparative research across cultures and nations*, ed. Stein Rokkan, pp. 67–81. Publication of the International Social Science Council, no. 8. Paris: Mouton.

Benjamin, Roger W.; and Blue, Richard N.; with Coleman, Stephen. 1971. Modernization and political change: A comparative aggregate data analysis of Indian political behavior. *Midwest Journal of Political Science* 15:219–61.

Beshers, James M. 1965. *Population processes in social systems*. New York: Free Press.

Betz, Michael. 1974. Riots and welfare: Are they related? *Social Problems* 21: 345–55.

Billings, Dwight. 1974. Culture of poverty in Appalachia: A theoretical discussion and empirical analysis. *Social Forces* 53 (December):315–23.

Blevins, Audie, Jr. 1971. Socioeconomic differences between migrants and nonmigrants. *Rural Sociology* 36 (December):509–20.

Bogue, Donald J. 1957. *Components of population change, 1940-1950: Estimates of net migration and natural increase for each standard metropolitan area and state economic area.* Scripps Foundation Studies in Population Distribution, no. 12. Oxford, Ohio: Miami University; Chicago: Population Research and Training Center, University of Chicago.

———. 1959. *The population of the United States*. Glencoe, Ill.: Free Press.

Bogue, Donald J.; Shyrock, Henry S., Jr.; and Hoermann, Siegfried S. 1957. *Subregional migration in the U.S., 1935-40*. Vol. 1. *Streams of migration between subregions*. Scripps Foundation Studies in Population Distribution, no. 5. Oxford, Ohio: Miami University.

Boland, Barbara. 1973. Participation in the Aid to Families with Dependent Children program (AFDC). In *Studies in public welfare*, pp. 139–79. Washington, D.C.: U.S. Government Printing Office.

Bonjean, Charles M.; Browning, Harvey L.; and Carter, Lewis F. 1969. Toward comparative community research: A factor analysis of United States counties. *Sociological Quarterly* 10:157–76.

Bramhall, David F., and Bryce, Harrington I. 1969. Interstate migration of labor-force age population. *Industrial and labor relations review* 22 (July):576–83.

Brazer, Harvey E. 1958. The role of major metropolitan centers in state and local finance. *American Economic Review, Papers and Proceedings* 48:305–16.

Break, George F. 1967. *Intergovernmental fiscal relations in the United States*. Washington, D.C.: Brookings Institution.

Briggs, Asa. 1961. The welfare state in historical perspective. *Archives Européennes de Sociologie* 2:221–58.

Broach, Glen T. 1973. Interparty competition, state welfare policies, and nonlinear regression. *Journal of Politics* 35:737–43.

Brown, James S.; Schwarzweller, Harry K.; and Mangalam, Joseph J. 1963. Kentucky mountain migration and the stem-family: An American variation on a theme by Le Play. *Rural Sociology* 28 (March):48–69.

Burch, Genevieve. 1974. Role preference of AFDC women. Paper presented at the annual meetings of the American Sociological Association in Montreal, Canada (August).

Burnside, Betty. 1971. The employment potential of AFDC mothers in six states. *Welfare in Review* 9 (July–August):16–20.

Carmines, Edward G. 1974. The mediating influence of state legislatures on the linkage between interparty competition and welfare policies. *American Political Science Review* 68:1118–24.

Chambers, Donald E. 1969. Residence requirements for welfare benefits: Consequences of their unconstitutionality. *Social Work* 14 (October): 29–37.

Clement, M. O. 1962. Interstate fiscal equity and federal grants-in-aid: An empirical method and its applications, fiscal 1952. *Southern Economic Journal* 29:279–96.

Cloward, Richard A., and Piven, Frances Fox. 1966. A strategy to end poverty. *Nation* 202 (May 2):510–17.

———. 1968. Workers and welfare: The poor against themselves. *Nation* 207:558–62.

Clynch, Edward J. 1972. A critique of Ira Sharkansky's "The utility of Elazar's political culture." *Polity* 5:139–41.

Cnudde, Charles F., and McCrone, Donald J. 1969. Party competition and welfare policies in the American states. *American Political Science Review* 63:858–66.

Collins, Laura S. 1967. Public assistance expenditures in the United States. In *Studies in the economics of income maintenance*, ed. Otto Eckstein, pp. 97–174. Washington, D.C.: Brookings Institution.

Coulter, Philip B. 1970. Comparative community politics and public policy: Problems in theory and research. *Polity* 3 (Fall):22–43.

Coulter, Philip B., and Gordon, Glen. 1968. Urbanization and party competition: Critique and redirection of theoretical research. *Western Political Quarterly* 21:274–88.

Coward, Barbara E.; Feagin, Joe R.; and Williams, J. Allen, Jr. 1974. The culture of poverty debate: Some additional data. *Social Problems* 21 (June):621–34.

Cowart, Andrew T. 1969. Anti-poverty expenditures in the American states: A comparative analysis. *Midwest Journal of Political Science* 13:219–36.

Crew, Robert E., Jr. 1969. Dimensions of public policy: A factor analysis of state expenditures. *Social Science Quarterly* 50 (September):381–88.

Crittenden, John. 1967. Dimensions of modernization in the American states. *American Political Science Review* 61:989-1001.

Cutright, Phillips. 1974. Region, migration, and the earnings of white and black men. *Social Forces* 53 (December):297-305.

Dahrendorf, Ralf. 1974. Citizenship and beyond: The social dynamics of an idea. *Social Research* 41:673-701.

Danzger, Herbert M. 1968. A quantified description of community conflict. *American Behavioral Scientist* 12:9-15.

Davidson, Chandler, and Gaitz, Charles M. 1974. "Are the poor different?" A comparison of work behavior and attitudes among the urban poor and nonpoor. *Social Problems* 22:229-45.

Dawson, Richard E., and Gray, Virginia. 1971. State welfare policies. In *Politics in the American states: A comparative analysis*, ed. Herbert Jacob and Kenneth N. Vines, pp. 433-75. Boston: Little, Brown.

Dawson, Richard E., and Robinson, James A. 1963. Inter-party competition, economic variables and welfare policies in the American states. *Journal of Politics* 25 (May):265-89.

DeJong, Gordon F., and Ahmad, Zafar M. N. 1974. Motivation for migration of welfare clients. Paper presented at the 8th World Congress of the International Sociological Association. Toronto (19-23 August).

De Jong, Gordon F., and Donnelly, William L. 1972. AFDC payment levels and nonwhite migration to cities. In *Proceedings of the Social Statistics Section, 1971*, pp. 187-91. American Statistical Association, Washington, D.C.: American Statistical Association.

———. 1973. Public welfare and migration. *Social Science Quarterly* 54 (September):329-44.

Derthick, Martha. 1968. Intercity differences in administration of the public assistance programs: The case of Massachusetts. In *City politics and public policy*, ed. James Q. Wilson, pp. 243-66. New York: John Wiley.

———. 1970. *The influence of federal grants.* Cambridge, Mass.: Harvard University Press.

———. 1975. *Uncontrollable spending for social services grants.* Washington, D.C.: Brookings Institution.

Downey, E. H. 1924. *Workmen's compensation.* New York: Macmillan Company.

Duncan, Greg J., and Morgan, James N. eds. 1975. *Five thousand families—Patterns of economic progress. Vol. 3. Analyses of the first six years of the panel study of income dynamics.* Ann Arbor: Institute for Social Research, University of Michigan.

Durbin, Elizabeth. 1973. Work and welfare: the case of Aid to Families with Dependent Children. *Journal of Human Resources* 8 (supplement): 103-25.

Durkheim, Emile. 1964. *The division of labor in society.* Trans. George Simpson. New York: Free Press.

Durman, Eugene. 1973. Have the poor been regulated? Toward a multivariate understanding of welfare growth. *Social Service Review* 47 (September):339–59.

Dye, Thomas R. 1965. Malapportionment and public policy in the states. *Journal of Politics* 27 (August):586–601.

———. 1966. *Politics, economics and the public: Policy outcomes in the American states.* Chicago: Rand McNally.

———. 1969a. Income inequality and American state politics. *American Political Science Review* 63:157–62.

———. 1969b. Inequality and civil-rights policy in the states. *Journal of Politics* 31:1080–97.

———. 1969c. *Politics in states and communities.* Englewood Cliffs, N.J.: Prentice-Hall.

Eckstein, Otto. 1966. Strategies in the war against poverty. In *Poverty amid affluence*, ed. Leo Fishman, pp. 200–211. New Haven: Yale University Press.

Elazar, Daniel J. 1972. *American federalism: A view from the states.* 2d ed. New York: Thomas Y. Crowell.

Elesh, David. 1973. Poverty theories and income maintenance: Validity and policy relevance. *Social Science Quarterly* 54 (September):359–73.

Elliott, James R. 1965. A comment on inter-party competition, economic variables, and welfare policies in the American states. *Journal of Politics* 27:185–91.

Elman, Richard M. 1966. *The poorhouse state: The American way of life on public assistance.* New York: Dell Publishing Co.

Eppley, David B. 1970. The AFDC family in the 1960's. *Welfare in Review* (September–October):8–17.

Ernst, Charles F. 1938. New trends in public welfare legislation. *State Government* 11 (May):85–88.

Fabricant, Solomon. 1952. *The trend of government activity in the United States since 1900.* New York: National Bureau of Economic Research.

Feagin, Joe R. 1972. America's welfare stereotypes. *Social Science Quarterly* 52 (March): 921–23.

Featherman, David L. 1971. Residential background and socioeconomic achievement in metropolitan stratification systems. *Rural Sociology* 36 (June):107–24.

Fine, Sidney. 1964. *Laissez-faire and general welfare state: A study of conflict in American thoughts, 1865–1901.* Ann Arbor: University of Michigan Press.

Fisher, Glenn W. 1964. Interstate variation in state and local government expenditures. *National Tax Journal* 17 (March):57–74.

Frazier, Franklin. 1957. *Black bourgeoisie: The rise of a new middle class in the United States.* Glencoe, Ill.: Free Press.

Frederickson, H. George. 1974. Social equity and public administration: Introductory comments. *Public Administration Review* 34 (January–February):1–2.

Freedman, Donald, and Freedman, Deborah. 1968. Farm-reared elements in the non-farm population. *Rural Sociology* 21 (March):50–61.

Fry, Brian R., and Winters, Richard F. 1970. The politics of redistribution. *American Political Science Review* 64:508–22.

Gallaway, Lowell E.; Gilbert, R. F.; and Smith, P. E. 1967. The economics of labor mobility: An empirical analysis. *Western Economic Journal* (June).

Gans, Herbert T. 1962. *The urban villagers.* Glencoe, Ill.: Free Press.

Garfinkel, Irwin, and Orr, Larry L. 1974. Welfare policy and the employment rate of AFDC mothers. *National Tax Journal* 27:275–84.

Gary, Lawrence E. 1973. Policy decisions in the Aid to Families with Dependent Children program: A comparative state analysis. *Journal of Politics* 35:886–923.

Gayer, David. 1972. The effects of Medicaid on state and local government finances. *National Tax Journal* 25:511–19.

Gendell, Murray, and Zetterberg, Hans L. 1964. *A sociological almanac for for the United States.* New York: Charles Scribner's Sons.

George, K. M. 1961. Association of selected economic factors with net migration rates in the southern Appalachian region, 1935–1957. M.A. Thesis, University of Kentucky.

Gist, Noel P., and Clark, C. D. 1938. Intelligence as a selective factor in rural-urban migrations. *American Journal of Sociology* 44 (July):36–58.

Gist, Noel P.; Pihlblad, C. T.; and Gregory, Cecil L. 1941. Selective aspects of rural migrations. *Rural Sociology* 6 (March):3–15.

Glazer, Nathan. 1969. Beyond income maintenance—a note on welfare in New York City. *Public Interest* 16 (Summer):102–20.

Godwin, William. 1820. *Of population: An enquiry concerning the power of increase in the numbers of mankind, being an answer to Mr. Malthus's essay on that subject.* London.

Goering, John M., and Coe, Rodney M. 1971. Cultural vs. situational explanations of the medical behavior of the poor. *Social Science Quarterly* 51 (September):309–19.

Gold, Ronald B. 1969. Fiscal capacities and welfare expenditures of states. *National Tax Journal* 22:496–505.

Goode, William J. 1962. Marital satisfaction and instability. *International Social Science Journal* 14:507–26.

Goodrich, Carter L., et al. 1936. *Migration and economic opportunity.* Philadelphia: University of Pennsylvania Press.

Goodwin, Leonard. 1972. *Do the poor want to work? A social-psychological study of work orientations.* Washington, D.C.: Brookings Institution.

Gordon, David M. 1969. Income and welfare in New York City. *Public Interest* 16 (Summer):64–88.

Gordon, Laura K. 1972. The intake process: Application and decision in a public welfare bureaucracy. Ph.D. diss., Department of Sociology, State University of New York at Stony Brook.

239   Bibliography

Gordon, Margaret S. 1963. *The economics of welfare policies*. New York: Columbia University Press.

Gramlich, Edward M. 1968. Alternative federal policies for stimulating state and local expenditures: A comparison of their effects. *National Tax Journal* 21 (June):119-29.

Greenleigh Associates. 1965. *Study of services to deal with poverty in Detroit, Michigan*. New York: Greenleigh Associates.

Greenston, Peter M., and MacRae, C. Duncan. 1974. A diffusion analysis of participation in the Aid to Families with Dependent Children (AFDC) program by states. Paper presented at meetings of the annual American Sociological Association, Montreal, Canada (August).

Grønbjerg, Kirsten A.; Street, David P.; and Suttles, Gerald D. *Poverty and social change*, forthcoming.

Gruber, Murray. 1972. The nonculture of poverty among black youths. *Social Work* 17 (May):50-58.

Grumm, John G. 1971. The effects of legislative structure on legislative performance. In *State and urban politics: Readings in comparative public policy*, ed. Richard I. Hofferbert and Ira Sharkansky, pp. 298-322. Boston: Little, Brown.

Gusfield, Joseph R. 1963. *Symbolic crusade, status politics and the American temperance movement*. Urbana: University of Illinois Press.

Halper, Thomas. 1973. The poor as pawns: The new "deserving poor" and the old. *Polity* 6 (Fall):71-86.

Handler, Joel F., and Hollingsworth, Ellen Jane. 1971. *The "deserving poor": A study of welfare administration*. Chicago: Markham.

Hannerz, Ulf. 1969. *Soulside: Inquiries into ghetto culture and community*. New York: Columbia University Press.

Hanson, Robert C., and Simmons, Ozzie G. 1969. Differential experience paths of rural migrants to the city. *American Behavioral Scientist* 13: 14-35.

Harlow, Robert L. 1968. Sharkansky on state expenditures: A comment. *National Tax Journal* 21:215-16.

Hart, David K. 1974. Social equity, justice and the equitable administration. *Public Administration Review* 34 (February):3-11.

Hauser, Philip M. 1964. Labor force. In *Handbook of modern sociology*, ed. Robert E. L. Faris, pp. 160-90. Chicago: Rand McNally.

Hausman, Leonard J. 1969. Potential for financial self-support among AFDC and AFDC-UP recipients. *Southern Economic Journal* 36 (July): 60-66.

————. 1970. The impact of welfare on the work effort of AFDC mothers. In *Technical studies*, ed. the President's Commission on Income Maintenance, pp. 83-104. Washington, D.C.: U.S. Government Printing Office.

Havens, Elizabeth M. 1973. Women, work and wedlock: A note on female marital patterns in the United States. *American Journal of Sociology* 78 (January):975-81.

Hawley, Amos A., and Zimmer, Basil. 1961. Resistance to unification in a metropolitan community. In *Community political systems*, ed. Morris Janowitz, pp. 146-84. Glencoe: Free Press.

Heffernan, W. Joseph, Jr. 1969. Research notes on the conventional political behavior of the poor. *Journal of Human Resources* 4 (Spring): 253-59.

————. 1973. Variations in negative tax rates in current public assistance programs: An example of administrative discretion. *Journal of Human Resources* 8 (supplement):56-68.

Helfgot, Joseph. 1974. Professional reform organizations and the symbolic representation of the poor. *American Sociological Review* 39 (August): 475-91.

Henriques, Fernando. 1953. *Family and colour in Jamaica*. London: Eyre and Spottiswoode.

Herrnstein, Richard. 1971. IQ. *Atlantic Monthly*, September, pp. 43-64.

Herzog, Elizabeth. 1963. Some assumptions about the poor. *Social Service Review* 37 (December):391-400.

Hill, Reuben; Stycos, J. Mayone; and Back, Kurt. 1959. *The family and population control*. Chapel Hill: University of North Carolina Press.

Hodge, Robert W., and Zald, Mayer N. 1963. Charity and community: A review of inter-city variation in welfare expenditures. Unpublished paper, National Opinion Research Center and Department of Sociology, University of Chicago.

Hofferbert, Richard I. 1966a. Ecological development and policy change in the American states. *Midwest Journal of Political Science* 10:464-83.

————. 1966b. The relation between public policy and some structural and environmental variables in the American states. *American Political Science Review* 60 (March):73-82.

————. 1968. Socioeconomic dimensions of the American states: 1890-1960. *Midwest Journal of Political Science* 12:401-18.

————. 1970. Elite influence in state policy formation: A model for comparative inquiry. *Polity* 2 (Spring):316-44.

Honig, Marjorie. 1973. The impact of welfare payment levels on family stability. In *Studies in public welfare*, pp. 37-53. Washington, D.C.: U.S. Government Printing Office.

————. 1974. AFDC income, recipient rates and family dissolution. *Journal of Human Resources* 9:303-22.

Hopkins, Anne H. 1974. Opinion publics and support for public policy in the American states. *American Journal of Political Science* 18:167-77.

Horan, Patrick M., and Austin, Patricia Lee. 1974. The social bases of welfare stigma. *Social Problems* 21 (June):648-57.

Howell, Joseph T. 1973. *Hard living on Clay Street: Portraits of blue collar families*. Garden City, N.Y.: Doubleday; Anchor Books.

Huntington, Samuel P. 1973. Political modernization: America vs. Europe. In *State and society: A reader*, ed. Reinhard Bendix, et al., pp. 170–200. Berkeley: University of California Press.

Hurry, Jamieson Bond. 1917. *Poverty and its vicious circles*. London: Jared A. Churchill.

Inkeles, Alex. 1969. Participant citizenship in six developing countries. *American Political Science Review* 63:1120–39.

International Labor Organization. 1958. Cost of non-statutory Social Security schemes. *International Labor Review* (October):388–403.

————. 1961. *The cost of Social Security, 1949–57*. Geneva: International Labor Organization.

Irelan, Lola M.; Moles, Oliver C.; and O'Shea, Robert M. 1969. Ethnicity, poverty, and selected attitudes: A test of the "culture of poverty" hypothesis. *Social Forces* 47 (March):405–13.

Jacob, Herbert, and Lipsky, Michael. 1971. Outputs, structure, and power: An assessment of changes in the study of state and local politics. In *State and urban politics: Readings in comparative public policy*, ed. Richard I. Hofferbert and Ira Sharkansky, pp. 14–40. Boston: Little, Brown.

Janowitz, Morris. 1961. Converging perspectives in community political analysis. In *Community political systems*, ed. Morris Janowitz, pp. 13–17. Glencoe: Free Press.

————. 1976. *Social control of the welfare state*. New York: Elsevier.

Jenkins, J. Craig. 1975. Farm workers and the powers: Insurgency and political conflict (1946–1972). Ph.D. diss., Department of Sociology, State University of New York at Stony Brook.

Jennings, M. Kent, and Zeigler, Harmon. 1970. The salience of American state politics. *American Political Science Review* 64:523–35.

Jensen, Arthur R. 1967. Estimation of the limits of heritability of traits by comparison of monozygotic and dizygotic twins. *Proceedings of the National Academy of Science* 58:149–56.

————. 1969. How much can we boost IQ and scholastic achievement? *Harvard Educational Review* 39:1–123.

————. 1970. IQs of identical twins reared apart. *Behavioral Genetics* 1: 133–46.

Johnston, J. 1963. *Econometric methods*. New York: McGraw-Hill.

Jones, E. Terrence. 1974. Political change and spending shifts in the American states. *American Politics Quarterly* 2 (April):159–78.

Kain, John F., and Persky, Joseph J. 1968. The North's stake in southern rural poverty. In *Rural poverty in the U.S.* Washington, D.C.: U.S. Government Printing Office.

Kallen, David J., and Miller, Dorothy. 1971. Public attitudes toward welfare. *Social Work* 16 (July):83–90.

Kaplan, H. Roy, and Tausky, Curt. 1972. Work and the welfare Cadillac: The function of and commitment to work among the hard-core unemployed. *Social Problems* 19 (Spring):469–83.

Kasper, Hirschel. 1968. Welfare payments and work incentive: Some determinants of the rates of General Assistance Payments. *Journal of Human Resources* 3 (Winter):86–110.

Kerbo, Harold R.; Silberstein, Fred B.; and Snizek, William E. 1974. Welfare recipients and system blaming for poverty. Paper read at the annual meetings of the American Sociological Association, Montreal, Canada (August).

Key, V. O., Jr. 1949. *Southern politics*. New York: Vintage Books.

———. 1956. *American state politics*. New York: Knopf.

Komarovsky, Mirra. 1964. *Blue-collar marriage*. New York: Random House.

Kornhauser, William. 1959. *The politics of mass society*. Glencoe: Free Press.

Kriesberg, Louis. 1970. *Mothers in poverty: A study of fatherless families*. Chicago: Aldine.

Kroeger, Naomi. 1971. Organizational goals, policies, and output: The dilemma of public aid. Ph.D. diss., Department of Sociology, University of Chicago.

Kurnow, Ernest. 1964. Determinants of state and local expenditures reexamined. *National Tax Journal* 17 (March):55–74.

Lansing, John B., and Morgan, James N. 1967. The effect of geographic mobility on income. *Journal of Human Resources* 2 (Fall):449–60.

Lansing, John B.; Morgan, James N.; and Mueller, Eva. 1967. *The geographic mobility of labor*. Ann Arbor, Mich.: Survey Research Center, Institute for Social Research.

Lee, Everett S. 1966. A theory of migration. *Demography* 3:47–59.

Lee, Everett S.; Miller, Ann Ratner; Brainerd, Carol P.; Easterlin, Richard A.; and Kuznetz, Simon. 1957. *Population redistribution and economic growth U.S. 1870–1950*. Vol. 1. *Methodological considerations and reference tables*. Philadelphia: American Philosophical Society.

Lewis, Hylan. 1967. *Culture, class and poverty*. Washington, D.C.: Health and Welfare Council of the National Capital Area.

Lewis, Oscar. 1966. *La Vida: A Puerto Rican family in the culture of poverty—San Juan and New York*. New York: Random House.

———. 1968. *Pedro Martinez*. New York: Random House.

Liebow, Elliot. 1967. *Tally's Corner: A study of Negro street corner men*. With a foreword by Hylan Lewis. Boston: Little, Brown.

Long, Harry H. 1974. Poverty status and receipt of welfare among migrants and nonmigrants in large cities. *American Sociological Review* 39 (February):46–56.

Lowi, Theodore J. 1969. *The end of liberalism: Ideology, policy, and the crisis of public authority*. New York: W. W. Norton and Co.

Lowry, Ira S.; DeSalvo, Joseph S.; and Woodfill, Barbara M. 1971. *Rental housing in New York City.* Vol. 2. *The demand for shelter.* New York: New York City Rand Institute.

Lurie, Irene. 1968. *An economic evaluation of Aid to Families with Dependent Children.* Washington, D.C.: Brookings Institution (mimeographed).

———. 1974. Estimates of tax rates in the AFDC program. *National Tax Journal* 27:93-107.

Lurie, Melvin, and Rayack, Elton. 1966. Racial differences in migration and job search: A case study. *Southern Economic Journal* 33 (July): 81-95.

Luttbeg, Norman R. 1971. Classifying the American states: An empirical attempt to identify internal variations. *Midwest Journal of Political Science* 15:703-21.

Lynch, John M. 1967. Trend in number of AFDC recipients, 1961-65. *Welfare in Review* 5 (May):7-14.

Malthus, Thomas R. 1817. *An essay on the principles of population.* Vol. 3. 5th ed. London.

Marshall, T. H. 1961. The welfare state: A sociological interpretation. *Archives Européennes de Sociologie* 2:284-300.

———. 1964. *Class, citizenship and social development.* Garden City, New York: Doubleday.

Martin, George. 1972. Emergence and development of social movements organization among the under class: A case study of the National Welfare Rights Organization. Ph.D. diss., Department of Sociology, University of Chicago.

Masters, Stanley H. 1972. Are black migrants from the South to the northern cities worse off than blacks already there? *Journal of Human Resources* 7 (Fall):411-23.

Merriam, Ida C. 1957. Trends in public welfare and their implications. *American Economic Review, Papers and Proceedings* 47:400-489.

Meyers, Samuel, and McIntyre, Jennie. 1969. *Welfare policy and its consequences for the recipient population: A study of the AFDC program.* Washington, D.C.: U.S. Government Printing Office.

Miller, Walter. 1958. Working class culture as a generating milieu of gang delinquency. *Journal of Social Issues* 14:5-19.

Mizruchi, Ephraim Harold. 1967. Aspirations and poverty: A neglected aspect of Merton's anomie. *Sociological Quarterly* 8:439-46.

Mohl, Raymond A. 1972. Poverty, pauperism, and social order in the preindustrial American city 1780-1840. *Social Science Quarterly* 52:934-48.

Moles, Oliver C. 1969. Predicting use of public assistance: An empirical study. *Welfare in Review* 7 (November-December):13-19.

———. 1971. The relationship of family circumstances and personal history to use of public assistance. *Social Work* 16 (April):37-47.

————. Forthcoming. Marital dissolution and public assistance payments: Variations among American states. *Journal of Social Issues.*

Moles, Oliver; Hess, Robert F.; and Fascione, Daniel. 1968. Who knows where to get public assistance? *Welfare in Review* 6 (September–October):8–13.

Monahan, Thomas P. 1955. Divorce by occupational level. *Marriage and Family Living* 17 (November):322–24.

Morehouse, Sarah McCally. 1973. The state political party and the policy-making process. *American Political Science Review* 67:59–72.

Morgan, David, and Lyons, William. 1975. Industrialization and affluence revisited: A note on socioeconomic dimensions of the American states, 1970. *American Journal of Political Science* 19 (May):263–76.

Morgan, James N.; Dickinson, Katherine; Dickinson, Jonathan; Benus, Jacob; and Duncan, Greg, eds. 1974. *Five thousand families—Patterns of economic progress.* Vol. 1. *An analysis of the first five years of the Panel Study of Income Dynamics.* Ann Arbor: Institute for Social Research, University of Michigan.

Morss, Elliott R. 1966. Some thoughts on the determinants of state and local expenditures. *National Tax Journal* 19:95–103.

Morss, Elliott R.; Fredland, J. Eric; and Hymans, Saul H. 1967. Fluctuations in state expenditures: An econometric analysis. *Southern Economic Journal* 33 (April):496–517.

Moynihan, Daniel P. 1965. *The Negro family: The case for national action.* Washington, D.C.: U.S. Department of Labor.

————. 1966. What is "community action"? *Public Interest* 5 (Fall):3–8.

————. 1969. *Maximum feasible misunderstanding: Community action in the war on poverty.* New York: Free Press.

Nie, Norman H.; Hull, C. Hadlai; Jenkins, Jean G.; Steinbrenner, Karin; and Bent, Dale H. 1975. *SPSS: Statistical Package for the Social Sciences.* 2d ed. New York: McGraw-Hill.

Nie, Norman H.; Powell, G. Bingham, Jr.; and Prewitt, Kenneth. 1969. Social structure and political participation: Developmental relationships, I, II. *American Political Science Review* 63:361–78; 808–32.

Nisbet, Robert. 1974. Citizenship: Two traditions. *Social Research* 41: 612–37.

Offe, Claus. 1972. Advanced capitalism and the welfare state. *Politics and Society* 2 (Summer):479–88.

Olsen, Marvin E. 1968. Multivariate analysis of national political development. *American Sociological Review* 33 (October):699–712.

Osman, Jack W. 1966. The dual impact of federal aid on state and local government expenditures. *National Tax Journal* 19:362–72.

Owen, Robert. 1817. *Report to the Committee of the Association for the Relief of the Manufacturing and Laboring Poor,* laid before the Committee of the House of Commons on the Poor Laws. London.

Paine, Thomas. 1894. "Rights of man." Part 2 in *The writings of Thomas Paine*, vol. 2, ed. Moncure Daniel Conway. New York: G. P. Putnam's Sons.

Palley, Marian Lief, and Palley, Howard A. 1972. A call for a national welfare policy. *American Behavioral Scientist* 15 (June):681-95.

Patterson, Samuel. 1968. The political culture of the American states. *Journal of Politics* 30 (February):187-209.

Paulson, Wayne; Butler, Edgar W.; and Pope, Hallowell. 1969. Community power and public welfare. *American Journal of Economics and Sociology* 28 (January):17-26.

Perry, Joseph B., and Snyder, Eldon E. 1971. Opinions of farm employers toward welfare assistance for Mexican American migrant workers. *Sociology and Social Research* 55 (January):161-69.

Pihlblad, C. T., and Gregory, C. L. 1957. Occupations and patterns of migration. *Social Forces* 36 (October):56-64.

Pilisuk, Marc, and Pilisuk, Phyllis. 1973. *How we lost the war on poverty.* New Brunswick, N.J.: Transaction Books.

Piven, Frances Fox, and Cloward, Richard A. 1971. *Regulating the poor: The functions of public welfare.* New York: Random House.

Podell, Lawrence. 1967. Mothers' nativity and immigration. In *Preliminary report no. 4: Families on welfare in New York City.* New York: Center for Social Research, Graduate Center, City University of New York.

Pogue, Thomas F., and Sgontz, L. G. 1968. The effect of grants-in-aid on state-local spending. *National Tax Journal* 21:190-99.

Powers, Edward A., and Bultena, Gordon L. 1974. Correspondence between anticipated and actual uses of public services by the aged. *Social Service Review* 48 (June):245-54.

President's Commission on Income Maintenance Programs. 1970. *Background papers.* Washington, D.C.: U.S. Government Printing Office.

Prothro, James W. 1972. Stateways versus folkways revisited: An error in prediction. *Journal of Politics* 34:352-64.

Pulsipher, Allan G., and Weatherby, James L., Jr. 1968. Malapportionment, party competition, and the functional distribution of governmental expenditures. *American Political Science Review* 62:1207-19.

Rainwater, Lee. 1967. The lessons of Pruitt-Igoe. *Public Interest* 8 (Summer):116-26.

———. 1970a. *Behind ghetto walls: Black family life in a federal slum.* Chicago: Aldine.

———. 1970b. Neutralizing the disinherited: Some psychological aspects of understanding the poor. In *Psychological factors in poverty*, ed. Vernon L. Allen, pp. 9-28. Chicago: Markham.

Raymond, Richard. 1972. Determinants of non-white migration during the 1950s: Their regional significance and long-run implications. *American Journal of Economic Sociology* 31 (January):9-20.

Reid, William J., and Smith, Audrey D. 1972. AFDC mothers view the Work Incentive Program. *Social Service Review* 46 (September):347-62.

Rein, Martin, and Heclo, Hugh. 1973. What welfare crisis?—A comparison among the United States, Britain, and Sweden. *Public Interest* 33 (Fall): 61–83.

Rein, Mildred, and Wishnov, Barbara. 1971. Patterns of work and welfare in AFDC. *Welfare in Review* 9 (November–December):7–12.

Ricardo, David. 1821. *On the principles of political economy and taxation*. London.

Rieger, Jon M., and Beagle, J. Allen. 1974. The integration of rural migrants in new settings. *Rural Sociology* 39 (Spring):42–55.

Riley, Dennis D. 1971. Party competition and state policy making: The need for a reexamination. *Western Political Quarterly* 24:510–13.

Rischin, Moses, ed. 1968. *The American gospel of success: Individualism and beyond*. With an introduction by Moses Rischin. Chicago: Quadrangle Paperback Edition.

Ritchey, P. Neal. 1974. Urban poverty and rural to urban migration. *Rural Sociology* 39 (Spring):12–27.

Robinow, I. M. 1913. *Social insurance. With special reference to American conditions*. New York: Henry Holt.

Rodman, Hyman. 1971. *Lower class families: The culture of poverty in Negro Trinidad*. New York: Oxford University Press.

Rodman, Hyman; Voydanoff, Patricia; and Lovejoy, Albert E. 1974. The range of aspirations: A new approach. *Social Problems* 22 (December): 184–98.

Rokkan, Stein, ed. 1968. *Comparative research across cultures and nations*. Publication of the International Social Science Council, no. 8. Paris: Mouton.

Rutman, Gilbert L. 1970. Migration and economic opportunity in West Virginia: A statistical analysis. *Rural Sociology* 35 (June):206–17.

Sacks, Seymour, and Harris, Robert. 1964. The determinants of state and local government expenditures: Intergovernmental flows of funds. *National Tax Journal* 17 (March):75–85.

Sauber, Mignon, and Rubinstein, Elaine. 1965. *Experiences of the unwed mother as a parent: A longitudinal study of unmarried mothers who keep their first-born*. New York: Community Council of Greater New York.

Savitz, Leonard. 1960. *Delinquency and migration*. Philadelphia: Commission on Human Relations.

Scanzone, John A. 1970. *Opportunity and the family: A study of the conjugal family in relation to the economic-opportunity structure*. New York: Free Press.

Schiller, Bradley R. 1973. Empirical studies of welfare dependency: A survey. *Journal of Human Resources* 8 (September):19–32.

Schiltz, Michael E. 1970. *Public attitudes towards Social Security 1935–65*. Washington, D.C.: U.S. Government Printing Office.

Schultz, T. W. 1960. A policy to redistribute losses from economic progress. Research Paper no. 6008, University of Chicago Office of Agricultural Economics.

Schwartz, Joel J., and Tabb, David. 1972. Social welfare: Changing policies and changing priorities. *American Behavioral Scientist* 15 (June):645–64.

Schwarzweller, Harry K. 1964. Education, migration and economic life chances of male entrants to the labor force from a low-income rural area. *Rural Sociology* 29:152–67.

Seager, Henry R. 1921. *Social insurance: A progress of social reforms.* New York: Macmillan Co.

Seufert, Robert L. 1974. The utility of social disorder as a social indicator of state welfare policy formation. Paper presented at the 8th World Congress of Sociology, International Sociological Association, Toronto, Canada (August).

Sharkansky, Ira. 1967a. Economic and political correlates of state government expenditures: General tendencies and deviant cases. *Midwest Journal of Political Science* 11 (May):173–92.

———. 1967b. Regional patterns in the expenditures of American states. *Western Political Quarterly* 20:955–71.

———. 1967c. Some more thoughts about the determinants of government expenditures. *National Tax Journal* 20:171–79.

———. 1968a. Economic development, regionalism and state political systems. *Midwest Journal of Political Science* 12 (February):41–61.

———. 1968b. Regionalism, economic status and the public policies of American states. *Social Science Quarterly* 49 (June):9–26.

———. 1970a. *Regionalism in American politics.* New York: Bobbs-Merrill.

———. 1970b. The utility of Elazar's political culture: A research note. *Polity* 2 (Fall):66–83.

———. 1971a. Economic development, representative mechanisms, administrative professionalism and public policies: A comparative analysis of within-state distributions of economic and political traits. *Journal of Politics* 33:112–32.

———. 1971b. Economic theories of public policy: Resource-policy and need-policy linkages between income and welfare benefits. *Midwest Journal of Political Science* 15:722–40.

Sharkansky, Ira, and Hofferbert, Richard I. 1969. Dimensions of state politics, economics and public policy. *American Political Science Review* 63:867–79.

Shea, John R. 1973. Welfare mothers: Barriers to labor force entry. *Journal of Human Resources* 8 (supplement):90–102.

Shils, Edward A. 1956. *The torment of secrecy: The background and consequences of American security policies.* New York: Free Press.

———. 1975. *Center and periphery: Essays in macrosociology.* Chicago: University of Chicago Press.

Simmel, Georg. 1965. The poor. *Social Problems* 13 (Fall):118–40.

Smith, David L. 1968. The response of state and local governments to federal grants. *National Tax Journal* 21:349–57.

Sommers, Paul M., and Suits, Daniel B. 1973. Analysis of net interstate migration. *Southern Economics Journal* 40 (October):193–201.

Spall, Hugh, and McGoughran, Edward. 1972. AFDC in Michigan during the twentieth century. *Review of Social Economy* 32 (April):70–85.

Spilerman, Seymour. 1970. The causes of racial disturbances: A comparison of alternative explanations. *American Sociological Review* 35:627–49.

Startup, Richard. 1971. A sociology of migration? *Sociological Quarterly* 12:177–90.

Steiner, Gilbert Y. 1966. *Social insecurity: The politics of welfare*. Chicago: Rand McNally.

————. 1974. Reform follows reality: The growth of welfare. *Public Interest* 34 (Winter):47–82.

Stephens, G. Ross. 1974. State centralization and the erosion of local autonomy. *Journal of Politics* 36:44–76.

Stewart, James C., Jr.; Lauderdale, Michael; and Shuttlesworth, Guy E. 1972. The poor and the motivation fallacy. *Social Work* 17 (November): 34–37.

Strouse, James C., and Jones, Philippe. 1974. Federal aid: The forgotten variable in state policy research. *Journal of Politics* 36:200–207.

Stuart, Archibald. 1975. Recipient views of cash versus in-kind benefit programs. *Social Service Review* 49 (March):79–91.

Sullivan, John L. 1973. Political correlates of social, economic, and religious diversity in the American states. *Journal of Politics* 35:70–84.

Suttles, Gerald D. 1968. *The social order of the slum: Ethnicity and territory in the inner city*. Chicago: University of Chicago Press.

Sutton, Francis X.; Harris, Seymour E.; Kaysen, Carl; and Tobin, James. 1956. *The American business creed*. Cambridge: Harvard University Press.

Sutton, Richard L. 1973. The states and the people: Measuring and accounting for "state representativeness." *Polity* 5 (Summer):451–76.

Taeuber, Karl E., and Taeuber, Alma F. 1965. *Negroes in cities*. Chicago: Aldine.

Tanzi, Vito. 1968. Governments' approaches to income redistribution: An international comparison. *National Tax Journal* 21:483–86.

Tompkins, Gary L. 1975. A causal model of state welfare expenditures. *Journal of Politics* 37 (May):392–416.

Tripi, Frank. 1974. The inevitability of client alienation: A counter argument. *Sociological Quarterly* 15 (Summer):432–41.

Tropman, John E. 1973. The welfare gap allocations and utilization within the American states. Paper read at the annual meetings of the American Sociological Association, New York City (August).

Tropman, John E., with Gordon, Alan. 1974. The welfare threat: AFDC coverage and closeness in the American states. Paper read at the annual meetings of the American Sociological Association, Montreal, Canada (August).

Udry, Richard J. 1966. Marital instability by race, sex, education, and occupation using 1960 census data. *American Journal of Sociology* 72 (September):203-9.

————. 1967. Marital instability by race and income based on 1960 census data. *American Journal of Sociology* 72 (May):673-74.

Uhlenberg, Peter. 1973. Noneconomic determinants of nonmigration: Sociological considerations for migration theory. *Rural Sociology* 38 (Fall):296-311.

United States Bureau of Labor. 1910-13. *Report of conditions of woman and child wage earners in the United States.* 19 vols. Washington, D.C.: U.S. Government Printing Office.

United States Bureau of the Census. 1961-63. *U.S. census of population: 1960.* Washington, D.C.: U.S. Government Printing Office.

————. 1963. *U.S. census of population, 1960: Mobility for states and state-economic areas,* PC (2)-2B. Washington, D.C.: U.S. Government Printing Office.

————. 1971. Characteristics of the low-income population, 1970. *Current Population Reports,* series P-60, no. 81. Washington, D.C.: U.S. Government Printing Office.

————. 1971-73. *U.S. census of population: 1970.* Washington, D.C.: U.S. Government Printing Office.

————. 1972a. Characteristics of the low-income population, 1971. *Current Population Reports,* series P-60, no. 86. Washington, D.C.: U.S. Government Printing Office.

————. 1972b. Social and economic characteristics of students: October, 1971. *Current Population Reports,* series P-20, no. 241. Washington, D.C.: U.S. Government Printing Office.

————. 1973a. *Characteristics of Negro inmigrants to selected metropolitan areas: 1970,* PC(S1)-47. Washington, D.C.: U.S. Government Printing Office.

————. 1973b. *Statistical abstracts of the United States, 1972,* 93d ed. Washington, D.C.: U.S. Government Printing Office.

————. 1973c. *U.S. census of population: 1970, PC(S1)-48, interstate migration by state: 1970.* Washington, D.C.: U.S. Government Printing Office.

United States Congress House Committee on Ways and Means. 1969. *Report on findings of special review of AFDC in New York City.* Transmitted by U.S. Department of H.E.W. and the New York State Department of Social Services 91st Congress, 1st Session (17 October).

United States Social and Rehabilitation Service. 1968. *Source of funds extended for public assistance payments and for the cost of administration, services and training, fiscal year ended June 30, 1967.* Washington, D.C.: U.S. Government Printing Office.

————. 1970. Applications, cases approved, and cases discontinued for public assistance, January-March 1970. NCSS Report A-9, 1-3/70. Washington, D.C. (mimeographed).

———. 1971*a*. Applications, cases approved, and cases discontinued for public assistance, April–June 1970. NCSS Report A-9, 4-6/70. Washington, D.C. (mimeographed).

———. 1971*b*. Applications, cases approved, and cases discontinued for public assistance, July–September 1970. NCSS Report A-9, 7-9/70. Washington, D.C. (mimeographed).

———. 1971*c*. Applications, cases approved, and cases discontinued for public assistance, October–December 1970. NCSS Report A-9, 10-12/70. Washington, D.C. (mimeographed).

———. 1971*d*. OAA and AFDC: Standards for basic needs for specified types of assistance groups, July 1970. NCSS Report D-3, 7/70. Washington, D.C. (mimeographed).

———. 1971*e*. Compilations based on *Characteristics of state plans: General provisions—eligibility, assistance, administration* in effect June 1, 1970. Unpublished Report, State Plan and Program Characteristics Branch, U.S. Department of Health, Education, and Welfare. Washington, D.C. (September).

———. 1971*f*. *Characteristics of state public assistance plans under the Social Security Act: General provisions—Eligibility, assistance, administration*. Public Assistance Report no. 50, 1970 ed. Washington, D.C.: U.S. Government Printing Office.

———. 1971*g*. Aid to Families with Dependent Children, special characteristics relating to unemployment of the father, based on review of approved state plans, July 1971. Washington, D.C. (November) (mimeographed).

———. 1972. State maximums and other methods of limiting money payments to recipients of the special types of public assistance, July 1971. NCSS Report D-3, 7/71. Washington, D.C. (mimeographed).

United States Social Security Administration. 1960. *Characteristics of state public assistance plans under the Social Security Act: General provisions—Eligibility, assistance, administration*. Public Assistance Report no. 50, 1959 ed. Washington, D.C.: U.S. Government Printing Office.

———. 1962. Monthly cost standards for basic needs used by states for specified types of old-age assistance cases and families receiving AFDC, January 1961. Washington, D.C. (mimeographed).

Uslaner, Eric M., and Weber, Ronald E. 1975. The "politics" of redistribution. *American Politics Quarterly* 3 (April):130–70.

Valentine, Charles A. 1968. *The culture of poverty: Critique and counterproposals*. Chicago: University of Chicago Press.

Van Til, Jon. 1973. Becoming participants: Dynamics of access among the welfare poor. *Social Science Quarterly* 54 (September):345–58.

Verba, Sidney, and Nie, Norman H. 1972. *Participation in America: Political democracy and social equity*. New York: Harper and Row.

Walker, Helen M., and Lev, Joseph. 1953. *Statistical inference*. New York: Holt, Rinehart and Winston.

Walker, Jack L. 1969. The diffusion of innovations among the American states. *American Political Science Review* 63:880–99.

Weber, Max. 1962. *The city*. Trans. and ed. Don Martindale and Gertrud Neuwirth. New York: Collier Paperback.

Weber, Ronald E., and Schaffer, William R. 1972. Public opinion and American state policy-making. *Midwest Journal of Political Science* 15: 683–99.

Weiss, Harry. 1918–35. Employer liability and workmen's compensation. In *History of labor in the United States*, ed. John R. Commons et al., 3:564–610. New York: Macmillan Co.

Wertheimer, Richard F., II. 1970. *The monetary rewards of migration within the U.S.* Washington, D.C.: Urban Institute.

Wilensky, Harold L. 1975. *The welfare state and equality: Structural and ideological roots of public expenditures*. Berkeley: University of California Press.

Wilensky, Harold L., and Lebeaux, Charles N. 1965. *Industrial society and social welfare*. New York: Free Press (paperback ed.).

Williamson, John B. 1973. Beliefs about the welfare poor. *Sociology and Social Research* 58 (October):163–75.

————. 1974a. Beliefs about the motivation of the poor and attitudes toward poverty policy. *Social Problems* 21 (June):635–48.

————. 1974b. The stigma of public dependency: A comparison of alternative forms of public aid to the poor. *Social Problems* 22 (December): 213–28.

Winegarden, C. R. 1973. The welfare "explosion": Determinants of the size and recent growth of the AFDC population. *American Journal of Economics and Sociology* 32 (July):245–56.

Periodicals

Book of the States, vol. 24 (1962–63); vol. 29 (1972–73).

Social Security Bulletin, vol. 23 (1960); vol. 24 (1961); vol. 33 (1970); vol. 34 (1971); vol. 36 (1973).

Welfare in Review.

Author Index

Subject Index

Administration. *See* Welfare administration
AFDC program. *See* Aid to Families with
Dependent Children program;
Welfare
Age limits, 42–43, 137, 213, n.14
Aid to Dependent Children (ADC), 14
Aid to Families with Dependent Children
program (AFDC): administrative costs
of, 40; criticism of, 32; effect on family
structure, 61; federal requirements for,
38; growth of, 32, 162; history of, 38–
40, 209 n.29; local contributions to,
212 n.12; reason for studying, 31–32,
163; size of, 32, 209 (*see also* Welfare
rolls); states' participation in, 40–41,
156. *See also* Welfare
Aid to the Aged, Blind, and Disabled
(ABD), 213 n.16
Aid to the Blind (AB), 212 n.12, 213 n.16,
215 n.31
Aid to the Permanently and Totally Disabled (APTD), 210 n.32, 212 n.12,
213 n.16, 215 n.31
Alabama, 52
Alaska, 41, 212 n.9, 216 n.37
Application, rate of, 144, 145, 149, 150,
229 n.22
Applications, approval of, 144–45, 149,
150, 229 n.22
Arizona, 47, 52, 141, 213 n.18
Arkansas, 47, 141
Autonomy of states, 11–13, 20, 38, 50

Benefit level: and cost of living, 136–37;
and eligibility requirements, 136; and
extent of need, 28, 148; limitations on,
47–48; and mass society status, 72–73,
136; and state fiscal capacity, 27, 136,
207 n.12; and Total Eligibility Score,
136, 137; use as variable, 23–24, 136,
217 n.39, 229 n.17; and welfare rolls,
54, 61, 113–14, 217 n.40
Blacks: discrimination against, 84, 85,
156, 158, 205 n.18; extension of rights
to, 25, 73, 130–31, 156. *See also*
Blacks, number of; Minority groups;
Race
Blacks, number of, 25, 75; and broken
families, 82, 225 n.6; use as variable,
75; and welfare policies, 75, 83–84,
131, 134–35, 140, 156, 163; and welfare
rolls, 74–75, 82, 225 n.6. *See also*
Blacks; Minority groups; Race
Broken homes. *See* Families, broken

California, 125, 137, 215 n.28, 229 n.15
Caseworkers, 137, 143, 144, 149, 229
n.23, 230 n.25
Center and periphery, 10–11, 13, 22, 33,
128, 161, 165, 205 n.14
Cheating, welfare, 49, 54, 74, 112, 152
Citizenship: civil, 10, 25, 161; duties of,
31, 118, 130–31, 153, 230 n.2; economic, 3, 11, 84–85, 118, 159, 161;
extension of, 2–3, 8–16, 23, 31, 84, 85,
94, 118, 119, 127, 130–31, 156, 158,
161, 163, 164–68; meaning of, 118,
153, 158, 165; of migrants, 91–92, 130,
163; of minority groups, 25, 73, 84, 85,
130–131, 156, 158, 163–64; political,
9–10, 118, 159, 161; rights of, 10, 13,
31, 118, 130, 145, 148, 153, 159–161,
230 n.2; social, 2–3, 10–11, 13–15, 16,
23, 25, 31, 118, 158–59, 161, 165; types
of, 9–11, 159, 161
Civil rights. *See* Citizenship; Civil rights
movement
Civil rights movement, 31, 118, 122, 158,
159, 160, 161–62
Cold War, 158
Composite factor, 69, 82, 86, 93, 105, 129
Connecticut, 212 n.9
Correlation: coefficients of, 221 nn.3, 5;
223 n.16; explanation of, 216 n.37
Cost of living, 136–37. *See also* Cost
standard
Cost standard: definition of, 47, 214
n.23; and economic conditions, 136–
37, 214 n.25; and mass society status,
72–73, 136; regional variations in, 47,
136–37, 214 n.25; relation to poverty
level, 47, 59; relation to welfare rolls,
54, 217 n.40; use as variable, 136
Cross-sectional analysis, 30–31
Culture: diffusion of, 10–11; fragmentation of, 33, 163, 168; political (*see* Politics; State governments, structure of);
variation between states, 13
Culture of poverty theory, 4–7, 74, 112,
130–31, 204 n.4

Decentralization, political and administrative, 11–12, 20, 153, 163, 164,
230 n.1
Delaware, 52
Demographic characteristics of recipients, 42–43, 162, 216 n.35
Dependency, economic, 119, 127, 128,
140, 145, 148, 150. *See also* Need,
extent of; Poverty, Welfare rolls

Desegregation, school, 25, 159
Deservedness, concepts of, 14–16, 122–23, 126, 130–31; criteria for determining, 26, 28, 43, 143, 148, 157, 163. *See also* Eligibility requirements; Public opinion; Total Eligibility Score; Welfare policies
Design, research, 30–35. *See also* Statistical techniques
Discrimination, 6, 83–84, 85, 94, 122, 123, 152, 156, 158, 205 n.18
Disregards, income, 48–49, 137, 215 n.27
Domestic affairs, focus on, 158, 162

Economic development: dimensions of, 69–71; and poverty, 9; and voter participation, 28–29; and welfare system, 14, 15, 20–29, 114, 129, 136–40, 152, 156, 166, 207 n.12. *See also* State fiscal capacity
Economics literature, 21, 22, 26, 112, 207 n.11
Education, level of, 25, 33; and eligibility requirements, 128–29, 134–35; use as variable, 33, 63, 207 n.11, 218 nn. 13, 14; and welfare rolls, 68, 85, 86, 96, 97, 101, 104
Eligibility requirements: age, 42–43, 137, 213 n.14; court decisions on, 43, 45, 122, 160; demographic, 42–43; durational, 43–44, 160, 213 n.17, 228 n.8; economic, 42–49, 72, 140 (*see also* Benefit level; Cost standard; Income, limitations on); effect of federal regulations on, 38, 41–42, 50, 122, 164; effect of politics on, 28, 54, 135, 140, 157; and extent of need, 14–16, 27–28, 50, 127, 128, 145, 148; family status, 43, 137; indexes of, 215 n.33; (*see also* Total Eligibility Score); interpretation of, 45, 143; liberalizing of, 141, 145, 149, 156; and mass society status, 127, 131, 134, 135, 140, 165; noneconomic, 14, 137; and presence of blacks, 75, 83–84, 131, 134–35, 140, 156, 163; and property limitations, 41, 49, 137, 215 nn.29, 30; residence, 43–44, 90, 130, 160, 211 n.5, 213 nn.16, 17, 228 n.8; restrictiveness of, 41, 50, 71–72, 122, 137 (*see also* Total Eligibility Score); social, 42–46; and state fiscal capacity, 21–24, 27, 28, 129; variations among states, 41, 50–51, 124, 168; variations within states, 211 n.5; and welfare rolls, 21, 35, 54, 80, 117–18,

125–26, 140–41, 157, 216 n.35. *See also* Total Eligibility Score; Welfare policies
Employment: female, 69, 86, 105–6, 110–11, 228 n.5; nonfarm, 65, 67; opportunities for, 83, 112–14; of welfare recipients, 112–14; and welfare rolls, 86, 105–6, 110–11. *See also* Occupations; Underemployment; Unemployment
Environment. *See* Culture of poverty theory
Equality, 165–66. *See also* Inequality
Expenditures. *See* Welfare expenditures

Factor analysis, 68–70, 81, 100; explanation of, 220 n.24; results of, 181–86; uses of, 209 n.26
Families, broken, 33, 67, 218 n.9; causes of, 108–11; correlation with race, 82, 225 n.6; use as variable, 108; and welfare rolls, 61–62, 81, 85, 86, 87, 92, 97, 100–101, 104, 105, 108–9, 110, 225 n.3
Family Assistance Plan (FAP), 162
Family size, 32, 33, 60
Family status: and economic conditions, 218 n.9, 220 n.23; and eligibility requirements, 43, 137. *See also* Families, broken
Fathers: absent, 43, 45, 163, 218 n.8, 225 n.3 (*see also* Families, broken); substitute, 44, 45, 46, 214 n.19; unemployed, 44, 45, 218 n.8
Federal financial participation (FFP), 212 nn.6, 7
Federal government: authority of, 12, 20, 38, 42; role in welfare programs, 15, 21, 39–41, 158–59, 164, 207 n.15, 211 n.6; and welfare policies, 12, 20, 38, 41–42, 50, 122, 164, 215 n.29
"Federal medical assistance percentage," 212 n.7
Fetus, eligibility for AFDC, 42–43, 213 n.15
Finances, state. *See* State fiscal capacity
Fiscal capacity. *See* State fiscal capacity
Florida, 47, 148, 212 n.9, 215 n.26
Foster care, 46
Fragmentation, cultural, 33, 163, 164, 168
F-statistic, 222 n.5

General Assistance program (GA), 210 n.33, 212 nn.12, 13

Regression coefficients, explanation of, 222 n.6

Residency requirements, 43, 160, 211 n.5, 213 n.17; durational, 43–44, 211 n.5, 213 n.16, 228 n.8; and migration, 90, 130

Resource-policy analysis, 27

Resources. *See* Economic development; Need, extent of; State fiscal capacity

Revenue, per capita, 66, 114, 129; and welfare rolls, 97, 101, 104, 105, 114, 156, 225 n.3

Revenue, state. *See* State fiscal capacity

Rights. *See* Citizenship; Political rights; Social citizenship

Riots, 160, 163

Satisfaction, as cause of poverty, 5

Scandals, *See* Cheating, welfare

Shapiro v. *Thompson*, 43, 160, 228 n.8

Significance levels, 219 n.22, 222 n.5

Social citizenship, 2–3, 10–11, 13–15, 16, 23, 25, 31, 118, 158–59, 161, 165

Social factors: and citizenship rights, 158–62; and poverty, 4–8

Social Security program: number of recipients, 210 n.32; and welfare policies, 31, 38–39, 42, 48, 122, 158, 211 n.5

Social-welfare constituency, 158

South: determinants of welfare rolls in, 224 n.17; racial composition of, 75; shift toward mass society status, 226 n.8; socioeconomic characteristics of, 69, 223 n.17; welfare policies in, 134. *See also* Regional variation

South Carolina, 51, 52

South Dakota, 212 n.9

Southerners, presence of, 75. *See also* Blacks; Blacks, number of; Migrants; Migration

Standard Metropolitan Statistical Areas (SMSAs), 219 n.17

Standard of living, 152, 166. *See also* Cost standard

State fiscal capacity: use as variable, 33, 65, 66; and welfare programs, 21–24, 27, 28, 66, 114, 129, 135, 156–57, 166. *See also* Economic development

State governments: autonomy of, 11–13, 20, 38, 50; centralization of, 205 n.15; structure of, 13, 22–23, 135, 140, 206 n.3

States: attitude toward welfare, 148–49, 154–55; fiscal capacity of (*see* State

fiscal capacity); mass society status of, 13–14, 69, 153–55, 223 n.17 (*see also* Mass society status); political cultures of, 13, 22, 23, 206 n.3 (*see also* State governments)

Statistical techniques: cross-sectional analysis, 30–31; factor analysis, 68–70, 81, 100, 181–86, 209 n.26, 220 n.24; *F*-statistic, 221 n.5; regression analysis, 30, 31, 35, 70, 81–83, 85–87, 92–93, 101, 108, 110, 124, 129, 131, 208 n.25, 209 n.28, 221 n.1, 222 nn.5, 7; time-series analysis, 31, 111, 155

Stepwise regression analysis, 30, 31, 35, 70, 85, 87, 92–93, 101, 108, 110, 125, 129, 131; advantages of, 222 n.7; explanation of, 209 n.28, 221 n.1; limitations of, 222 n.5

Stigma of welfare, 14, 94, 122–23, 148–49, 165, 167, 210 n.30, 227 n.1

Stratification, class, 164, 230 n.5

Stratification approach, 14–16, 25–26, 33–35, 58–77

Stratification variables, 58–62, 67–69, 72–73, 76, 80–83, 92–93, 97, 100, 101, 104–6, 107–8, 115, 117, 131, 140

Substitute fathers, 44, 45, 46, 214 n.19

Suitable home clause, 28, 46, 205 n.18, 214 n.21

Supplemental Security Income program (SSI), 164, 211 n.5

Surveys, data from, 208 n.22

Taxation: and eligibility requirements, 129, 131–34; income limitations as, 215 n.27; inequities in, 24, 164, 207 n.18; relation to welfare expenditures, 24; and Total Eligibility Score, 129; use as variable, 65, 66; and welare policies, 156; and welfare rolls, 86, 97, 114, 156, 224

Tennessee, 148

TES. *See* Total Eligibility Score

Texas, 42, 148, 212 n.9

Threat variables, 58, 75, 76, 77, 86–87, 91–92, 100, 104–5, 107, 115, 131, 135, 156

Time period, choice of, 30, 31

Time-series analysis, 31, 111, 155

Title XIX (Medicaid), 39–40, 204 n.1

Total Eligibility Score (TES): and benefit level, 136, 137; construction of, 174–77; explanation of, 50, 135–36, 228 n.2; and extent of need, 72, 136; and industrialization-urbanization,

136, 228 n.3; and mass society variables, 126-28, 136, 156; and stratification variables, 72; and threat variables, 131, 156; variations in, 51, 117-18, 129, 216 nn.34, 36, 229 nn.14, 15, 20; and voter participation, 128-29; and welfare rolls, 54, 72, 117-18, 125, 126-28. *See also* Eligibility requirements; Welfare policies

Underemployment: and broken families, 110, 220 n.23; definition of, 217 n.5; and extent of need, 59; female, 59-60, 62, 68, 82, 97, 101, 104-5, 106, 110, 112, 114, 225 n.2; and industrialization, 225 n.2; male, 59, 86, 87, 92, 96, 105, 110; and welfare rolls, 68, 80-81, 82, 86, 87, 92, 96, 97, 101, 104-5, 106, 110, 112, 114
Unemployed Parent Program, 41, 44-45, 52, 53-54, 212 n.13
Unemployment: and broken families, 108-9; causes of, 6-7; definition of, 44-45, 59, 213 n.18; as determinant of status, 73; female, 59-60, 112, 217 n.6; male, 44, 45, 80-81, 85, 218 n.8; and welfare rolls, 33, 80-81, 85, 112, 210 n.35
Unrest, civil, 144. *See also* Riots
Urbanization: as cause of poverty, 6-7, 8-9, 26-27; index of, 64, 69, 219 n.16; and mass society status, 33; and modernization, 64, 154; and Total Eligibility Score, 136, 228 n.3; and voter participation, 67; and welfare policies, 26; and welfare rolls, 26-27, 68, 96, 122
Urbanization-industrialization factor, 86

Variables: mass society, 62-76, 84-86, 97, 100-106, 115, 131, 135; selection of, 33-35, 58, 221 n.1; stratification, 58-62, 67-69, 72-73, 76, 80-83, 92-93, 97, 100, 101, 104-6, 107-8, 115, 117, 131, 140; threat, 58, 75, 76, 77, 86-87, 91-92, 100, 104-5, 107, 115, 131, 135. *See also specific variables*
Vermont, 141
Virginia, 212 n.9
Voter participation: and citizenship, 29, 33, 62-63, 159, 161; and economic development, 28-29; eligibility for, 9, 161, 205 n.13; measures of, 218 n.12; and Total Eligibility Score, 128-29;

and underemployment, 68; and urbanization, 67; and welfare policies, 22, 62-63; and welfare rolls, 62-63, 85, 86, 87, 92, 96, 97, 105
Voting Rights Act, 159, 161

Waiting period, 43-44
Wallace, George, 160
War on Poverty, 5-6, 158-59
Washington, D.C., 45, 216 n.37
Welfare: applications for (*see* Application, rate of; Applications, approval of); attitudes toward, 38, 49, 83-84, 106, 123, 143, 145, 148-49, 160 (*see also* Public opinion); benefits (*see also* Benefit level; Payments, welfare); as cause of broken families, 108-9 (*see also* Families, broken); cheating in, 49, 54, 74, 112, 152; discrimination in, 83-84, 94, 122, 123, 205 n.18; eligibility for (*see* Eligibility requirements; Total Eligibility Score; Welfare policies); need for (*see* Need, extent of); Public opinion on, 28, 109, 112, 122-23, 148-49, 160-61; stigma of, 14, 94, 122-23, 148-49, 165, 167, 210 n.30, 227 n.1; utilization of, 94, 143 (*see also* Welfare rolls). *See also* Welfare administration; Welfare expenditures; Welfare policies; Welfare recipients; Welfare rolls; Welfare system
Welfare administration: attitude toward recipients, 148-49; costs of, 40; effect on welfare rolls, 167; and political influence, 135, 143; problems in, 137, 141-43; requirements for, 211 n.2; vested interests of, 158; and welfare policies, 135. *See also* Welfare policies
"Welfare crisis," 2, 16, 31, 154, 204 n.1
Welfare expenditures: and economic development, 21, 22, 24, 26-27, 129, 135, 136, 140, 143, 152, 166, 207 n.12; effect of politics on, 22-23, 140, 152, 157, 207 n.13; federal government's share of, 21, 39-40, 211 n.6, 212 n.7; and mass society status, 14, 21-22, 26; as proportion of all expenditures, 24. *See also* Benefit level; Payments, welfare
Welfare legislation. *See* Legislation, welfare
Welfare payments. *See* Benefit level; Payments, welfare; Payment standard
Welfare policies: and economic conditions, 14, 15, 20-29, 129, 136-40, 166;